SUPERMARKET
Buying Guide

SUPERMARKET
Buying Guide

Kent B. Banning, Mary Weber,
and the Editors of Consumer Reports Books

CONSUMER REPORTS BOOKS
A DIVISION OF CONSUMERS UNION
YONKERS, NEW YORK

Copyright © 1994 by Kent B. Banning
Consumers Union of United States, Inc.,
Yonkers, New York 10703

LIBRARY OF CONGRESS CATALOGING-IN-PUBLICATION DATA

Banning, Kent B.
Supermarket buying guide / Kent
B. Banning, Mary Weber, and the Editors of Consumer Reports Books
p.   cm.
Includes index.
ISBN 0-89043-631-2
1. Marketing (Home economics) I. Weber, Mary. II. Consumer
Reports Books. III. Title.
TX356.B36   1994
641.3'1—dc20   93-29244
CIP

Design by Kathryn Parise

First printing, March 1994

Manufactured in the United States of America

This book is printed on recycled paper ♲

Supermarket Buying Guide is a Consumer Reports Book published by Consumers Union, the nonprofit organization that publishes *Consumer Reports*, the monthly magazine of test reports, product Ratings, and buying guidance. Established in 1936, Consumers Union is chartered under the Not-for-Profit Corporation Law of the State of New York.

The purposes of Consumers Union, as stated in its charter, are to provide consumers with information and counsel on consumer goods and services, to give information on all matters relating to the expenditure of the family income, and to initiate and to cooperate with individual and group efforts seeking to create and maintain decent living standards.

Consumers Union derives its income solely from the sale of *Consumer Reports* and other publications. In addition, expenses of occasional public service efforts may be met, in part, by nonrestrictive, noncommercial contributions, grants, and fees. Consumers Union accepts no advertising or product samples and is not beholden in any way to any commercial interest. Its Ratings and reports are solely for the use of the readers of its publications. Neither the Ratings, nor the reports, nor any Consumers Union publications, including this book, may be used in advertising or for any commercial purpose. Consumers Union will take all steps open to it to prevent such uses of its material, its name, or the name of *Consumer Reports*.

CONTENTS

Acknowledgments   vii

Introduction   1

1. How to Save Money at the Supermarket   4

2. The Poultry Counter   29

3. The Meat Counter   42

4. The Fish Market   63

5. The Produce Section: Vegetables   71

6. The Produce Section: Fruits   92

7. The Dairy Case   112

8. Shopping the Aisles: Food Staples   125

9. How to Prepare and Store Food Safely
   by Lisa Y. Lefferts   159

   Appendix: Consumer Reports Ratings of
   Brand-Name Food Products   178

   Index   285

ACKNOWLEDGMENTS

The information in this book could not have been compiled without the cooperation of many people in the food field, including supermarket personnel, government agencies, and consumer organizations. Equally important has been my association with institutional, hotel, and restaurant chefs, who freely shared their knowledge and experiences with me.

I also wish to thank Julie Henderson, my editor at Consumer Reports Books, for her patience and assistance.

—*Kent B. Banning*

SUPERMARKET
Buying Guide

Introduction

In uncertain economic times, most consumers have to pay close attention to the household budget. Every expense has to be carefully weighed to ensure that, first, it's necessary and, second, it's the best deal in town. Often, major expenditures can be delayed, such as repairing the roof or buying a new car; other expenses can be canceled entirely, like dining out, theater tickets, or a vacation trip.

One type of expenditure, however, cannot be postponed or forgotten: food. For this essential, consumers have no choice whether to buy or not. Nevertheless, they can save a considerable amount of money by buying selectively and knowledgeably. No category offers as much of an opportunity to save as those products found in your local supermarket.

In the battle for your dollar, the supermarket giants use sales, coupons, marketing strategies, and advertising blitzes to convince you that their stores offer you the best deal for your money. This competitive arena provides you, the consumer, with the opportunity to shave hundreds, even thousands of dollars off your annual food bills—*if* you can cut through all the advertising hype and retail ploys that surround you the moment you enter the supermarket. Knowledge is your secret weapon—knowledge about merchandising techniques that stimulate impulse buying, about when a sale is not really a sale, and about the different varieties of foods and how one can be substituted for another.

You can "cherry pick"—comparison shop in several stores, buying only those items on special in each store. You can "coupon," too: American consumers saved $4 billion in 1991 by using coupons. You can also use the advertised specials in your daily newspapers to plan your next week's menu. But again, none of these money-saving techniques will help unless you have the knowledge to compare the same types of product, or unless you use coupons wisely as a part of your overall shopping strategies. And what about those specials? Often, a supermarket will put a certain cut of meat on sale, but the store's method of cutting and preparation results in more waste from bone and fat than do other cutting methods. Consequently, the so-called special may be actually more expensive than the same cut not on sale but available in another store. Again, knowledge is your weapon against paying higher prices and getting less value.

How to Use This Book

The *Supermarket Buying Guide* provides information you will need to shop wisely and economically. In many cases, you will be able to buy better quality for less money because you have learned about product pricing and how the many varieties of the same type of food can be utilized to suit your purposes.

You'll find out about supermarkets and how they work in chapter 1. Merchandising techniques and selling ploys are discussed, as well as how to curb impulse buying, plan a menu, and make smart buys. A unique feature is a 1992 *Consumer Reports* survey that rated supermarkets for cleanliness, service, and awareness of consumer needs.

Chapters 2 through 8, the heart of the book, describe and discuss the foods most frequently purchased in a supermarket, including poultry, meats, variety meats, fish, vegetables, fruits, dairy foods, and staples such as cereals, flour, pasta, and beverages. These chapters offer hints and tips on purchasing and using these products, always with the emphasis on cutting costs and getting the most for your money.

Chapter 9 tells you how to store and use food products safely. Written by Lisa Y. Lefferts, an expert on food safety and risk assessment, this chapter can help you avoid contaminants in your food and prepare healthier, safer meals.

The Appendix features *Consumer Reports* buying advice and brand-name Ratings of 15 food products. The Ratings are usually based on tests by a trained panel of taste-testers, or on nutritional comparisons or other key characteristics. Where appropriate, supplementary analyses are provided.

At times, references are made in this book to "informal" tests. Readers should be aware that these tests were neither conducted nor supervised by *Consumer Reports* food scientists.

1

How to Save Money at the Supermarket

Are you a shopper or a spender? There is a difference. A shopper is an intelligent buyer, one who buys with a purpose in mind. A spender, on the other hand, buys on impulse, yielding to the many stimuli provided by every newspaper, magazine, sign, TV or radio commercial, and salesperson. The shopper buys to satisfy a specific need; the spender allows advertising to create the need. Most important, the shopper understands the purpose of advertising and uses it, rather than being used by it.

Every time you enter a supermarket, you are assailed by the combined efforts of the advertising executive, the graphic artist, the market researcher, the sales psychologist, and many other specialists whose sole purpose is to convince you that their product is the only one for you. The size, shape, and color of the package is designed to tug at your purse strings, and the tone and content of the store ads and floor displays are directed at any doubts you may have about your status, your appearance, or even your sex appeal. Considering that the cost of these combined selling techniques is estimated at over $5 billion per year, it's no wonder that there are probably more spenders than shoppers in today's supermarkets.

You are not without resources, however. You can become a smart shopper by learning

- how supermarkets foster impulse buying
- how to buy to meet *your* needs and pocketbook
- how to comparison shop
- how to know which product is best

The first three items are not difficult to master—they involve paying attention to a few basic rules of food buying. The last one, however—how to know which product is best—is more complicated, and much of this book is devoted to that topic.

Let's first take a look at today's supermarkets, their selling strategies, and what you can do to use their marketing techniques to your advantage.

The Supermarket as Selling Machine

Supermarkets have historically operated on profit margins as low as one-half cent on every dollar of sales. The scant profits made on staples like milk, flour, coffee, and bread are offset by heftier markups on impulse buys like potato chips or a new cereal, on special goods from the deli or bakery, and on fancy fare.

Here are some ways that supermarkets try to influence your buying decisions.

ADVERTISING AND MARKETING

You're the target of endless ads for brand-name products before you even set foot in the store. Marketers also give millions in "street money" to supermarkets that will tout particular brands in newspaper ads and store circulars and then place them prominently on store shelves.

A newer tactic is in-store marketing. As you wheel your cart along, big-name brands want you to think not soup but *Campbell's*, not canned fruit but *Del Monte*. So they spend some $450 million a year putting billboards on carts, installing instant-coupon machines, and arranging talking shelf displays, product demonstrations, and the like.

"Micromarketing," the electronic targeting of individual consumers, has also caught the grocery industry's fancy. With the help of electronic scanners, shopper surveys, and information you provide when you apply for and use a check-cashing or preferred-shopper card, a supermarket can learn a lot about you. It can mail a cat owner coupons for cat litter, for example. At the checkout counter, it can give the single shopper instant discounts on frozen dinners or hot deli foods. It can further target occasional shoppers, frequent shoppers, or shoppers who buy a lot of store brands.

COUPONS

When manufacturers offer coupons for high-profit impulse items like peanuts or a new rice mix, people buy 50 percent more

---

BONUS AND WAREHOUSE PRICE CLUBS

Supermarkets still promote one-stop shopping, but they have added other inducements to capture their share of the shopping dollar. All of these programs are designed to build customer loyalty to a particular chain of stores rather than to specific brands.

Bonus clubs

These programs offer a no-cost membership card that allows you to take advantage of special discounts on various items. You present your membership card when checking out, and the discounts are automatically subtracted from your bill. Bonus clubs supplement or replace store coupons but do not alter the value of coupons issued by manufacturers.

Preferred-shopper programs

These programs are intended to provide retailers with certain demographic information about their customers. Preferred-shopper programs entitle you to discounts and other store services in exchange for information about yourself and your shopping preferences.

Warehouse price clubs

First came the warehouse stores—bare-bones operations that put lower prices ahead of ambience, service, and product variety. Then came the membership clubs, which offer no frills and good prices for a $25 to $35 annual fee. The clubs pile groceries on pallets or on long rows of metal shelving; the products themselves come in large containers or multipacks. Many clubs have meat, produce, and bakery sections, while most sell appliances, office supplies, and even clothing.

To get an idea of the possible savings, a reporter from *Consumer Reports* shopped at a Pace membership warehouse in Bergen County, New Jersey, and at an A&P in Yonkers, New York. He had to buy in bulk at the warehouse: a 24-can pack of *Coke* rather than the supermarket's 6-pack; a 35-ounce box of *Cheerios* rather than a 15-ounce box; a 50-pound bag of *Purina Dog Chow* rather than a 5-pound bag. Nothing he bought in either store was on sale.

The reporter found considerable savings in the lower unit costs at the warehouse. Unit prices on regular sizes of *Purina Dog Chow*, *Palmolive* detergent, *Oscar Mayer* bacon, and *Plumrose* boiled ham were up to 100 percent higher at his local supermarket. The differences were smaller on other products, including *Coca-Cola* and *Lipton* tea bags—but the warehouse prices were always lower: Buying in quantity at the warehouse cost $76.71; buying in the same quantity at the supermarket would have cost $128.53.

than they would if the product weren't promoted. That's why manufacturers find it worthwhile to distribute some 310 billion cents-off coupons per year, in full knowledge that 292 billion of them will wind up in a landfill, unredeemed.

Coupons also convey the impression that shoppers are getting a bargain, a false impression if coupon clipping leads you to buy products you wouldn't ordinarily buy. Many coupons are for new products, which the industry considers the lifeblood of stores. New products are appearing at a rate of nearly 17,000 a year, up 60 percent since 1987.

Why the proliferation? It's certainly not necessity. We consumers like variety, but we could do with something less than

147 brands and types of cereal, or 22 brands and types of peanut butter. Manufacturers use product differentiation to grab shelf space from competitors and ring up incremental sales by adding anything shoppers are willing to pay for—from the latest action-hero cereal to the convenience of a squeeze bottle to the glamour of a foreign name.

LAYOUT AND DESIGN

The fact that you must often go from one end of the store to the other to pick up a quart of milk is part of a carefully executed plan to stretch out your shopping trip and, hence, your exposure to the pitch. But supermarkets that try to slow traffic by erecting an obstacle course of aisle-clogging merchandise displays, for example, run the risk of alienating their customers. Indeed, in a 1992 *Consumer Reports* survey of readers (see page 25), one of the biggest complaints about supermarkets was that the aisles were congested.

The store itself can be used to project an image. A few supermarket chains cultivate a warehouse look—steel shelving, industrial-type lighting, pipes crisscrossing the ceiling, and huge bins overflowing with dry goods—but sometimes without the low prices to match the image.

PRODUCT PLACEMENT

With shelf space at a premium, retailers have gone into the real estate business, renting their shelf space to the highest bidder. To get the products on the shelves, manufacturers may offer stores a temporary discount, which the store can either pocket or turn into an opportunity to run a sale. Chains also sometimes require manufacturers to pay a premium, or "slotting allowance," of as much as $50,000 to stock a new item. Some also demand a "failure fee" for products that don't make it. And even if a product becomes successful, manufacturers may have to keep stuffing the chain's coffers to keep a product on the shelf.

Critics say such promotional practices drive up the cost of brand-name goods, even if only by pennies per package. The

HOW TO SAVE (UP TO) $2,423 A YEAR

To see how the pennies mount up when you buy by price, some *Consumer Reports* staffers shopped for a list of items two ways at a nearby A&P. They filled one cart without regard to price; they filled the other with store brands (A&P has a very full line of such brands).

When they bought national brands and "value-added" goods (prepeeled and shredded carrots and celery trimmed of excess greenery, for example), they ran up a tab of $114.36; when they shopped with a more price-conscious eye, the bill totaled $67.76. Overall savings: $46—or, if you make a similar shopping trip each week, $2,423 a year.

In shopping, the *Consumer Reports* staffers bought comparable sizes of both national and store brands. They didn't use coupons, and they didn't buy items on sale. Their list included items most people buy every week—vegetables, snacks, soda, cold cuts, bread. It also included items you might buy only once every two weeks, or every month, but it didn't include milk or other items that might be on your weekly list. In fact, it didn't include everything you might buy during the course of a year. But the list points the way to real savings.

Of course, you may not want to save the last penny at the supermarket. Perhaps you prefer an expensive brand of cereal or bathroom tissue. The point is that over the course of a year, significant savings—even if somewhat less than $2,423—are available if you buy by price whenever you have no strong preference otherwise.

Product, size	Name brand	Store brand
Carrots, 1 lb.	Verdelli, shredded $2.58	Bagged whole ....$.59
Celery, bunch	Dole "Hearts" 1.89	Plain bunch .... .99
Mayonnaise, qt.	Kraft 2.79	A&P 1.19
Black olives, 5¾ oz.	S&W 1.99	A&P 1.19
Ketchup, 2 lb.	Heinz 1.69	A&P .... .79

Product, size	Name brand	Store brand
Steak sauce, 10 oz.	Lea & Perrins 3.55	A&P 1.69
Tea, 100 bags	Lipton 2.79	A&P 1.39
French-roast coffee, 12 oz.	Folgers 2.79	A&P Eight O' Clock 1.59
Dill pickles, qt.	B&G 2.19	A&P 1.59
Microwave popcorn, 10 ½ oz.	Orville Redenbacher's 2.29	A&P .... .99
Soda, 6-pack	Coca-Cola Classic 2.79	A&P Cola 1.64
Honey-roasted peanuts, 12 oz.	Planters 3.79	A&P 2.39
Solid white tuna fish, 6⅛ oz.	Bumble Bee 1.59	A&P 1.19
Baked beans, 1 lb.	B&M 1.39	A&P .... .39
Cling peach halves, 1 lb.	Del Monte 1.19	A&P .... .83
Bleach, 1 gal.	Clorox 1.49	A&P 1.09
Cat litter, 10 lb.	Tidy Cat 2.45	A&P 1.87
Dog food, 5 lb.	Purina Dog Chow 3.69	A&P Munchy Meal 1.29
Aluminum foil, 200 ft.	Reynolds Wrap 4.39	A&P 3.69
Tissues, 250 count	Kleenex 1.59	A&P 1.29
Paper towels, 90 sheets	Brawny 1.39	A&P .... .50
Extra-strength acetaminophen, 100	Tylenol 6.37	A&P 3.59
Ice cream, ½ gal.	Breyers 3.99	Ann Page 2.39
Frozen flounder fillets, 1 lb.	Van de Kamp's 9.00	A&P 4.19
Boiled ham, 1 lb.	DAK 5.69	A&P 3.99
Bacon, 1 lb.	Oscar Mayer 3.49	A&P 2.09
Creamy peanut butter, 28 oz.	Skippy 3.29	A&P 2.89
Pancake syrup, 24 oz.	Log Cabin 2.89	A&P 1.49
American cheese, 1 lb.	Kraft Singles 3.99	A&P Ched-O-Bit 2.99

Product, size	Name brand	Store brand
Thin spaghetti, 1 lb.	Creamette ..... .89	A&P .... .53
Toasted oat cereal, 15 oz.	Cheerios 2.99	A&P 1.49
White rice, 5 lb.	Uncle Ben's ... 3.99	A&P 1.59
Butter, 1 lb.	Land O Lakes 2.39	A&P 1.69
Dishwashing liquid, 22 oz.	Palmolive 1.89	A&P 1.39
Baby shampoo, 20 oz.	Johnson & Johnson 3.29	A&P 2.79
Canned green beans, 1 lb.	Del Monte ..... .95	A&P .... .75
Vegetable oil, qt.	Crisco 2.19	A&P 1.69
Vanilla extract, 2 oz.	McCormick ... 4.09	A&P 2.27
Cream cheese, 8 oz.	Kraft Philadelphia 1.39	A&P .... .99
Frozen lemonade concentrate, 12 oz.	Minute Maid 1.29	A&P .... .79
Total	**$114.36**	**$67.76**

stores deny it. But there's no denying that the high cost of the real estate can squeeze out smaller manufacturers.

In a typical store, high-traffic areas like the dairy and meat sections, end-aisle displays, and checkout stands are prime property. The top or bottom run of shelving along an interior aisle, where canned fruit resides, is less desirable. Products whose purchase is generally driven by necessity are often banished to such positions. Retailers know you'll reach or bend to pick up what you need.

Some stores use checkout scanning data to keep track of which products are in greatest demand. They constantly refine their product mix—to add more high-profit perishables, or to eliminate lackluster performers. The scanning data also help stores devise more effective promotions by tracking sales. Do shoppers buy more potato chips, for instance, when dip goes on sale?

Product tie-ins stimulate sales, too: Set up a theme display of everything the shopper will need for a cookout. Price the hamburgers and hot dogs low, then make up the difference with the barbecue sauce and charcoal and paper plates. Or sell fresh-baked French bread at cost, but make sure there's a nearby display of wine and Brie.

But today a shopper rebellion is under way in America's supermarkets. Highly advertised, high-priced national brand names have fallen on hard times as value-conscious shoppers look past advertising and fancy labels to stock up on store brands.

Battle of the Brands

As consumers search for bargains in a sluggish economy, sales of store-brand goods have risen steadily. Discount brands developed by supermarket chains now account for 18 percent of all grocery purchases. In 1976, 76 percent of all supermarket shoppers considered themselves brand-loyal. Today, only 23 percent of shoppers do. More sophisticated than ever before, and constrained by a tougher economic climate, consumers have begun to ignore big-brand advertising and to shop for commodities by price.

As the image of the national brands has slipped, the supermarket industry has begun to pay increasing attention to the quality and image of store brands. Gone are the plainly labeled generics, creatures of the double-digit inflation of the late seventies. Today's store brands enjoy prominent shelf placement, more promotion, and most important, generally higher manufacturing standards.

The big brands are feeling the pressure. Procter & Gamble, for example, is girding itself for a price war against the cheaper store goods. It says it will soon cut the prices of some of its detergent products by as much as 15 percent. Industry analysts expect that big-brand competitors like Unilever and Colgate-Palmolive will soon follow. The irony is that quite a few store brands are supplied by the big-name makers—Borden, Bausch & Lomb, Chock Full o'Nuts, Dole, Jergens, H. J. Heinz, Ralston-Purina, and Campbell.

When you buy a big-brand cereal, you pay for a lot more than you can eat—the enormous advertising and marketing costs that made the brand a household word. When you buy a store brand, you save because the chain hasn't spent much on advertising and marketing the product, or on intermediate handlers. For the retailer, however, store brands can bring higher profits than brand names—50 percent or more on pricey items such as breakfast cereals. Store brands also build customer loyalty.

Some 64 percent of *Consumer Reports* readers who responded to a questionnaire in 1992 said they believe supermarket brands are about as good in quality as national brands. Half of these readers routinely purchased their supermarket's own dairy products; 4 in 10 bought store-brand canned or frozen vegetables; and 1 in 4 relied on their store's paper goods, trash bags, and bread.

Whenever *Consumer Reports* tests supermarket products, from foods to paper goods to soaps and personal-care items, store brands are included. Often, those store brands have done as well as the big-name brands (see box pages 9–11). And consistently buying store brands can save money at the checkout counter.

Buyer Beware: Supermarket Pricing Practices

Manufacturers, processors, and supermarket retailers increasingly use on-sale or "special" pricing as a method to introduce new products and to stimulate the sales of existing products and brands. Although many of the special pricing methods are legitimate and can save you money, there are some that call for caution.

For example, some stores post a false regular retail price and then mark the item down to give the impression of a bargain. Always compare, if possible, the sale price with the price of the same item of a different brand. Other stores sometimes mark down an item that is supposed to be of equal quality or packaging with competitive products but, in reality, is not. "Family pack chicken parts," for one, actually may contain a few extra wings and legs. A cut of meat on special may not be as closely trimmed as the regularly priced cut. Also look out for mislabeling—a practice often used with packaged meats, fish, and poultry. For example, a package of bone-in chicken breasts may not note on the label that the backbone is included, or a fish fillet may be labeled with the name and price of a more expensive variety.

A common practice in pricing is the *loss leader*. A chain will deliberately price an item below cost to build traffic in the stores. Thanksgiving turkey sales are an excellent example, since many turkeys are sold far below cost to the supermarket. However, many related items such as cranberry sauce, stuffing, and fresh vegetables may have temporarily been increased in price to make up the difference.

The increased use of electronic price scanners at checkout stations has created another opportunity for price gouging, particularly in those stores in which individual items are no longer priced on the shelves. Studies have shown that the rate of error—instances where the price charged at the checkout counter is not the same as the price marked (usually on the shelf below the item)—is higher in stores with scanners than in those that still shelf-price individual items.

CAN YOU TRUST THE SCANNER?

Automated checkout systems, with their electronic bar-code scanners, have been hailed as labor-saving wonders that shorten lines and speed service.

Recent highly publicized reports, however, contend that the systems err more often than most shoppers realize—and that mistakes are usually in the store's favor. According to *Information Week*, a trade publication for computer systems managers, scanner overcharges that typically amount to just a few cents per transaction cost consumers an estimated $2.5 billion a year.

Consumer Reports magazine did its own informal check, sending out a small panel of shoppers to various supermarkets around the country to buy their weekly order and check for scanner mistakes. Most found no errors. A few found nickel-and-dime mistakes, sometimes for the shopper, sometimes against. One reported a $2.29 container of Parmesan cheese scanned in at $2.99—along with three other smaller mistakes in his favor. Another didn't get the new sale price on a jar of peanut butter, paying $2.39 instead of $1.66.

How do mistakes happen? Many chains, especially larger ones, have a central data base that electronically sends anywhere from several hundred to several thousand weekly price changes to each store. But store employees may not update supermarket shelf tags or the computer listings correctly or quickly enough to avoid errors.

Scanners engendered widespread suspicion when they appeared in the mid-1970s, mainly because it seemed stores would stop marking prices on individual items. That's happened, alas: Only a handful of states and municipalities still have item-pricing statutes on the books. Instead of marking items, many stores use shelf tags placed below the product. The labels tend to be small and hard to read. Sometimes they're in the wrong place—or missing entirely.

To avoid paying for scanner mistakes, do what the *Consumer Reports* panel did: Note prices carefully as you fill your cart. If the items are not individually marked, write the prices down, perhaps right on your shopping list. Then check the scanner as it rings up the prices, or check the groceries against the register tape as you unload your bags at home. Many stores will give you the item at no charge or otherwise reward you if you can prove that the scanner has given an incorrect price.

OTHER EFFECTS ON PRICING

Several other factors must be taken into consideration when planning menus and making a shopping list. These conditions can double or triple the price of food items almost overnight.

▪ *Seasons.* Fresh fruit and vegetable prices fluctuate according to the season, particularly in areas where certain varieties are locally grown. Even fruits and vegetables shipped across the country are low in price when the growing season is at its peak. Meats and poultry are also subject to seasonal price variations, not because of the growing season but because of fluctuating demand. Steaks such as porterhouse, T-bone, and top sirloin are more expensive during the summer months because of an increase in backyard barbecuing, for example. Around the Christmas holidays, steak and prime rib prices go up because more people choose these more expensive cuts in restaurants and for parties. In some areas, briskets cost more in February because meat packers are corning briskets for St. Patrick's Day. Knowing these trends can help you avoid items that are more costly because of seasonal demand.

- *Unusual conditions.* Food items can be priced artificially high because of freak weather conditions. A snowstorm in the Midwest will have an immediate impact upon the level of meat prices. Heavy rains or a drought in California will affect fruit and vegetable prices, and killing frosts in Florida will boost citrus prices. International events can also influence prices—crop failures in foreign countries will increase U.S. exports and prices, and large harvests will force prices down. Strikes by truckers or agricultural workers will raise price levels of certain foods. In short, any event that affects the chain of food production and distribution will impact on price levels. In most cases, you can substitute one food item for another to avoid paying more.

- *High price, low quality.* A reverse relationship usually exists between price and quality in the fresh fruit and vegetable market. When crops are good and supplies abundant, the price is lower and the quality excellent. If, however, much of the crop is damaged or lost because of weather conditions, the price will go sky-high even when the remaining crop that is shipped is in poor condition. In this situation, prices for other varieties of the same fruit or vegetable will also increase because of demand. For example, if the iceberg lettuce crop is hit by adverse weather conditions, not only will the iceberg variety increase in price but so will the romaine, Boston, Bibb, and red-leaf varieties. Often, however, the other varieties come from another growing area and therefore may be of much better quality.

Smart Shopping Strategies

Now that you know and understand how supermarkets are organized to make you buy, you have some of the necessary tools to become a shopper and not a spender. The following buying strategies will further reinforce better shopping habits:

BE OBJECTIVE

Evaluate a product logically on its own merits. Advertising and marketing ploys will try to convince you that a particular product has superior value and is the best buy. The truth is, most of us develop biases about various brands and products: The constant repetition of a brand name eventually sets up a preconceived notion in our minds about its relative quality. To compete for available shelf space, advertisers may claim the product is "new" or "improved," or they reach out to new customers by redesigning the package. The cost of such promotions, of course, is built into the price—and you pay for it.

Generic or store-brand products don't carry that overhead because they are not nationally advertised (see page 9). But are they of similar quality? In an informal test, cans and packages of like products, with the labels removed, were judged on the basis of color, texture, size, and taste. The results indicated that only one fact was consistent—and that was the absence of consistency. At times, the generic or store brands were equal to, or superior to, the brand-name product; at other times, this was not the case. Obviously, it pays to adopt the attitude that no product is better than another unless you have seen and tasted the difference. *Buy the product because it is the right one for your purpose and pocketbook,* not because of the color of the package, the appeal of a commercial, or the blandishments of a salesperson.

GUARD AGAINST IMPULSE BUYING

Studies have shown that almost two-thirds of purchases made in a supermarket are not planned. Many are the result of impulse buying. As noted previously, anything a store does to make you notice a product is likely to increase its sales. Just moving an item from the lowest shelf to an eye-level position increases sales as much as 50 percent.

STORE LAYOUT

Supermarkets plan their product layout not to speed you on your way but to stop you in your tracks, both with offers you can't refuse and with physical impediments. Here's how the typical supermarket is laid out, and why.

- Just inside the door, a wall of "bargains" on seasonal fare, like cookout supplies in summer, is meant to slow you down.
- The produce department is usually close to the entrance, since fruits and vegetables are often impulse buys and an attractive display showcases a store's image.
- Related products are displayed together, partly for your convenience and partly to stimulate impulse buying. You're more likely to buy salad dressing if it's located next to the lettuce and tomatoes.
- A floral display also attracts impulse buyers.
- Island-shaped refrigerated cases not only let shoppers buy from all sides, they slow traffic.
- You probably buy milk every trip. That's why dairy products are likely to be inconveniently located at the rear of the store. No sense letting customers rush in and out for a quart of milk.
- Products on sale go on special display at the end of the aisle. You know that. And the store knows you know. So the "endcaps" are also used for products not on sale.
- The bakery serves best near the front of the store, so the enticing aroma hits you as you walk in, before you've had a chance to steel yourself against the fresh French bread.
- For one last shot, high-margin items like batteries, gum, candy, and magazines get in the way at the checkout counter.

THINK ONLY OF COST PER POUND

The efficient shopper always thinks in terms of yield when buying food products. The term *yield* refers to the amount of edible food that is left *after* you have accounted for losses from bone, trim, fat, peel, water, other packing mediums, and cooking. The yield of a product is always expressed in percentages. For example, a cut of meat weighs a pound. But it will lose 4 ounces of bone and trim and another 4 ounces during cooking, so it has a yield of 50%—only 8 ounces will be left to serve. An armbone chuck roast weighing 2 pounds 13 ounces will contain 7 ounces of bone, 3½ ounces of fat and sinew, and will lose 14 ounces during cooking. If the roast originally cost $1.89 a pound, it will cost you $4.15 a pound when served. A 16-ounce can of green beans costs 69 cents, but because the can contains only 10 to 11 ounces of beans (the remainder is water), the actual cost of the beans, once on your plate, is approximately $1 per pound.

When you compare the actual cost of cooked and served food, it is easier to compute the cost per pound than the cost per serving. Serving sizes vary considerably according to a person's age and appetite, the type of meal, and the way the food is used.

It's important to know and understand yields when comparing food prices, because almost every type of food costs more on the plate than it did when purchased. The opportunity to save money by knowing yield percentages is based on the fact that the percentages can vary considerably. It is not unusual to see a product that yields 95 percent priced the same or only slightly above a product that can be used for the same purpose but yields only 40 percent. This is particularly true of meats, poultry, seafood, and fresh produce.

KNOW YOUR NEEDS

Most foods are available in several different forms and, in most cases, each style is priced differently. For example, pineapple can be purchased fresh or canned as slices, chunks, tidbits, or crushed. Tomatoes can be bought fresh or canned as whole, sliced, crushed, or pureed. Why pay more for whole tomatoes if you are going to puree them? In another example, buying a USDA Choice top round for pot roast is simply throwing money away. A bottom round or rump makes an excellent pot roast and costs 30 to 40 cents less per pound.

Buying the correct quantity is also important. If you are like

BETTER FOOD LABELS—AT LAST

It took an act of Congress, years of research, and some last-minute government wrangling, but now new nutrition labels for all processed foods must appear on the products on supermarket shelves by May 1994.

The U.S. Food and Drug Administration (FDA), which developed the labeling rules, successfully resisted industry pressure and held to its plan to present nutrition information as percentages of "daily values." That will help people compare different foods to see how they fit into an overall diet.

The final label format has several refinements over earlier drafts. Most significantly, the label lists daily values for a 2,000-calorie diet. (Earlier versions had used a 2,350-calorie diet.) The label also lists nutrient limits for a 2,500-calorie diet, useful mainly for larger men but helpful to other consumers who want to extrapolate nutrition information for other caloric intakes.

The 2,500-calorie diet was a concession to the U.S. Department of Agriculture (USDA), which feared that people would shun meats seemingly too high in fat in a 2,000-calorie diet. But the USDA also made a major concession by agreeing to use the FDA's label format for processed foods under its jurisdiction. That's a boon for consumers, who might have faced two different labels in the stores—one for meat lasagna (USDA) and another for cheese lasagna (FDA), for example.

The FDA's daily values for fat—no more than 65 grams in a 2,000-calorie diet—equal approximately 30 percent of calories from fat. (Many experts, however, feel that a limit of 20 to 25 percent would be healthier.)

The FDA's regulations also standardize meanings for claims: A food that derives more than half its calories from fat, for example, can't be called "light" unless it has at least 50 percent less fat than the product with which it's compared. Foods labeled "fresh" cannot have been frozen, processed, heated, or chemically preserved.

Finally, the new rules limit the labels' health claims to only a few, well-substantiated facts, such as the link between fiber and prevention of some types of cancer.

The following is a sample label format for processed macaroni and cheese:

Nutrition Facts

Serving Size ½ cup (114 g)
Servings per Container 4

Amount per Serving

Calories 260   Calories from Fat 120

*% Daily Value**

Total Fat 13 g	**20%**
Saturated Fat 5 g	**25%**
Cholesterol 30 mg	**10%**
Sodium 660 mg	**28%**
Total Carbohydrate 31 g	**11%**
Dietary Fiber 0 g	**0%**
Sugars 5 g	—
Protein 5 g	—
Vitamin A 4% •	**Vitamin C 2%**
Calcium 15% •	**Iron 4%**

*Percent daily values are based on a 2,000-calorie diet. Your daily values may be higher or lower depending on your caloric needs.

	Calories: 2,000	*2,500*
Total Fat	Less than 65 g	80 g
Saturated Fat	Less than 20 g	25 g
Cholesterol	Less than 300 mg	300 mg
Sodium	Less than 2,400 mg	2,400 mg
Total Carbohydrate	300 g	375 g
Fiber	25 g	30 g

Calories per gram:

Fat 9   •   Carbohydrates 4   •   Protein 4

QUICK TIPS FOR BETTER BUYING

- Clip coupons only for products you would buy anyway.
- Carry a list, and stick to it. If you have an impulse to buy something that's not on the list, write it down for next week's list (unless it's on sale).
- Check prices, and comparison shop carefully.
- Stock up on high-priced items like cereal and aluminum foil when they're on sale. Retailers do the same thing when manufacturers offer them limited-time discounts on certain brands. They call the practice "forward buying."
- Check the unit prices of products and buy some in larger sizes or in quantity from a warehouse club, if that means a lower price per unit. The savings can be substantial. Because of pressure from the clubs, many conventional supermarkets have special sections that offer big "club packs."
- Cherry-pick "hot specials" on items you stock regularly. Many chains heavily discount one or another popular item (like orange juice or mayonnaise) each week.
- Buying some foods in bulk is not wise if the products have a short shelf life. Cereals can go stale and mayonnaise can turn rancid, for example, unless they are used up within a certain period of time (check expiration dates on jars and packages).
- Consider joining a preferred-shopper club. It entitles you to bonus discounts and to coupons for items that you might buy anyway. Note, however, that the application typically requires you to give the store some personal information—your age, marital status, number of kids and pets, and income level— that the chain can use for its own marketing purposes.
- Finally, shop for store brands whenever you have no decided brand preference.

most people, a third of your refrigerator space is filled with left-overs. Most of these bits and pieces will be either thrown away or "downgraded." *Downgrading* is a food industry term that means you are using a food item for a purpose that would or-dinarily require a less expensive product. One example: using leftover roast beef ($2.89 a pound) for stew beef ($1.89 a pound). On the other hand, don't waste food. Leftovers can be incorporated into casseroles and other dishes. Most meats, canned goods, and frozen foods come in a variety of sizes. Purchase whatever you need in a size appropriate for a single meal or multiples of a single meal. If you have purchased an item that is larger, separate or cut the item into the correct size before cooking. A cut of top round for roast beef may be larger than necessary for one meal, so cut some steaks off the face of the roast and freeze them for later use.

TAKE ADVANTAGE OF THE DISCOUNTS

Many people plan their menus first and make a shopping list from their menus. But weekly specials, bonus club discounts, and coupons are now a major weapon in the battle among the giant supermarkets. Therefore, shopping the specials and using discounts wisely can often save you a substantial sum.

Develop a routine of planning your weekly menus and preparing your shopping list around the combination of advertised specials (making sure they really *are* specials), store discounts, and coupons. You'll be amazed at how fast the savings add up.

Rating the Supermarkets

Consumer Reports readers were asked to rate their primary supermarket for the period between April 1991 and March 1992. More than 10,000 readers described their shopping habits and rated their satisfaction with their supermarket's cleanliness, competitive prices, employee courtesy, and checkout speed, among other things.

- Image counted when it came to why readers chose certain stores. Although only one of three readers cited price as a key consideration in choosing a store, two-thirds of those who shopped at Food Lion, ShopRite, Lucky, Meijer, and Pathmark considered price critical. Those chains cultivate a low-price image. Harris-Teeter, which showcases fresh

foods, drew shoppers largely on the strength of its produce. And Publix, whose motto is "where shopping is a
pleasure," was twice as likely as any other chain to draw
customers for its helpful, courteous service.

- Many of the low-rated chains—Finast (now called Edwards), Acme, Pathmark, Grand Union, and A&P—are in
the East. Was that because the East is more urbanized and
it's tougher to operate in large cities? No: Stores in large
cities in other parts of the country fared well, overall.
What's more, most eastern stores used by *Consumer Reports*
readers are located in suburbs, not within a city's bound-
aries. Further, chains with stores in the East and another
region didn't do consistently better outside the East.

A little more than half of the *Consumer Reports* readers were
highly satisfied with their supermarket. According to the survey,
Publix did the best job of pleasing its customers—three out of
four shoppers were highly satisfied with the Florida-based chain.
At the bottom of the Ratings were Grand Union and A&P, with
only one in three shoppers saying they were highly satisfied.

SERVING THE INNER CITY

Among the rated stores in the *Consumer Reports* survey, Pathmark,
Lucky, and Vons have been especially active in moving into the
inner cities. Poor urban neighborhoods have long been under-
served, with far fewer supermarkets than middle-class urban
areas. The poor have also been paying anywhere from 5 to 25
percent more for their groceries, according to various studies. Until recently, their neighborhood choices have been limited to
overpriced convenience stores or small supermarkets with poor-
quality produce, little product variety, few sale items, and fewer
services. In recent years, Pathmark and Lucky have been working
with community groups and developers to build more full-size
inner-city stores, noting that the effort makes good business sense.
Some other rated stores, including Jewel, Safeway, and Giant, also
have large stores in inner cities.

RATINGS Supermarkets

As published in the *September 1993* issue of Consumer Reports

WHO'S GOOD, WHO'S NOT

Attribute	Satisfied Most	Satisfied least
Clean store	Publix Harris-Teeter	Pathmark
Courteous staff	Publix	Pathmark
Competitive prices	Meijer	Giant Food Grand Union
Fast checkout	Publix	A&P
Produce quality	Publix Smith's Meijer Harris-Teeter	Food Lion Pathmark A&P
Specials in stock	Publix Giant Food Food Lion	Acme Pathmark ShopRite
Good price labeling	Giant Food	Pathmark

WHAT'S GOOD, WHAT'S NOT

Attribute	Readers highly satisfied
Clean supermarket	67 percent
Product variety	54
Quality of meat/poultry	53
Special departments	52
Quality of produce	52
Courteous employees	51
Competitive prices	43
Fast checkout	32

PROFILES OF TWO TOP PERFORMERS

Publix

Founded: 1930.

Headquarters: Lakeland, Fla.

Stores: 407 supermarkets, mostly in Florida. A few in South Carolina. Expanding into Georgia.

Chief competitors: Winn-Dixie and Kroger.

1992 sales: $6.7-billion; 8th largest chain in U.S. and largest employee-owned chain.

New stores: 40,000 to 65,000 square feet.

Special departments: Full-service bakery, pharmacy, seafood, florals, one-hour photo processing, deli-café.

Motto: Where shopping is a pleasure.

Claims to fame: Company built reputation on service, and service is a key reason people keep coming back, our readers say. Chain stood well above pack for helpful and courteous employees.

Smith's Food & Drug Centers

Founded: 1948.

Headquarters: Salt Lake City.

Stores: 123 combination food and drug stores in Arizona, California, Idaho, Nevada, New Mexico, Texas, Utah, and Wyoming. Expanding into Southern California.

Chief competitors: Albertson's, Furrs, Lucky, Vons, Food 4 Less.

Sales: $2.7 billion; 28th largest chain in U.S.

New stores: 70,000 to 75,000 square feet.

Special departments: "Big-deals" warehouse section, photo lab, video rental, pharmacy, hot foods to go, bakery, fresh seafood, full-service bank, cosmetics boutique, box office for local events.

Motto: A better way to run a supermarket.

Claims to fame: Family-owned chain has tripled in size in decade. Committed to one-stop-shopping concept and everyday-low-price program. Prides itself on clean supermarkets. Our readers agree.

Listed in order of readers' overall satisfaction

Better ○ ◐ ● Worse

Chain, main location	Satisfaction score	Clean	Prices	Courtesy	Checkout	Readers rate other attributes — Above Average	Below Average
Publix South	~80	◑	○	●	●	Produce, variety, special departments, clear aisles & price labeling, advertised specials in stock.	—
Smith's Food & Drug West	~78	◐	◐	●	◐	Produce, variety, special departments, clear aisles, advertised specials in stock.	—
Harris-Teeter South		◑	○	◐	○	Produce, meats & poultry, special departments, clear aisles & price labeling, advertised specials in stock.	—
Meijer Midwest		○	◑	○	○	Produce.	Clear aisles, advertised specials in stock.
Ralphs West		○	●	○	○	Advertised specials in stock.	—
Giant Food South		◐	◐	◐	◐	Variety, special departments, clear aisles & price labeling, advertised specials in stock.	—
Albertson's South, West		○	○	◐	◐	Clear aisles & price labeling, advertised specials in stock.	—
Giant Eagle Northeast, Midwest		○	◐	○	○	—	—
Dominick's Midwest		○	○	○	○	—	—
Shaw's Northeast		◐	○	○	○	—	—
Stop & Shop Northeast		○	○	○	○	Clear aisles.	—
Vons West		○	○	○	○	—	Clear aisles.

Readers rate main attributes: Clean, Prices, Courtesy, Checkout

			Satisfaction			Better/Worse than average	
Kroger South, Midwest		↟	○	○	○	—	—
ShopRite Northeast		↟	◐	◐	●	—	Clear aisles & price labeling, advertised specials in stock.
Lucky West		↟	○	○	○	Advertised specials in stock.	—
Jewel Midwest		↟	○	○	○	—	—
Food Lion South		↟	◑	○	○	Advertised specials in stock.	Produce, variety, meat & poultry, special departments.
Finast East, Midwest		↟	◑	○	○	—	Advertised specials in stock.
Acme Northeast		↟	○	◐	○	—	Variety, clear aisles, advertised specials in stock.
Safeway South, West		↟	○	○	○	—	—
Winn-Dixie South		↟	◐	○	○	Advertised specials in stock.	—
Pathmark Northeast		↟	◐	●	○	—	Produce, meats, & poultry clear aisles and price labeling, advertised specials in stock.
Grand Union Northeast		↟	●	○	◐	—	Variety, special departments, clear price labeling, advertised specials in stock.
A&P Northeast, South		↟	◐	◑	●		Produce, variety, special departments, clear price labeling, specials in stock.

Notes on the table: Ratings are based on 10,000 reader responses to CU's 1992 Annual Questionnaire. Each chain was evaluated by at least 200 readers; some chains, such as Kroger and Safeway, were evaluated by more than 1,500 respondents. Chains include only stores that bear corporate name. For example, we rated Kroger stores but not King Soopers, a Kroger Co. division. Results reflect the experience of our readers, not necessarily that of all supermarket shoppers.

The overall **satisfaction score** summarizes readers' average satisfaction with store quality, using the following scale: 100 = completely satisfied, 80 = very satisfied, 60 = fairly well satisfied, 40 = somewhat dissatisfied, 20 = very dissatisfied, 0 = completely dissatisfied. Differences of less than four points are not meaningful.

In the next columns are reader judgments on major attributes. The judgments are relative—even the lowest-rated store satisfied most customers.

The last pair of columns note whether stores were above or below average in other areas, such as the number of advertised specials in stock, the openness of aisles, or the quality of produce.

Other highlights of the findings:

- *Consumer Reports* readers most often chose a supermarket for its closeness to home, although product and brand variety and low prices were also important considerations.
- Fast checkout and courteous staff were also important, but cleanliness was the most predictive of readers' overall satisfaction with their supermarkets.
- Readers were especially aggravated by congested aisles and damaged goods on shelves.
- Women readers were generally more careful shoppers than men—more likely to check ads and flyers, compare nutrition labels, and check expiration dates. Shoppers older than 55 also tended to shop more carefully.

2

The Poultry Counter

Over the last few decades, the growth in popularity of poultry as a staple food has been spectacular: Per capita consumption has increased almost 300 percent. As consumers continue to be health and diet-conscious, sales of poultry products will almost certainly continue to rise.

Unlike beef, pork, and lamb, most poultry accumulates fat on the underlying surface of the skin instead of between the muscles and fibers. If the skin is removed before cooking or serving, poultry becomes a dieter's dream—a tender, flavorful meat with fewer calories than red meat.

Chickens, turkeys, geese, capons, rock cornish game hens, and ducks are all included under the term *poultry*, and are usually available all year long. Modern distribution and storage techniques have eliminated any seasonal fluctuations in supply and have stabilized the pricing of most poultry products.

Chicken is usually classified by both age and quality. Younger chickens are marketed as broiler-fryer, roaster, or capon, whereas older birds are sold as hen, fowl, or stewing chicken. Quality grades are U.S. Grade A, B, or C. Turkeys, geese, and ducks are also marketed by age and quality, using the same general criteria as chickens.

Poultry is also available both whole and cut up into parts, or sold precooked for the busy homemaker. You should be aware, however, of the extra cost and the possible differences in quality when deciding between fresh and chilled poultry and the various frozen convenience products.

STORING AND PREPARING POULTRY

Today's factory-bred poultry is particularly prone to contamination from salmonella, a group of bacteria that can cause food poisoning. The following precautions should be taken when handling or preparing fresh poultry:

- All poultry should be refrigerated or frozen as soon as possible after purchase. Do not let poultry sit in a warm car for two or three hours while you shop. If you are going to be out for the afternoon, buy your poultry just before returning home, or use an insulated cooler packed with ice to store your poultry and frozen foods until you can refrigerate or freeze them.
- Store fresh poultry for only a day or two after purchase in the coldest part of your refrigerator.
- Refrigerate or freeze leftover poultry immediately after the meal.
- Always clean the cutting board (preferably made of wood— see page 169) and the counter with hot water and detergent after cutting or preparing fresh poultry. This step will avoid cross-contamination of other foods. Any utensils and dishes used in preparing fresh poultry should also be thoroughly washed with detergent and hot water.
- If you plan to refrigerate chicken stock, do not remove the melted fat floating on top. The fat will solidify and act as a sealer, thus prolonging the safe storage time. Remove the solidified fat just before reheating.
- If you stuff a chicken or turkey, put the stuffing inside the bird just *before* you cook it. Do not pack it in too tightly; stuffing expands as it cooks. After the meal, remove the leftover stuffing from the bird and refrigerate. Reheat it thoroughly before eating. You might take a tip from the experts (James Beard among them) and cook the stuffing separately in a baking dish. You'll find stuffing tastes even better that way— it's crispier, less soggy, and easier to serve.

Chicken

Chicken is the most popular variety of poultry found in the supermarket. Although available in many forms, fresh whole chicken or chicken parts constitute the bulk of retail sales. The delicate flavor of chicken blends well in casseroles and skillet meals yet makes a satisfying main dish. Chicken also provides more flexibility in menu planning than does any other meat, because it can be prepared in a variety of ways.

GRADING CHICKEN

All poultry is inspected by federal or state agencies, according to USDA standards. As with beef, "inspected" poultry refers only to the health of the bird and the conditions under which it is processed, not to its comparative quality. The grading of chickens is based on the following standards:

Grade A. The bird is free of any major deformities and has a well-developed covering of flesh, particularly in the breast area. The breast has a well-rounded appearance, and the flesh carries along the entire length of the breastbone. There is a well-developed layer of fat under the skin, particularly behind the thighs. No flesh is exposed on the breast or the legs, and any other cuts or tears or areas of missing skin are minor. There are no broken bones, nor is there any major discoloration of the skin or flesh.

Grade B. These chickens may have slightly crooked breasts or legs. These deformities do not affect the distribution of flesh, however, and the chicken will still meet Grade B standards as long as there is a moderate distribution of flesh over the breastbone. There should be enough fat in and under the skin to prevent the flesh from showing through, especially on the legs and breasts. The chicken should be free of serious or major discolorations of the skin and flesh, and it should have only a moderate amount of tears, cuts, or exposed flesh. Parts may be disjointed but have no broken bones.

Grade C. Most of the chickens that are Grade C are actually Grade A or B birds that have substantial tears and cuts or are missing parts. From a nutritional viewpoint, these chickens are perfectly acceptable.

Most chickens found in supermarkets are Grade A. Often, however, some markets will sell Grade B chickens as "specials," and the comparative value can be determined only by comparing one grade against the other. Usually the Grade B variety has less meat weight to bone weight than does the Grade A, so a saving of 10 cents a pound is not worth the loss in yield. On the other hand, a difference of 30 cents a pound is worth the loss in weight.

PRICING CHICKEN PARTS

Fresh chilled or thawed chicken is available whole or precut, and in specific cuts: legs, thighs, wings, breast (bone in or boneless), and breast with backbone. The price per pound varies considerably from store to store and from region to region. Some chicken parts are more popular in one part of the country than another. Again, consumer demand sets the prices.

PRICING FORMULAS FOR FRESH CHICKEN

Bones, fat, and giblets make up about 50 to 60 percent of the weight of a whole chicken. To arrive at the actual cost of the uncooked meat, double the retail selling price per pound. To arrive at the actual cost of the meat when cut up into parts, use the following formulas:

Legs—multiply cost by 2.
Thighs—multiply cost by 1.7.
Legs and thighs—multiply cost by 1.8.
Breasts, bone in—multiply cost by 1.53.

Other pricing tips:

- "Family packs," often promoted by supermarkets as an economical way of buying chicken, can be misleading.

Often the package contains extra wings or legs for the same price, or more, as a whole chicken.

- Breasts are often sold in supermarkets as "breasts with backbone." The backbone adds 2 to 3 ounces of bone weight with no additional meat, and therefore is seldom a good buy.
- If you want four breasts and four legs and thighs, it is considerably more economical to buy two whole 2½ pound chickens and separate the parts yourself (it's easy). You will save approximately 20 percent.
- The cost of chicken parts fluctuates more than any other meat, so shop carefully. For example, in an informal test, the following packages of chicken were found in the same supermarket:

Breasts, bone in—$1.39 per pound
Breasts with rib meat—$1.59 per pound
Chicken fryer breasts—$1.19 per pound

Upon examination, the parts were the same cut from birds in the same weight category. They were then boned and found to yield the same amount of meat. Therefore, the best advice is to check the chicken cases carefully, because you'll find good buys.

- Generally, chickens weighing from 2½ to 4½ pounds will have the same bone-to-meat ratio, because the chicken is still growing during that period. Chickens under 2½ pounds tend to be sparsely fleshed and therefore have a higher bone-to-meat ratio.
- The appearance of the breast is the best clue to choosing a meaty bird within the same weight range. Broiler-fryers weigh between 2 and 3½ pounds, roasters weigh between 3½ and 4½ pounds, and stewing hens weigh between 4½ and 6 pounds. Grade A birds in any of these categories should have plump, fleshy breasts extending over the entire breastbone. To check out a bird, feel just in back of the peak of the breastbone and compare the thickness of the flesh.

- Some whole chickens are sold split in half, without the giblets and the neck. Since the average weight of the giblets and the neck is 5 to 6 ounces, it's worth it to pay 10 to 15 cents more a pound for the split halves. You still pay the same dollar amount as you would for the whole chicken with giblets.

- Range-growth birds, better known as free-range chickens, usually take 12 weeks to reach the normal market weight of 3½ pounds, whereas the commercially grown bird reaches that weight in seven to eight weeks. A range-grown chicken usually has a bigger skeleton, and the flesh is distributed differently; consequently, the ratio of meat to bone will be less.

THE COST OF CONVENIENCE: PRECOOKED CHICKEN

In supermarkets today, more and more freezer space is devoted to frozen chicken in all its many forms. Chicken is batter-dipped, breaded, and fried. It also comes prebaked or prefried as legs, legs and thighs, thighs, assorted pieces, breasts, cubes, nuggets, and sticks. In most cases, all you have to do is heat up the chicken in a conventional or microwave oven and it's ready for the table. Of course, the taste and texture of the product differs widely, as does the price. Many times there is no correlation between price and quality. An informal survey of a wide range of frozen and precooked chicken found differences of as much as 90 cents a pound between products of the same size, type, and pack—but with no significant differences in quality.

Admittedly, the convenience of frozen precooked chicken parts makes them attractive to working people. Time is money, and the added cost of convenience may be a necessity for some. Few shoppers realize, however, just how much they pay for convenience.

Some frozen precooked convenience items were purchased for comparison purposes. In order to compare equal products, the breading or coating was removed from the frozen precooked pieces. (The breading constituted 20 to 25 percent of the total weight.) The fresh chicken parts were then cooked, and a cost-per-pound comparison was made with the frozen items.

TABLE 2.1
Price Comparisons: Precooked vs. Fresh

Size	Item	*Frozen, Precooked Chicken* Cost	Cost, Unbreaded	*Fresh, Chilled Chicken* Cost, Uncooked	Cost, Cooked
32 oz.	Legs and thighs	$1.76/lb.	$2.35/lb.	$.76/lb.	$.91/lb.
32 oz.	Assorted pieces	$1.92/lb.	$2.56/lb.	$.89/lb.	$1.02/lb.
12 oz.	Boneless/skinless breast fillets	$4.96/lb.	$6.61/lb.	$3.69/lb.	$4.34/lb.

In the first two samples, the cost of the chicken pieces—including the bone, skin, and meat—are being compared, not the meat alone. As a general rule, then, the convenience of having chicken prepared and precooked will cost you between $1.50 and $2.00 per pound.

Boneless cooked chicken is also available in cans. At 90 cents for a 5-ounce can (½ ounce broth, 4½ ounces of mixed chicken meat), the actual cost is $3.20 per pound. Although the cost seems to be about a dollar a pound more than the frozen (see previous table), remember that the canned meat is boneless. Of course, the taste and quality of the canned chicken may be disappointing.

STEWING CHICKENS

Hens and fowls are generally more than 10 months old and usually weigh between 3 and 6 pounds. (Many hens are produced for the egg industry and are considerably older.) Because of their advanced age, these birds must be cooked by a moist heat method, hence the term *stewing chicken*. The demand for stewing hens and fowl is low, and consequently most of these birds are sold frozen. Once cooked, they yield about 45 to 48 percent meat and skin—not much more than a 3- or 4-pound roaster—despite their plump appearance. The presence of 9 to 12 ounces of cavity fat reduces the yield to the point that hens and fowls are usually not a good buy.

HOW TO COOK A CHICKEN

Chicken should always be cooked to an internal temperature of 180°F. This temperature is important for two reasons: First, the flavor and texture of a well-cooked (but not overcooked) chicken is infinitely superior to the dried-out, stringy, tough texture of an overdone bird. Second, overcooked chicken shrinks dramatically—a plump, juicy leg, thigh, or breast eventually turns into bone and a hunk of tasteless, dried-out meat.

Chickens—and all types of poultry except for ducks—contain a high percentage of tissue water and little fat, so overcooking dries out the bird and destroys its flavor and succulence. Unlike beef grades, the grade of a chicken has little to do with the amount of shrinkage; the fat is all under the skin, not within the tissue.

Broiler-fryers and roasting chickens—generally weighing from 2½ to 4½ pounds—can be cooked in a variety of ways, either whole or in parts. Again, the shrinkage will be about the same, so long as you do not overcook the bird.

Roasting. It's best to truss a chicken before roasting it. This helps retain the bird's shape and appearance. Use soft twine and tie the wings and legs close to the body. If the bird is stuffed, skewer or tie the vent closed. (Remember, do not stuff the chicken until just before cooking.) Using a moderate cooking temperature (350°F), roast the bird until the center of the breast or the inside of the thigh area reaches 185°F. As with other types of meats, a high temperature will dry out the meat and even burn some parts before the bird is done. Usually there is sufficient fat under the skin to self-baste, but a melted butter or margarine baste can be used if a darker browning is desired. Chicken parts can also be roasted or baked, but because chicken parts cook so much faster, brown them in a skillet first if a richer or deeper color is desired.

Frying. Chickens weighing 2 to 4 pounds can be panfried using several different methods. Cut the chicken into parts and brown, uncovered, in a skillet, using a small amount of oil. Turn the parts periodically to ensure even browning. Reduce the heat to medium low until the chicken is done. Chicken parts can also be breaded or batter-dipped and either fried in deep oil or panfried in ¼ to ½ inch of oil. To ensure that the fried chicken is done and to speed up the frying process, poach the parts first for 10 minutes, pat dry, and then bread. The poaching method also reduces shrinkage and results in a more tender and juicy chicken. Note, however, that breading and frying chicken parts increases the fat content by as much as 40 percent.

Braising. When chicken is to be used in casseroles or stews, remove the skin beforehand. Chicken skin cooked in a liquid becomes tough and rubbery. If you braise chicken with the skin on, always brown the parts first to retain some of the crispness. When stewing chicken parts or braising them in a moderate amount of liquid, always bring the liquid to a boil and then reduce the heat just below the point where bubbles form in the liquid. Rapid boiling may overcook the meat, resulting in toughness and increased shrinkage.

Barbecuing or grilling. Many outdoor cooks try to cook chicken parts entirely over the coals, sometimes ending up with barbecued chicken that is raw on the inside and charred on the outside. An alternative method of barbecuing is to poach or microwave the chicken parts first. By partially precooking the chicken, you can be assured of the meat being cooked through. You can also control the layering of the sauce to build up a flavorful coating that is also pleasing to the eye. Again, to obtain the best results, do not overcook. Use a meat thermometer or, if cooking chicken parts, separate a little flesh near the bone and look for the typical white color of fully cooked chicken.

Microwaving. Poultry is more adaptable to microwave cooking than red meat—the microwaves help to moisten and tenderize the more delicate meat of a chicken and turkey, whereas other methods of cooking tend to remove the moisture. If you prefer the bird to have a brown, crisp skin, however, use a conventional oven or grill; the microwaved bird can also be put under the broiler for a few minutes to brown. Casseroles that use chicken or turkey as a base do very well in the microwave, although many cooks first brown the poultry parts in a frying pan or dutch oven before assembling the casserole.

Duck

Ducks are usually marketed when they are eight to nine weeks old and weigh between 3½ and 5½ pounds. Despite their weight, ducks are not meaty birds. The entire undersurface of the duck's skin has a thick layer of fat, and although the edible yield of a duck is about 45 to 50 percent, less than half is actually meat.

Ducks are graded A, B, and C, but because of modern methods of production, most of the birds sold today are Grade A.

HOW TO COOK A DUCK

Because most lovers of duck like the skin crisp, the birds are almost always cooked by dry heat methods, such as baking or roasting. Some recipes recommend roasting the bird first and then cutting up and simmering the parts in a spicy sauce. As with any poultry, the internal cooking temperature for duck must be at least 185°F.

Cornish Game Hens

Cornish game hens are specially bred to be ready for market when weighing between 16 and 30 ounces. Because a whole or half bird can serve one person, the game hen is a favorite for special dinners, banquets, and gala occasions. All Cornish game hens in supermarkets are top grade in quality. They are usually distributed frozen, since fresh game hens are available only near growing or processing areas.

The Cornish game hen is not an inexpensive bird. Typical prices range from $1.59 to over $2.00 for a 22-ounce hen. Moreover, the ratio of edible meat to bone and trim is considerably less than any other type of chicken; a 22-ounce hen consists of only about 8 ounces of meat and skin.

HOW TO COOK A CORNISH GAME HEN

Usually, a Cornish game hen is stuffed and roasted in a 325°F oven. Sometimes larger birds are cut in half, and each half is placed over a scoop of stuffing in a roasting pan. The hens are done when their internal temperature reaches 185°F. Again, do not overcook because the meat will become tough and stringy.

Capons

The capon, another member of the chicken family, is usually marketed when over 10 months old and weighing 4 to 8 pounds. A capon is actually a castrated male bird that develops a large amount of white meat in the breast area. The meat is tender, juicy, and flavorful, and the accumulation of fat under the skin is less than that of stewing hens in the same weight range.

The capon is generally sold frozen, and practically all of these birds fall into the Grade A category. Capons cost from $1.50 to $2.00 a pound, considerably more than a fryer-broiler or a roasting chicken. It has always been assumed that the extra cost was justified because a capon yields so much more meat per pound. Actually, however, the capon yields only 5 to 10 percent more than a chicken weighing 2½ to 4 pounds, and the cost is usually double per pound when purchased.

HOW TO COOK A CAPON

Since the meat is tender, the capon can be prepared using any of the methods suitable for fryer-broilers or roasters.

Turkeys

Today, turkey equals chicken in the variety of promotional efforts used to increase its appeal in the supermarket. Whole frozen turkeys, turkey parts, fresh chilled turkeys, ground turkey, turkey ham, turkey bologna, turkey frankfurters and sausages, and a variety of turkey frozen dinners have made this a food staple in many homes. Since turkey meat contains less fat than other meats, it has also gained in popularity with weight-conscious consumers.

Whole young turkeys are usually frozen, although many supermarkets have fresh turkeys available upon special order, or during the holidays. All turkeys are inspected by the U.S. Department of Agriculture, and most retailers offer only Grade A turkeys to their customers. Grade B and C birds are sold to processors, where appearance is not important. Young turkeys can be labeled as fryer-roasters, young toms, young hens, or just young turkeys. A *self-basting* turkey is one that is injected with a butter, broth, or oil solution equal to 3½ to 5½ percent of the bird's total weight. If the label indicates a self-basting bird, it must also list all the ingredients in the solution.

PRICING

Turkey parts are also popular, although the pricing sometimes bears little relationship to the actual yield of edible meat and skin. For example, in 1992, on the same day and in the same supermarket, one shopper noted the following prices:

Turkey legs—89 cents per pound

Turkey legs and thighs—89 cents per pound

Turkey breast with rib cage—$1.99 per pound

Turkey legs are about one-half bone, tendon, and cartilage and one-half meat and skin. Turkey thighs are 35 percent bone and 65 percent meat and skin, although the percentage of skin on the thighs is less than that found on the legs. Thigh meat is lighter and more tender, so from every viewpoint the legs and thighs were a much better buy than just the legs. Since the breastbone with rib cage is about 26 percent of a turkey breast's total weight, the actual cost of the breast meat is about $2.65 a pound—but the meat is 100 percent white meat and easier to slice. Incidently, the same store had boneless turkey breasts for $2.49 a pound.

Frozen whole turkeys, with necks and giblets, are available in weights from 6 to 24 pounds, although 24-to-32-pound birds are available on special order. The young hens, weighing 6 to 8 pounds, yield 50 to 53 percent meat; young toms, at 10 to 12 pounds, yield about 45 percent meat. The ratio of meat to bone then increases as the turkeys become heavier. For example, a turkey weighing 18 pounds yields 50 to 54 percent meat, but a 26-to-28-pound bird will yield over 60 percent. All sizes of turkeys produce 60 to 65 percent white meat and 35 to 40 percent dark.

HOW TO COOK A TURKEY

Turkeys, like other poultry, should be roasted at a moderate heat until the internal temperature reaches 185°F. Normal shrinkage from cooking is 25 to 30 percent, but overcooking will lead to even more shrinkage. One method is to buy a whole turkey, then either cut it in two or separate the breasts and the legs and thighs from the back. Roast these parts and the stuffing separately, and you will reduce both cooking time and shrinkage considerably.

Because a turkey is a large bird without much fat, the breast meat has a tendency to dry out during cooking. Most recipes for roast turkey suggest basting the bird frequently or covering the breast with a piece of cheesecloth saturated with butter or margarine. Regardless of the method used, preventing or reducing the loss of moisture is important if you want to preserve the flavor and texture of the white meat.

3

The Meat Counter

For years nutritionists and national health agencies have been reporting that the typical American diet contains too much fat. They claim, based on current scientific evidence, that reducing our fat intake could decrease the incidence of coronary heart disease, hypertension, and some types of cancer prevalent in the United States. Evidently, many Americans have received the message. Over the past two decades, the consumption of red meat, a prime source of dietary fat, has decreased by 10 percent. Meanwhile, the consumption of chicken, fish, and turkey has increased substantially. Red meat, however, continues to be an important source of protein, and many families serve such an entrée at least once or twice a week.

Although limiting red meat is one way to reduce the consumption of saturated fats, the *choice* of meats and the way they are cooked can reduce saturated fat levels even further. Making the proper choices among the dozens of packages of meat found in supermarkets today is not an easy task, however.

Solving the Mystery of the Meat Counter

Our parents or grandparents never had to cope with the meat-counter maze. They simply went to the neighborhood butcher, told him what they wanted, and let him pick out the best cut for their purposes. His choices, though, were not always the best—most butchers knew how to cut meat but few knew how to cook it.

Today, in this era of self-service, *you* must do the choosing. One problem is that each cut is different. The blade chuck roast, top sirloin roast, and top round roast all differ in terms of tenderness, flavor, and actual serving cost.

The mystery of the meat counter can be solved by learning and understanding a few simple facts about meat and the way it is merchandised. Like most commodities, meat is priced according to consumer demand. Because this demand is created mostly by shoppers who do not know how to buy meat, the knowledgeable consumer has the advantage. Let's take the example of a chuck steak. Chuck is usually the lowest priced steak available and the poorest-quality cut. It is, however, one of the most popular cuts because it is "cheaper" than any of the other types of steaks in the meat section.

Now let's separate the steak into edible and nonedible parts, that is, the lean meat from the bone and fat. If the steak weighs 2 pounds, 5 ounces when purchased, then let's say only 1 pound, 6 ounces is actually usable. If you paid $1.59 per pound for the steak (total cost $3.70), you really paid about $2.69 per pound of edible meat before cooking.

To compute the actual cost of the edible meat, divide the total cost of the cut as purchased ($3.70) by the total ounces of edible meat (1 lb., 6 oz. = 22 oz.) ($3.70 ÷ 22 = 16.8 cents per ounce). To convert to cost per pound, multiply the cost per ounce by 16 (16.8 × 16 = $2.69 per pound). Apply this formula to other cuts of meat to find out the real amount of money you have paid for the edible portions. Once you have mastered this calculation, you can almost visualize the edible and nonedible parts of a cut, and make a fairly accurate judgment of your actual costs.

Obviously, the chuck steak is not a good buy—there are better-quality and less costly steaks. A chuck steak also has an excessive amount of surface and intermuscular fat, a primary source of saturated fat. Other types of steak can be trimmed to eliminate most of the fat.

EATING LEAN: CUTS OF BEEF

When you go to the supermarket to buy a roast or a steak, it pays to know which part of the animal yields the tenderest cut, which needs longer cooking, which is the most flavorful, and which is the leanest. In this case, ignorance may cost you a substantial sum of money, and even spoil a meal.

First, consider the animal as a whole. Each cut of beef includes bones, muscle, connective tissue (tendon), and fat.

STANDARD CUTS OF BEEF

Any cut of meat using the following terms in the description comes from the arm and shoulder of the animal and will be relatively tough.

- Shoulder roast or steak
- Arm roast or steak
- Blade roast or steak
- Brisket
- Cross rib
- Short rib
- Seven bone
- Plate
- Chuck
- Triangle
- Shoulder fillet
- London broil (chuck)

Unless these cuts are from high-quality beef, use a moist heat method such as stewing, braising, or simmering to ensure tenderness.

All of the cuts taken from the center muscles are tender if they come from medium- or high-quality beef. The key terms to memorize for the center section are

- Rib or standing roast
- Club steak
- Rib eye, roast, or steak
- Tenderloin
- Rib or spencer roll
- Loin, New York strip steak
- Sirloin steak, pinbone, or wedge bone
- Porterhouse steak
- T-bone steak
- Top sirloin butt
- Bottom sirloin butt
- Flank steak
- Fillet
- Contrafillet

All of these cuts should be cooked by dry heat methods, such as broiling, frying, oven roasting, or grilling.

The hind leg and the rump muscles can also be tough. The key terms here are

- Rump roast or steak
- Sirloin tip
- Top (inside) round
- Bottom (outside) round
- Eye of the round
- Full-cut round
- Shank
- London broil (round)

Most of these cuts are somewhat better than the foreleg and shoulder cuts because they contain less crossgraining and sinew. You can often use a dry heat method of cooking if the cuts are from high-quality beef. Marinating the cuts beforehand can also help.

Two of these four parts are edible—the muscle and the fat. Because fat is not desirable from a health viewpoint, your choice should be based on the amount of lean meat or muscle available. With a little practice, you can begin to visualize what proportion of the cut is muscle, and then mentally adjust the price per pound. Some cuts—the boneless round, for example—will not contain any bone or connective tissue and almost no intermuscular fat. Your only concern with this type of roast is the amount of surface fat left untrimmed by the butcher.

Aside from the cost, you are also concerned with the flavor and tenderness of the meat. These factors depend upon the part of the animal from which the meat was cut, the age of the animal, and how and what the animal was fed.

The cut. The lean meat of any animal is composed of thousands of muscle fibers bound together by connective tissue. Most of these muscles are attached to bone or cartilage at both ends. The closer to the point of attachment, the closer the connective tissue and the tougher the meat.

How the animal uses the muscle also affects tenderness. Muscles used in walking or jumping are stronger and tougher than those from other parts of the body. The tougher muscles are shank muscles in the hind legs and forelegs and the outer muscles of the legs (bottom round and armbone chuck) and the upper chest (boneless chuck). Muscles in the rib cage and the loin area are used much less and therefore are more tender (rib roast, sirloin steaks, T-bone, porterhouse, and tenderloin).

Unfortunately, in some supermarkets the name on the label doesn't clearly identify what part of the animal the cut came from. Names such as "California roast," "roto-roast," or "butcher's steak" give no clue. Many supermarkets are discontinuing this practice, however, and are using more standardized terminology that can be used to determine relative tenderness and quality. If you learn these key words, you can usually locate the source of the cut.

Age and feed. What exactly is "quality" beef? Quality is determined by several factors, and these factors must be taken into consideration when grading meat.

The age of the animal and what it's fed are important in producing tender, flavorful cuts—especially with beef. Older cows fed on grass will always be tough, no matter what cut you choose. Young, corn-fed steers have the highest number of tender cuts. You can tell whether the steak or roast came from an old cow or a young steer by paying attention to the color, texture, and placement of the fat.

In beef animals, the most important requirement for high quality is the presence of *marbling*, streaks of white, fatty tissue within the red muscle. The fat forms around the muscles themselves and around the muscle fibers, adding juiciness and flavor.

Too much fat is not desirable from a health standpoint, so you have to choose a happy medium between tenderness and flavor and a reasonable amount of fat in the diet. Remember also that there is a world of difference between "lean" beef and well-trimmed beef. Most butchers use a ¼-inch trim, meaning that all the surface fat in excess of ¼ of an inch is removed before the meat is packaged or displayed. If you further trim the cut before cooking—remove the remainder of the surface fat—you can reduce the total amount of saturated fat by as much as half.

The color and texture of the fat is another important clue to the quality of the meat. High-quality beef has a fat cover that is creamy white and almost flaky. The poorer the quality, the more yellow and oily the fat. Yellow fat means the cut is tough and will require a long cooking time.

Using these visual clues—the size and location of the muscle and the color and texture of the fat—you can pick out high-quality meat every time you shop.

In addition to the visual clues, the USDA provides two valuable services for the consumer.

MEAT INSPECTION

All animals marketed for human consumption must be inspected for harmful diseases by the U.S. Department of Agriculture. The inspectors also check out the processing plant to ensure compliance with sanitation requirements. If all the necessary requirements are met, then the meat is stamped with their seal of approval (see box).

The legend "INSP'D&P'S'D" is stamped on major cuts of beef carcass. However, you may not see it on the individual roast or steak you buy.

The "Inspected and Passed" symbol is stamped on every prepackaged, processed meat product that is federally inspected.

Note: Many supermarkets and freezer or food plans imply in their advertising that the USDA inspection stamp is a mark of the quality of the meat. This statement is false. The stamp indicates only that the meat is free from disease and contamination.

GRADES OF MEAT

- *USDA Prime.* The best grade, usually found only in fine restaurants and hotels as well as in some specialty meat markets.
- *USDA Choice.* The highest grade available in most supermarkets.
- *USDA Select.* The next highest grade, but found less in retail markets because it is more expensive than ungraded beef.
- *USDA Standard.* This grade is sold in markets under a private label such as Blue Ribbon, Best, or Quality. Such labels do not involve any government standards.
- *USDA Commercial.* Often used in hamburger but sometimes marketed by wrapping the cut in a piece of fat from a Choice carcass. Considerable amounts of this grade are also sold by food and freezer plans. It is an unsatisfactory grade for home use.
- *USDA Utility.* Used mostly for ground beef and processed meats.
- *USDA Canner/Cutter.* Used mostly in processed meats.

Approximately 80 percent of the beef cattle processed in the United States are graded by the USDA. The remainder is processed and sold by various packers as "no-roll" or "generic," which means the USDA has not classified the beef animal in terms of quality and yield.

If the beef is not graded by the USDA, then usually the retailer will assign some brand name to it that implies high quality but does not relate to USDA standards. This lack of consistency in the quality of ungraded beef makes it very difficult for average consumers to pick out high-quality meats with any degree of certainty—*unless* they use the visual clues described previously.

HOW TO COOK BEEF

Cook some of the round cuts—such as top round steak, bottom roast or steak, boneless rump roast, eye of the round, and top round roast—by dry heat methods (baking, roasting, grilling) if they are high-quality (USDA Choice or equivalent). In fact, using these cuts as roasts or steaks is economical because the price per pound is often considerably less than that of traditional roasts such as rib or tenderloin. Moreover, the round cuts produce considerably less waste from bone and fat than do the rib roasts. Using dry heat rather than a moist heat method will also reduce cooking shrinkage by 20 to 25 percent. Best results are obtained by cooking these cuts at 250° to 300°F to an internal temperature of 145°F for medium rare. If the roasts are cooked at a higher temperature until well done, they will be dry and tough.

NEW COOKING LABELS FOR MEAT

As of April 1994, the USDA requires all raw meat and poultry to carry labels stating that some meats may contain bacteria and need to be kept refrigerated or frozen. The labels will also emphasize the importance of keeping raw meat separate from other foods and the need to cook meat thoroughly.

Because of potential consumer confusion about the meaning of "cook thoroughly," the USDA said that the new labeling would be accompanied by an education campaign on how to cook meat.

Veal

Many veal cuts have almost disappeared from the meat counters of most supermarkets. The reason is cost—veal is expensive to produce and consequently the price is prohibitive for most shoppers.

Veal comes from very young calves and has very little fat but considerable connective tissue. Veal is neither very tender nor is it very flavorful, so cooking methods and recipes tend to add flavor by adding stuffings, sauces, and gravies to the meat.

Cook most cuts of veal to an internal temperature of 170°F, usually by roasting or braising. Only a few cuts, such as thin cutlets or chops, can be sautéed or panfried.

The government grades most veal and the grades are the same as beef.

The flesh of high-quality veal is a delicate pink with a shading of gray; it is finely textured with no marbling. The fat cover on the outside and between the muscles should be white.

Much of the veal produced today goes to restaurants. However, a few cuts, including cutlets, chops, veal loin steaks, and ground veal, show up regularly on retail counters.

VEAL AND ANIMAL RIGHTS

As more and more meat and poultry products are raised by so-called factory-farming techniques, pressure is being put on state and federal regulatory agencies to ensure that the animals are raised and slaughtered humanely.

One of the more objectionable practices, according to animal rights groups, is the placement of the animal in a crate or cage that restricts movement—sometimes to the point where it is unable to turn around. This technique is used mostly in veal production. Some states have already enacted legislation that establishes minimum sizes for these cages, and they prohibit other practices considered to be inhumane.

From the consumer's viewpoint, when the product reaches the supermarket, it is impossible to determine how the food animal was raised. Consequently, boycotting the meat counter seems to be largely ineffective in erasing any unacceptable animal-raising practices. Concerned consumers will probably be more successful if they lend their voices, votes, and support to any one of several lobbying efforts that call for more legislation in this area.

Lamb

Most self-service meat counters feature numerous cuts of lamb, such as shoulder chops, rib chops, leg of lamb, and loin roasts. Fortunately, retailers have not attached as many fancy titles to lamb cuts as they have to beef.

Much of the lamb produced domestically is graded by the USDA. Lamb is classified and graded according to two sets of criteria: (1) The carcass is classified as lamb, which means the animal was less than a year old. Older animals constitute the next category, which is yearling mutton or mutton. (2) Each cut is then graded for quality:

- U.S. Prime
- U.S. Choice
- U.S. Good
- U.S. Utility
- U.S. Cull

The most common grade of lamb found in self-service meat counters is U.S. Choice, at least in the case of domestic lamb. Much of the lamb sold in the United States is produced in New Zealand and Australia, however, and is not graded according to USDA standards of quality. Since all New Zealand and Australian lamb is shipped frozen, many retailers feature it in the frozen food section. Because of differences in feeding methods, the non-domestic lamb usually has a stronger flavor.

The lamb offered in supermarkets, particularly larger cuts such as leg of lamb or rack, will have the characteristic USDA shield and grade rolled on the outside surface. Packages of chops and cutlets should also carry the USDA label. If you cannot find any evidence of grading, ask the butcher or the store manager about the origin of the lamb.

Another clue is the color of the meat. High-quality domestic lamb is light in color, so the older the animal, the redder the meat. The fat on U.S. Choice lamb is creamy white or slightly pink in color and feels somewhat soft. The flesh of New Zealand or Australian lamb is reddish in color and the fat cover will be sparse and somewhat grayish.

HOW TO COOK LAMB

Almost all the cuts of good-to-high-quality domestic lamb can be cooked by a dry heat method, such as oven roasting, broiling, panfrying, or grilling. As with beef, the cooking temperature will affect the amount of shrinkage. Lamb should be cooked at low temperatures and served medium rare (still pink). Too many cookbooks still recommend cooking lamb to an internal temperature of 170° to 180°F. Europeans, however, have been serving lamb rare to medium rare (140° to 150°F) for centuries, a practice that only recently has gained in popularity in the United States. When cooked the European way, the lamb does not shrink as much and is much more flavorful.

Lamb chops cut from the shoulder or chuck tend to have considerable surface and intermuscular fat. To reduce the amount of saturated fat retained by the meat, broil or grill the chops on a rack to allow the melted fat to drain away. Other lamb cuts contain mostly surface fat that can be trimmed before cooking.

The ratio of bone to meat is quite high in most chops and bone-in roasts, so the cost of lamb as served is higher than most cuts of beef or pork.

Pork

Many shoppers still think—erroneously—that pork is high in fat and dietary cholesterol. In fact, cooked lean pork has about the same amount of fat as lean beef or chicken and considerably less cholesterol than shrimp. Pork is also a food high in nutrient density, which means it contains many of the required daily nutrients as compared to calories.

Much of the pork produced today is marketed to the retail and restaurant trade as cured meat, including ham, bacon, and picnic ham. While there are many methods of curing meats, all fall within two basic categories: dry curing and brine curing. *Dry* curing uses salt as the basic curing ingredient. Other ingredients are also added, including sodium nitrate to develop color, and sugar, maple syrup, or honey for flavor. *Brine* curing involves pumping a salt and water solution through the arteries of the meat, thus distributing the cure throughout.

Pumping brine into the meat initially increases the weight. If the cured meat increases in weight by up to 10 percent, then its label must include the words "water added." But if the cured meat has been aged or dried to the point that the weight returns to the natural or original amount, it may be labeled "ham," although some processors use the expression "dry ham."

Some cured meats are then cooked or smoked to an internal temperature above 148°F. You must thoroughly cook any hams or cured meats that are not labeled "cooked," "fully cooked," "ready to eat," or "ready to serve."

Since most pork comes from animals 9 to 12 months old, very little of the meat is graded in the same manner as beef or lamb. Instead, pork processing plants and pork products are inspected for disease and proper sanitary conditions by the USDA.

HOW TO COOK PORK

It is traditional to cook any fresh pork products to an internal temperature of at least 170°F (well done) because of the possible existence of parasites in the meat that cause a disease called trichinosis. This disease is rarely encountered now in the United States, but many people still prefer their pork well done.

Unfortunately, because of the old fear of trichinosis, most people overcook pork. Pork is most flavorful and succulent when it is cooked only to the point where the meat turns from pink to white, particularly next to the bone. Overcooking not only increases shrinkage but also dries out and toughens the meat.

Selecting pork is easier than selecting good beef or lamb simply because almost all the pork marketed today is of high quality and is tender and flavorful. So the most important factor in selecting pork is the amount of trimming done by the butcher. Pork naturally develops a heavy fat cover, and the retailer should trim most of this excess fat from the cut before it is offered for sale.

How to Reduce Shrinkage in Meats

Any cooking method dehydrates meat, even when the meat is cooked in liquid. But you can reduce shrinkage to a minimum if you take the following precautions.

Rule #1. Buy good-quality cuts. The higher the quality or grade of the meat, the less the cooking loss.

Meat is composed mostly of water. The lower the quality or grade of meat, the higher the percentage of water. For example, a low-quality cut such as a USDA Standard or Commercial contains from 75 percent to over 85 percent water, while a higher-quality USDA Choice contains only 65 to 70 percent water. Young beef (or veal) also has a higher percentage of water and tends to shrink even more.

During the growth stages of the animal, unsaturated fats begin to replace some of the water. These increased fatty deposits are less susceptible to loss or dehydration during the cooking process, and thus the meat is subject to less shrinkage. In an informal test, two identically sized roasts, one a USDA Choice cut and the other a USDA Standard cut, were cooked at the same temperature and to a similar internal temperature as measured by meat thermometers. The USDA Choice grade had over 10 percent less shrinkage and was done in 20 percent less time than the USDA Standard grade. Based on many similar experiments, it is safe to say that ungraded beef, because it is usually equivalent to USDA Standard or Select, is subject to significantly higher shrinkage than USDA Choice or USDA Prime, regardless of the cooking method used.

Rule #2. Roast at a low temperature. The higher the cooking temperature, the greater the cooking loss.

Years ago it was common practice to preheat the oven to 450° to 500°F before starting to roast a cut of meat. After 20 to 30 minutes, the temperature was lowered to 350° to 400°. This method was thought to sear and "seal" the meat so it would remain juicy and tender. Continuing research, however, contradicts this long-held belief.

- Searing does not retain the juices and, in fact, dehydrates the meat at a rapid rate.
- The lower the cooking temperature, the less the cooking loss.
- Meat cooked at substantially lower temperatures still shows the characteristic browning of the surface, yet the meat is more tender.

- Flavor is enhanced by the greater retention of juices when the meat is cooked at a lower temperature.
- Lower cooking temperatures can reduce shrinkage from 28 percent to as low as 8 percent.

Despite all this evidence, most cookbooks still recommend oven roasting of meats at 325° to 375°F. But many restaurants roast meat at temperatures as low as 200°, and with excellent results. True, lower temperatures mean longer cooking time: As a general rule, if you roast at 225° to 250°F, you must allow about 20 percent more cooking time. Lower but longer cooking has the added advantages of saving energy and allowing the cook a more leisurely preparation period.

A word of caution: Timing your roast using minutes per pound is courting disaster. Each cut of meat has a different moisture and fat content, size, and thickness. The only way to obtain perfect results is to use a meat thermometer.

Lower temperatures when braising or cooking meats in liquids also affect shrinkage—a fast-rolling boil does not make meat more tender. All that is necessary is a slow simmer or even a temperature setting just below simmer to tenderize the meat. Test for tenderness with a fork.

Rule #3. Don't overcook. The more well-done the meat, the more the cooking loss.

In general, meat is considered to be rare at an internal temperature of 135°F, medium-rare at 145°F, and well done at 160°F and above. The internal temperature of meat cooked by moist heat methods (stewing, braising) will always be in excess of 200°F because of the temperature of the cooking medium and the length of cooking time. (Ground meat, because of danger of bacterial contamination, should always be cooked to an internal temperature of 160°F.)

In most cases, meat will shrink or lose about 5 percent of its weight for every 10 percent rise in internal temperature. The following table illustrates how much weight a USDA Choice cut of meat loses when cooked by various methods:

TABLE 3.1
Weight Loss vs. Internal Temperature of Cooked Meat

Cooking Method	Temperature Setting	Weight Loss or Shrinkage		
		Rare	Medium	Well-Done
Broiling	Medium	8–12%	15–20%	20–25%
Panfrying	Medium	10–12%	15–20%	20–30%
Oven roasting	225°–250°F	8–12%	14–18%	20–25%
Pot roasting	Low	—	—	25–35%
Stewing	Medium low	—	—	35–50%

Using grades below USDA Choice will increase the overall percentages. These results are based on cooking with a conventional oven.

Microwaving Meat

The microwave oven is very effective and efficient for defrosting foods and heating leftovers. It is also fast and efficient for cooking vegetables, both frozen and fresh.

Consumer acceptance of the microwave for meat cookery, however, has been less than enthusiastic. The cooking is very uneven, and many cuts of meat do not develop the characteristic browned appearance that makes meat appealing to most people. Some areas are overcooked while others are underdone.

Manufacturers provide variable power settings, carousels, diffusers, browning elements, and many other features to accommodate those cuts of meat requiring dry heat methods. All these added features may have improved the ovens' performance, but many cooks still feel that microwaving is best left to those jobs it does well.

It's easy to see why certain cuts of meat do not cook as well in the microwave oven. The microwaves themselves penetrate the food only about 1 or 1½ inches, and in some ovens the waves come from a limited number of directions. This means the roast has to be turned over and around to be evenly cooked. Because the interior of the roast is not cooked by the waves but by the transfer of heat from cooked to uncooked areas, the roast has to be allowed to stand periodically so that the heat may transfer properly. Some areas have to be covered to prevent overcooking. Moreover, the density and size of most roasts require approximately the same amount of time in a microwave as in a conventional oven. Some cooking instructions suggest the use of both ovens, conventional and microwave—one for browning and the other to finish cooking.

Cooking by microwave also results in similar or higher levels of shrinkage when compared to conventional methods. This is particularly true when low power settings are not available.

Sausages and Frankfurters

Sausage making for the commercial trade is strictly controlled in the United States. Because the product is made from either coarsely or finely ground meats that are often mixed with other ingredients for flavor and preservation, the opportunity to add forbidden animal by-products exists. Only through strict governmental regulation can consumers be assured that the sausages they buy are both wholesome and safe. (Unless otherwise stated, the term "sausages" refers to breakfast sausages, frankfurters, weiners, bologna, salami, and other similarly processed meat products.)

WHAT'S IN A HOT DOG

All varieties of sausages or frankfurters are made by grinding meat, adding enough water to blend the seasonings, and adding other ingredients to bind the mixture, preserve the color, and cure or preserve the finished product. The resulting mixture is then forced into casings for further processing.

Sausage casings may be either natural or artificial. Natural casings are made from the small and large intestines of cows, sheep, or pigs and have been carefully cleaned, salted, and chilled. Artificial casings are made from several different materials, including a type of cellulose. Many sausage products are sold as "skinless," meaning the artificial casing is mechanically removed after the product is processed.

Quality in sausage products is defined by the meats and fillers used. By law, manufacturers must list on the label all of the ingredients in their products. The ingredients must be listed in order of their total amount in the product—therefore, the highest amount is listed first, the second-highest listed second, and so forth.

The next time you pass the sausage counter in your local supermarket, take the time to read some of the product labels and the list of ingredients in several brands of frankfurters. The labels will give you some valuable information, sometimes more than you really wanted to know. The words "beef," "pork," "veal," or "chicken" can be used only when muscle meats are used. If meat by-products or variety meats are ingredients, this must be stated on the label. "Meat by-products" or "variety meats" refers to pork snouts and stomachs; beef, veal, lamb, or goat tripe; beef, lamb, pork, or goat hearts, tongues, lips, spleens, and partially defatted pork or beef fatty tissue.

All franks and wieners contain salt for both flavor and preservation. There is usually a long list of other ingredients, including binders, extenders, antioxidants, coloring, color fixatives, mold retardants, nitrites, artificial flavorings, and emulsifying agents. (All these additives or ingredients must be approved by the USDA. In fact, the recipes used by each processor must be individually approved.) Herbs and spices are listed, but almost never are they identified. This is to protect the processor's "secret" recipe.

BUY LOCALLY

Small, local frankfurter and sausage makers produce very limited amounts of each type of sausage at any one time. Consequently, they do not have to use as many additives as the larger manufacturers with multistate distribution. Many sausage makers take great pride in their products, using only quality meats and the finest of other ingredients. It is worth your time to search for this type of family-run business. True sausage making is an art. Of course, these products cost more, but many consumers are willing to pay the higher price for quality.

SUPERMARKET SAUSAGES

Commercially produced sausages are those products processed for wide distribution through chain supermarkets and other large retail outlets. As mentioned before, commercial producers use a number of different additives, fixatives, and preservatives to ensure the shelf life of their products. A look at the labels will enable you to judge for yourself the relative quality of the products. Here are a few other hints about buying commercial sausage products.

- It is not unusual for fluid to collect in the plastic packages containing frankfurters, knockwurst, and small bologna. The liquid should be clear, however. If it is cloudy or contains particles of residue, don't buy the product.
- Check the wrapping of any sausage product. Don't buy it if the plastic film is ruptured or inflated or the seal broken.
- Ready-sliced sausage products such as bologna, salami, and the minced loaves should be fresh-looking, with a characteristic bright color. There should be no signs of

ARE HOT DOGS GOOD FOR YOU?

As many health-conscious consumers know, hot dogs contain up to 30 percent fat and derive about 75 to 85 percent of their calories from fat. Obviously, some of the fat is lost during the cooking process—as well as some of the 3 to 10 percent water added by the manufacturer to help blend the ingredients. Nevertheless, the high fat and sodium content means that franks and wieners are not the healthiest of foods. Make them an occasional indulgence—a lunch on the run or a picnic treat. (For more information on the nutritional content of hot dogs, see Appendix.)

moisture collecting on the surface and no darkening of any area under the plastic wrap.

- Fresh franks should look fresh and have a characteristic bright color, and the casing should be dry, not slimy. Graying of the meat is an indication of age.

SPECIALTY AND ETHNIC SAUSAGES

Federal meat inspection regulations limit the number of sausages that can be imported into the United States. As a result, most so-called ethnic sausages found in supermarkets are actually made in this country, including beerwurst, bockwurst, bratwurst, kielbasa, knockwurst, mortadella, pepperoni, salami, and chorizo.

BACON: THE FOOD YOU HATE TO LOVE

Bacon certainly is not good for you. Three-quarters of its calories come from fat. Much of its good taste comes from salt. Bacon is also among the main dietary sources of nitrosamines, a suspected carcinogen. And bacon is expensive—as much as $7 a cooked pound, or even more.

So there's really no reason to eat bacon—except for the way it smells and tastes. For millions of Americans, that's reason enough. If you're among the millions who do eat bacon at least occasionally, here are some facts that may somewhat temper the guilt.

Bacon does contain lots of fat, but it's no more fatty than some other foods—just more visibly so. One egg, for instance, contains about as much fat as two slices of bacon. Whereas 74 percent of bacon's calories come from fat, that's the same as the percentage of calories from fat in cheddar cheese. Surprisingly, only about one-third of bacon's fat calories comes from saturated fat. Bacon contains twice as much unsaturated fats as saturated fat.

Bacon is clearly a salty food. Besides the salt that's used in curing, sodium occurs naturally in the meat. At 303 milligrams in a three-slice serving, bacon is not as bad as a hot dog or a few slices of American cheese, but it's something to avoid if you're on a sodium-restricted diet.

The nitrite present in bacon from the curing process is also a worry. But the connection between nitrite and cancer is far from clear.

Cost. It's the yield that determines bacon's true cost—the cost per pound after cooking. And it's often said that bacon shrinks less when baked in the oven or microwave than when panfried. To test that theory, *Consumer Reports* food scientists cooked samples of the same brands all three ways. The yields were practically the same. But bacon in an oven or microwave makes less mess than in a pan, and a conventional oven or even a microwave should be able to hold more slices at a time.

Recommendations. Don't eat bacon every day. It isn't especially good for you, and it costs too much. Save it for special occasions. And, when you do eat bacon, limit it to only one or two slices— and savor the aroma instead. Use just a bit of bacon to flavor foods like salads, quiches, and casseroles. One slice should be enough for a BLT. When you buy bacon, look for roughly even distribution of fat and lean to help ensure even cooking and crisp texture.

Some of the specialty types of sausages are sold in bulk and are not prewrapped, so the list of ingredients may be difficult to get. The ingredients may be posted near the display, or the retailer may have identifying labels.

Variety Meats

Variety meats include liver, brains, heart, kidneys, tongue, tripe, and sweetbreads. Although these by-products are highly nutritious, variety meats have never been as popular in the United States as they are in Europe or the Far East. Consequently, much of the variety meats produced in the United States are exported abroad.

Variety meats include beef, calf, pork, and lamb, so their sizes can vary. The taste, however, is quite similar. All of these meats are highly perishable and should be cooked as soon as possible after purchase.

- **Liver.** The most popular of the variety meats, liver, whether beef or calf's, is highly nutritious and flavorful. Sometimes it is sold with the outside membrane still intact. This should be peeled off before cooking. Liver can be braised, broiled, or panfried.

- **Brains.** All types are tender, with a delicate flavor, but they are highly perishable. If you are not going to use brains immediately, cook them before freezing or refrigerating. Wash them thoroughly, remove the membrane, then braise or fry.

- **Heart.** Another very flavorful variety meat, heart is not as tender as the others. Cook it with a moist heat—braise or simmer the meat completely immersed in the liquid.

- **Kidneys.** Kidneys are usually purchased whole, with the membrane intact. Remove the membrane and any cartilage still attached, and wash thoroughly. Braise, broil, or cook them in liquid.

- **Tongue.** Unlike other variety meats, tongue can be bought fresh, canned, smoked, corned, or pickled. If you purchase it fresh, ask the butcher to show you how much additional trimming is needed, because the skin and the roots should be removed before serving. Cook the meat very slowly in water or stock.

- **Tripe.** This variety meat is available fresh, canned, or pickled. So-called fresh tripe has been separated from the stomach lining and partially cooked. It is always necessary to continue to cook tripe at a low temperature before it is broiled, dipped in batter, or any other of the numerous methods of preparation.

- **Sweetbreads.** These are portions of the thymus gland of young beef cattle or veal calves. Very perishable, sweetbreads should be cooked as soon as possible. Remove the membrane and broil, fry, or braise.

4

The Fish Market

Americans are eating more fish. Over the last decade, consumption per person in the United States has risen nearly 25 percent—from 12½ to 15½ pounds a year.

Perhaps the most important factor in the increase of fish sales is the current interest in a high-protein, low-fat diet. Fish is one of the best sources of complete protein and is an integral part of almost every weight-loss regimen. As fish becomes more popular, however, it also becomes more expensive.

Demand Versus Supply

Consumer demand is only one reason for the increase in fish prices. Widespread overfishing by both foreign and domestic fleets has resulted in the virtual elimination of some varieties of seafood. Uncontrolled trawling near spawning grounds has also disrupted the normal cycle of feeding and spawning for some important food fish. Consequently, the cost of many traditional types of fish has increased significantly as supplies grow scarcer.

Some steps have been taken to remedy this bleak outlook. First, the establishment of the 200-mile fishing limit by the U.S. government in 1977 has curtailed overfishing in several critical areas. Unfortunately, the move was made too late to benefit current supplies.

Second, new markets have been developed for underutilized species of fish, including turbot, shark, squid, sablefish, tile, and monkfish. These "new" types of fish cost less than the traditional sole, bass, or salmon, and are readily available during most of the year. Squid, for example, is considered a delicacy in many parts of the world, and yet only recently has it been extensively marketed in this country.

Third, and perhaps the most significant development, is aquaculture or fish farming, an industry that has exploded over the past decade. In the early 1980's, aquaculture was limited to a few species of trout, catfish, and shrimp, and the farms produced only a very small percentage of the seafood sold at the retail level. Today, more than 30 percent of seafood products on the market are produced by aquaculture.

HOW TO BUY FRESH FISH

For most people buying fish, the biggest challenge is finding one that is both fresh and clean—and then cooking it properly. Here are some guidelines:

- When buying whole fish, look for bright, clear, bulging eyes. Cloudy, sunken, discolored, or slime-covered eyes often signal fish that is beginning to spoil.

  The skin of freshly caught fish is covered with a translucent mucus that looks a bit like varnish. The color is vivid and bright. Avoid fish whose skin has begun to discolor; shows depressions, tears, or blemishes; or is covered with a sticky, yellowish-brown mucus.
- When buying steaks or fillets, look for moist flesh that still has a translucent sheen. Watch out for flesh that's dried out or gaping (proof that the muscle fibers are beginning to pull apart). That's a sign of over-the-hill fish.
- Note how the fish is displayed, and look for any clues that the temperature may be too high. Fish piled high, displayed in open cases, or sitting under hot lights provide a perfect place for bacteria to grow. If fish fillets are displayed inside separate pans surrounded by ice, that's usually a sign the retailer is paying some attention to quality. Whole fish should be displayed under ice.

- Carefully evaluate store specials and price reductions. Specials may be a way to move older fish. Most retailers would rather reduce the price than throw away fish. A "Saturday-get-rid-of-it" special will be cheap but may not make the tastiest meal.
- Look for evidence that fish has been frozen and then thawed. Note which fish have "fresh" display signs on them. Look for chunks of ice floating in the fish liquid—a clue that the fish had been frozen. If you're not sure, ask. Although many shelf tags may not be honest, some of the clerks may be.

  There's nothing wrong with frozen fish, but if you unknowingly buy fish that had once been frozen and then refreeze it, its texture and flavor will suffer. It's probably better to buy frozen fish instead.
- Keep an eye out for pretty displays of cooked seafood sold next to raw fish. The proximity of the cooked item to the raw fish is a potential health hazard.
- Use your nose. Fresh fish smell like the sea, but they have no strong odor. Freshwater fish in good condition sometimes smell like cucumbers. Strong odors usually indicate spoilage.
- Once you buy fish, refrigerate it quickly. At home, store it in the coldest part of your refrigerator, keep it in the original wrapper, and use it fast—within a day. A lot of fish have little shelf life left.

HOW TO BUY FROZEN FISH

Frozen fish requires expert handling. If the product is allowed to thaw and refreeze, the overall quality has been diminished or destroyed. Even if the fish has been kept frozen, excessive storage time can affect quality. That's because some deterioration still takes place, even at low temperatures.

Here are a few hints about buying frozen fish:

- Gently squeeze the package, or, if buying a plastic-wrapped whole fish, squeeze the tail section or the thin side of the fillet. If there is any sign of softness or pliability, do not buy the product.

- If the fish is wrapped in see-through plastic, look for signs of dehydration—the flesh will have a white, spongelike appearance. If the fish is packaged and is not visible, inspect it at home for the same signs. If you notice any deterioration, return the product to the store as soon as possible.
- When opening packaged frozen fish, make sure that the wrapping fits tightly and is vaporproof. The flesh should be firm and glossy, and there should be no crystallization inside the package.
- If any part of the flesh has turned orange, return the product to the store. The color change is caused by the oxidation of fat in the fish, which indicates prolonged storage or a cycle of intermittent thawing and refreezing.

HOW TO BUY SMOKED OR SALTED FISH

Because of changing consumer tastes, most fish is only lightly smoked or salted. As a result, these products are now more susceptible to spoilage than they would be if salting or smoking were still the only method of preservation. Keep salted and smoked fish under constant refrigeration and away from high humidity. Hard-dried fish products need not be refrigerated, but before purchasing them, look for signs of mold or deterioration, particularly around the cavity and the gills.

Varieties of Finfish

Finfish are either roundfish or flatfish. *Roundfish* such as salmon, swordfish, and red snapper are not truly round but oval-shaped, with the backbone running down the center of the fish between two thick strips of flesh. *Flatfish* include flounder, sole, and haddock, and all of them swim horizontally along the sea bottom, with both eyes facing upward. Flatfish have two thin layers of flesh separated by small bones that fan out of the fish's backbone.

Whole finfish are available only close to their source of supply because whole fish are sold fresh, as they are caught. Avoid buying whole fish from anywhere but the dock or from a reputable fish market. Remove the entrails as soon as possible to avoid rapid spoilage.

Drawn fish. Drawn fish have been gutted (entrails removed)— either on board after being caught or as soon as the boat docks. Usually, drawn fish are the only type available as fresh whole fish.

Dressed fish. Fish are "dressed" when they are completely gutted and scaled but with the head left on. Most of the fresh whole fish featured in the retail market are supposed to be dressed, but always check to ensure that the scales have been completely removed. Dressed fish are available fresh, frozen, smoked, and salted.

Headed and gutted fish. These are dressed fish without the head and tail. In some cases, the dorsal fin has also been removed.

Chunks. A chunk is a cross-section of a dressed fish with the fins removed. The only remaining bone is the backbone.

Steaks. Thick slices taken from the cross-section of a fish.

Fillets. A fish fillet is the whole or half of a side that has been cut away from the fin and backbone. Although most fillets are boneless, some still contain the small vertical bones that grow out of the backbone. To ensure that a fillet is boneless, run your finger down the center seam of the fillet to feel any remaining bones.

Fish sticks. Thin strips of whole or minced fish are breaded and then frozen.

Fish portions. Pieces of whole or minced fish are cut into uniform portions, then breaded or dipped in batter before freezing.

Formed minced or flaked fish. Processed flaked, shredded, or minced fish can be formed into various shapes. The pieces are then breaded or dipped in batter, cooked, and frozen.

COMPARATIVE COST

The edible portion of finfish varies considerably. Some fish may yield only 20 percent flesh, and others have a yield as high as 60 percent. Based on a serving of 4 to 5 ounces of edible meat, use the following formulas to determine the actual cost per pound.

- Whole fish: one serving per pound—multiply the purchase price by three.
- Drawn or dressed fish: ¾ pound per serving—multiply the purchase price by 2½.

HIGH-RISK GROUPS: FISH TO AVOID

For pregnant women or those women who expect to become pregnant, there's little choice but to avoid many popular types of fish. Salmon, swordfish, and lake whitefish may well contain polychlorinated biphenyls (PCBs), which can accumulate in the body to the point where they pose a risk to the developing fetus. Swordfish and tuna also can expose women to mercury, which could also harm the fetus. Young children, too, should avoid those fish. However, it is still possible to enjoy such species as flounder, sole, and catfish.

Other people can pretty much eat what fish they like, but prudence would suggest varying the fish diet to no more than one portion a week of a food likely to contain PCBs or high levels of mercury. Depending on where it is caught, some salmon is unlikely to contain a high level of PCBs. Salmon from Alaska and the north Pacific generally have low PCB levels. But, as *Consumer Reports* found, it's hard for consumers to be certain where a fish really comes from. If you want Alaskan salmon, try to buy it from a merchant you know and trust.

- Chunks or steaks: two servings per pound—multiply the purchase price by 1½.
- Fillets: three to four servings per pound—the purchase price is the actual raw cost.

Shellfish

A large portion of the seafood marketed in the United States falls into the category of shellfish, a classification that includes both mollusks and crustaceans. *Mollusk* refers to any species that controls its shell with a series of valves and includes oysters, clams, mussels, and scallops. *Crustacean* includes any type of shellfish that is covered by a rigid or flexible, removable covering. These animals include crayfish, shrimp, prawns, crabs, lobsters, and turtles.

Unlike finfish, most members of the shellfish family must still be alive to be purchased as fresh. Clams, mussels, and oysters close their shells tightly when handled; any mollusk whose shell remains open after being tapped is dead and should be discarded. When purchased fresh, lobsters and crabs should be lively, with considerable movement in their head and claws. The tail of a live lobster should curl upward when the animal is held upright, for example.

Most shellfish are available canned or frozen. Lobsters and crabs may also be available cooked.

The combination of increasing demand and diminishing supplies has driven the price of most shellfish up fourfold in the past two decades. Unfortunately, many areas where shellfish were once abundant have been overharvested or polluted. Clams and scallops formerly covered the bottoms of many bays and rivers, but now these areas are practically barren. Another problem is that the natural enemy of mollusks, seagulls, have become a protected species, and gulls are now so abundant that they literally strip the shallow water of young clams, scallops, oysters, and mussels.

The farming of some species of shellfish has become profitable, however. Oysters and mussels are now extensively grown on marine farms. Although experimental farming of shrimp in Baja

California has been less than successful, some Asian and South American countries are extensively farming shrimp and other seafood.

Like finfish, the quality of shellfish is determined by the way they are handled along every step of the distribution process. At the retail level, already shucked (shelled) clams, mussels, and oysters should be kept refrigerated and have firm flesh and clear liquor. Shrimp should be firm, bright in color, and devoid of black spots.

FAVORITE FISH

Here, in order of preference, is a list of the seafoods Americans eat the most.

1. Tuna
2. Shrimp
3. Cod
4. Alaska pollock
5. Salmon
6. Catfish
7. Clams
8. Flounder and sole
9. Scallops
10. Crabs

Source: U.S. Department of Commerce

5

The Produce Section: Vegetables

The produce section of the typical supermarket appears to be a veritable cornucopia of the good things of the earth: fresh, colorful, wholesome vegetables in all their variety. The United States, with its wide range of climatic conditions and soil types, is capable of growing the greatest number of vegetables of any country in the world. We also have the agricultural, storage, and transportation technology to ensure that most types of produce are available practically everywhere in the country, regardless of season.

For the shopper, it seems that all that is needed is a basic knowledge of vegetables and a sense of culinary adventure. The bewildering variety, however, and the many ways each vegetable is processed and packaged raises questions and doubts for the comparison shopper: What is the best value—fresh, frozen, or canned? Should I buy them packaged or in bulk? What should I be looking for in a fresh vegetable?

USDA Grading of Vegetables

The U.S. Department of Agriculture has established quality standards for grading fresh vegetables. USDA grades consider quality based on maturity, color, surface blemishes, and size, as well as the condition of the product because of its storage and

GRADINGS FOR CANNED AND FROZEN VEGETABLES

Many shoppers are confused by canned food products that are labeled "Grade A" but do not show the typical USDA shield. These products must meet USDA Grade A standards, but they have not been continuously inspected or graded by USDA inspectors. Only those products that have been processed and packed under the ongoing supervision of the USDA can be labeled with both the grade and shield or the statement: "Packed under the continuous supervision of the USDA."

In fact, most frozen and canned vegetables are not officially graded. That's because food processors and supermarkets feel that shoppers buy frozen or canned products based on brand identification. Processors and stores alike prefer to rely on advertising to establish a reputation for quality.

This lack of reputable grade designations, and the fact that no correlation exists between the amount of advertising and quality, means you can find superior frozen or canned vegetables only through the process of elimination. Smart shoppers will pay careful attention to the condition, appearance, and taste of the product, and should judge them on the following government standards for frozen and canned vegetables.

U.S. Grade A or *Fancy* vegetables should be at their peak of quality, with excellent color and uniform size. There should be no blemishes or spots, and the texture should be firm and not deteriorated from overprocessing. Both the flavor and the appearance should be excellent.

U.S. Grade B or *Extra Standard* vegetables should have very good color and only slight variations in size and texture. There should be almost no blemishes and no broken pieces. There may be some indication of overmaturity or overprocessing, but not enough to change the characteristic shape. The flavor and appearance should be very good.

U.S. Grade C or *Standard* vegetables may have considerable variation in size and color. Some of the pieces may be broken or blemished. There may be signs of age, undermaturity, or overprocessing. The texture may be too firm or too soft and the appearance not pleasing.

handling. The grading service is voluntary and must be paid for by the companies requesting the service. Only about 50 percent of fresh vegetables are graded.

The USDA grades for fresh vegetables are: U.S. Fancy, U.S. Extra #1, U.S. #1, and U.S. #2.

"Overprocessed" basically refers to canned vegetables, because in most instances the product is cooked to destroy micro-organisms and to allow the product to be stored without refrigeration. If the product is overcooked, there will be a change in texture and appearance and usually some deterioration around the edges.

All grades should be wholesome and nutritious, so your choice of which grade to buy should be based on the way you intend to use the product. Use only the best if you are serving the item by itself or using it in dishes where color and appearance is important. If you are combining foods, then uniformity is not as important, and Grade B will be acceptable. Use Grade C vegetables for soups, stews, and casseroles.

Types of Fresh Vegetables

In the following section, the more popular types of vegetables are discussed, including how to determine quality and how to store the vegetables to maintain good taste and nutritional value. Unless otherwise stated, the nutritional content is based on fresh, raw vegetables.

ANISE

A spicy licorice-flavored vegetable, consisting of a bulb with stalks and leaves, anise (or fennel) is usually marketed only fresh. The bulb and the stalks should be white, crisp, and firm. The leaves should be green, with little or no sign of turning brown or yellow. If the bulb is overly mature, it will start to develop brown spots.

Raw anise makes a sparkling addition to salads. It can also be braised and served as a side dish. Store anise in the coldest part of the refrigerator. In terms of cost, about 65 to 75 percent of

CANNED VERSUS FROZEN: WHICH TO BUY?

Canned vegetables usually come packed in water or their natural juices. The label gives the net weight of the total contents, yet in most cases only the solids will be used. As a general rule, a 16- or 17-ounce can of vegetables will contain only 10 to 11 ounces of actual product. In comparisons of both national and store brands, informal tests show as much inconsistency in drained weights as in quality levels. Perform your own test: Always pour the liquid out after opening the can and check the fill level. You will then be able to identify the brands that are consistently short.

Although most frozen foods are individually quick-frozen and therefore do not contain any liquid, some types of frozen foods are susceptible to breakage. When you buy frozen products, check the packages carefully and avoid buying those brands that contain considerable broken material.

The canning process often causes some loss of vitamins and minerals. Frozen food, on the other hand, usually retains most of its nutritional value.

Here are a few other tips:

- When comparing the price of a canned vegetable to that of the frozen variety, remember that a 16-ounce can is roughly equivalent to a 10-ounce package of frozen vegetables. This discrepancy in weight is because most frozen products are packed dry.
- Loose foods that are frozen dry have a decided advantage over canned and fresh products because you can take exactly the amount you need and keep the remainder frozen.
- Taste is one of the most important considerations. Fresh, and then frozen vegetables, always have the edge over the canned variety.

this vegetable is edible. Anise is very low in calories—about 30 per cup. It's also a good source of vitamin A and niacin, and contributes small amounts of calcium and iron.

ARTICHOKES

One of the oldest foods, artichokes are grown extensively in northern California and distributed throughout the United States. A herbaceous plant with tightly clinging green leaves, it supplies moderate levels of vitamins A and C, calcium, and potassium.

Look for compact, plump globes with uniformly green-colored leaves. Signs of browning, fuzzy centers, and spreading leaves are a sign of overmaturity. Artichokes can be stored at 33° to 35°F, but only for a short period of time. About 50 percent of an artichoke is edible.

ASPARAGUS

A member of the same plant family as lilies and tulips, asparagus is available in both green and white varieties, although green asparagus is the most common. Look for stalks that are straight and firm, with a fresh appearance. The tips should be compact, and the stems should have only about 1 to 1½ inches of a woody-textured base, which must be trimmed off. Asparagus is one of the most perishable of vegetables, so store it in the coldest part of the refrigerator. About 60 to 65 percent of fresh asparagus is edible.

A serving of cooked asparagus contains relatively low amounts of calories and is a good source of vitamins A and C.

BEANS

More varieties of beans are available than any other vegetable. The easiest way to classify beans is to separate them into the edible *pod* type, such as the green and wax bean, and the *shell* type, which includes the lima, red kidney, white, and other varieties.

Green and wax beans. This is known as the string bean because the pod usually contains two tough stringlike filaments that have to be removed before cooking. Researchers have now developed a stringless variety. When fresh, they are known as snap beans, pole beans, or bush beans; when canned or frozen, the stringless variety is called green or wax (yellow) beans.

In both the green and the yellow variety, look for long, straight pods without the bulges found in oversized beans. The beans should snap easily when bent and should not have any spots or blemishes. The pod is edible, so the only waste is the stem. A serving of cooked string beans is low in calories and is an excellent source of vitamin A.

Shell beans. Usually available canned, dried, and (depending on the bean) frozen, this type of bean is always removed from the shell before it is sold. The principal varieties are *pea beans*, a small, whitish bean with a delicate flavor and used in some brands of pork and beans as well as soups; *white beans*, sometimes called navy beans and used in soup, salads, or canned plain or in a sauce; *red kidney beans*, either light or dark, and used in salads, soups, casseroles, and in various sauces; *pinto beans*, a favorite for Mexican-style dishes and, mixed with various spices, called ranch beans, Texas-style, barbecue, and other names associated with the Southwest and Mexico; *garbanzo beans* or *chick-peas*, used in salads, soups, and casseroles; and *lima beans*, the only bean in the group that is most often used as a vegetable in menu planning.

Beans are high in protein and are often used as meat substitutes. Relatively high in calories, they are a good source of dietary fiber and potassium.

BEETS

One of the few root vegetables with edible stems and leaves, beets are usually available fresh throughout the year. Beet tops from young plants are high in vitamin A and are sold as salad greens. Cook them as you would spinach.

Beets are relatively low in calories and contain a moderate amount of vitamin C.

Top-quality beets have a deep red color, and the root or globe is firm and smooth. Overmature beets have a tendency to become tough and fibrous, so look for ones that are small to medium-sized. Don't worry if the tops or leaves look wilted and brown— this will not hurt the quality of the root.

Store beets at between 33° and 38°F. Don't trim the roots or stems too close until just before cooking. Otherwise, the beet will lose considerable moisture and color. If you buy beets with the tops on, expect about 40 to 50 percent waste.

BROCCOLI

Broccoli is a cool-weather plant, and its supply and quality may diminish during the months of July and August. A member of the cabbage family, broccoli is high in vitamin C, fiber, and sulforaphane—a possible cancer-fighting chemical, according to recent studies.

Always look for deep green–colored buds, leaves, and stems. As the plant matures, the stems lighten and the buds turn yellow. Old broccoli is fibrous, and the buds turn bitter and tough. The bottom part of the stem of young broccoli is excellent for soup stock.

BRUSSELS SPROUTS

Available only whole, brussels sprouts look like tiny cabbages, although the taste is distinctly different.

A serving of steamed brussels sprouts is a good source of vitamins A and C and is high in fiber.

High-quality brussels sprouts are brightly colored with tight, compact leaves. Faded, soft sprouts are bitter, and yellowing leaves are an indication of age. Sprouts lose moisture quickly, so store them in the refrigerator and use them quickly.

CABBAGE

Four principal varieties of cabbage are available: the popular green head, the red head, the savoy, and the Chinese (sometimes called celery cabbage). Used extensively in salads, raw cabbage is rich in vitamin C and minerals. Cabbage is also sold commercially as sauerkraut, cabbage fermented in its own juices and salt.

The green- and red-head cabbages should be firm, with a bright color and crisp, compact leaves. If the leaves are blemished, discolored, or have separated from the base of the cabbage, it is either too old or has been in storage too long. Whereas the outer leaf is usually removed before using, the first layer of inner leaves should be usable, resulting in only 15 percent waste. Cabbage stores well in the refrigerator.

The savoy and Chinese varieties have less of a head, since the leaves tend to grow vertically. The leaves should be crisp (not limp) and bright in color, with no brown edges or other blemishes. Although used mostly for salads, Chinese cabbage is also used in many stir-fry oriental dishes.

CARROTS

A versatile vegetable, carrots store well and are resistant to damage from handling. They mix well with many types of vegetables and are available fresh, canned, and frozen.

Look for firm, well-formed, orange-to-deep-orange roots. Cracks and yellowing are signs of overmaturity, particularly around the tops. Old carrots have tough, fibrous cores. Carrots are high in beta carotene, another purported cancer-fighting substance, according to some studies.

CAULIFLOWER

A member of the same plant family as cabbage and broccoli, cauliflower is low in calories and is an excellent source of vitamin C.

Cauliflower is shipped whole with the stem, head, and covering leaves, or the head alone, wrapped in plastic film. A cauliflower head should be very dense—so much so that many cooks recommend soaking it in saltwater for an hour to force out any insects. The flowerets or "curds" should be creamy white, firm, and compact, and they should not show any discoloration or spots. Overly mature cauliflower will show signs of budding, resulting in a grainy texture.

CELERY

Practically all the celery sold today is Pascal, although occasionally you may find some of the golden heart variety, recognized by its bleached-white appearance. Almost all celery is marketed fresh. The only exception is very young stalks, hearts, and knobs canned by a few specialty packers. Celery is very low in calories and contains fiber.

Look for light green, brittle stalks and leaves that show no signs of wilting. If the celery does wilt, try this old trick to restore firmness: Cut the knob or base off the celery and stand the celery stalks upright in a jar or pitcher half-filled with water. Refrigerate. (Before refrigeration, celery was commonly kept in a special container in the kitchen called the celery glass.)

Practically all of the celery plant is usable: the stalks cut up in salads, cooked as a vegetable, or for relish trays, and the leaves for soup stock. If you keep celery more than two days, use the storage hint described above.

CORN

Over 200 varieties of corn are grown in the United States, and all fall within three groups: yellow, white, and multicolor or bicolor. The most popular group is yellow corn, although white corn is still marketed in the South. Dried, multicolored Indian corn is often sold for decoration. Corn contains a moderate amount of calories and vitamin A.

If corn is sold in its husks (the green covering leaves), the leaves should be a bright green color and the tassels (silk strands) should be turning brown. The kernels should be plump and smooth, and the ears should be filled with kernels. Peel back one or two of the leaves to check the ears for wormholes. As corn matures, the kernels turn a deeper and richer yellow, but many people prefer the taste of the smaller-kerneled young corn. The smaller the kernels and the lighter the tassel, the younger the corn.

Buy corn that is as fresh as possible, and do not store it for any prolonged period. The natural sugars convert to starch when fresh corn is kept at medium-to-high temperatures.

Considering the amount of leaves and the size of the cob, an ear of corn has considerable waste. But the taste of fresh corn on the cob is so distinctive when compared to canned or frozen corn that any price comparison is meaningless.

CUCUMBERS

A favorite for salads and relish trays, cucumbers are also a run-away winner for pickles. Low in calories, cucumbers contain a small amount of dietary fiber and are generally low in nutritional value.

Table or slicing cucumbers are mostly field-grown varieties, harvested when the color is deep, rich green and the shape is long and thick. Cucumbers are washed and then waxed to preserve the color and to prevent dehydration (peel before using). The outer covering or rind should be firm and show no signs of yellowing. Store cucumbers at moderately cool temperatures. Since all but the stem can be eaten, the cucumber has little waste.

EGGPLANT

Only fresh eggplant is available as a vegetable or as a meat substitute, although cans of baby pickled eggplants can also be found in some supermarkets. Several different types of eggplant exist, but the dark purple, pear-shaped variety is the most common.

The skin should be dark and glossy, smooth and firm. Size is an important clue to maturity, because both immature and overly mature eggplant can be bitter. They are best when between three and six inches in diameter. Eggplant, which is quite perishable, will keep the longest when stored at 45° to 50°F. One other variety, the Japanese eggplant, is gaining in popularity. It is much smaller than the common variety, and grows more in length than in thickness. Eggplant is low in calories and has some dietary fiber.

GARLIC

Prized by many civilizations more as a medicine than a vegetable, garlic is an important and popular seasoning ingredient. In fact, many dishes would lose much of their flavor and zest without it. A compound, bulbous root, it has an odor that is strong, pungent, and, as breath-sweetener commercials would have it, long-lasting. Three general types of garlic are grown: the Creole, with its large cloves; the Italian, with small cloves but a strong flavor; and the Tahitian, also with large cloves but darker in color.

Choose garlic cloves that are firm, particularly the tips. Store garlic by itself, because other foods can absorb the garlic odor. It is best stored in a jar in the refrigerator.

LEEKS

Leeks are often erroneously grouped with green onions, shallots, and scallions, but they are actually thought to be a form of cultivated oriental garlic. They can be cooked in much the same way as celery but are most often used for soups.

Look for flat, bright-green leaves and firm white stalks. Signs of age are wilting or limp leaves with brown edges and stalks that are soft and spotty. Leeks should be stored in a cool, humid environment.

LETTUCE

Once available only in season, lettuce is now available in all parts of the country and all year long. The same strategy that allows growers to keep lettuce fresh during shipment can also help you keep it longer in your own refrigerator: You have probably noticed that head or iceberg lettuce is sold wrapped in a plastic covering that has many small slits or perforations. These openings allow the lettuce to drain when it is periodically sprayed with water while on display or en route to the retailer. In this same manner, you can also keep lettuce moist until you are ready to use it.

There are numerous varieties of lettuce, but most fall into one of five general types: *crisphead*, of which iceberg is the leading variety; *Butterhead*, including Boston and Bibb; *romaine* or *cos; leaf*, which includes both red- and green-leaf varieties; and *stem* or celtuce, which is used in many oriental dishes.

Lettuce is low in calories and high in vitamin A, especially the greener varieties.

Iceberg. Iceberg lettuce has a compact head, with darker green leaves around the outside. Although it is the most popular lettuce sold in the United States, it is the lowest on the nutritional and taste scale. Look for firm heads with crisp outer leaves and no sign of wilting or "rust." The so-called rust is a sign of a wide variation in holding temperatures during shipment, or of over-maturity. Although harmless, this discoloration detracts from the vegetable's appearance.

Butterhead. A softer and less crisp type of lettuce, butterhead includes such varieties as big and white Boston, Bibb, and May-king. The butterhead is excellent for tossed green salads or as a garnish. Look for fresh-appearing leaves that show no sign of spotting or excessive wilting. The head should be stored in the same manner as iceberg.

Cos. Better known as romaine, this type has long, narrow, crisp leaves and a well-defined rib or stem. It is an excellent salad lettuce and, because it retains its crispness, it is often used for garnishing and for Caesar salad. The leaves look rough but are very tender and flavorful. Romaine that is overly mature or has lost its freshness will begin to turn brown along the small veins of the leaves.

Leaf. Also a favorite salad lettuce, the red- and green-leaf types have crinkly, crisp leaves that are not only tasty but also make a very attractive garnish. Watch for browning along the edge of the leaves.

Stem. The edible part is the large seed stalk. It can be eaten raw, but most stem lettuce is used in oriental cookery. Brown spots along the stem are a sign that it is too old.

MUSHROOMS

An edible fungus, mushrooms are now commercially cultivated in carefully controlled growing environments. One standard variety is sold fresh in the United States, although several oriental and European varieties are now available in many supermarkets, including the chanterelle, cremeni, oyster, enoki, and portobello.

These varieties are more expensive than the standard supermarket mushroom, but each lends a unique taste to certain dishes. Mushrooms are low in calories and have little nutritional value. Those of high quality should be white, with few bruises or dark spots.

Mushrooms cook rapidly, usually in two to four minutes, and will shrink considerably if overcooked. If you use them in stews, soups, or sauces, add them shortly before turning off the heat.

OKRA

Okra, a seed pod harvested in the immature stage, is most popular as a vegetable in the southern part of the United States. Used extensively in soups, especially chicken gumbo, okra is a good source of vitamin A.

Look for pods of less than 4 inches in length, with a bright green color and no blemishes. The tips should bend or snap easily. If the color is dull and the body tough and rigid, the product will be fibrous. If okra is overcooked, the texture changes to a gummy or pasty consistency disliked by many.

ONIONS

Shopping for onions can be confusing. Many varieties have typical yellow or white skins and are quite similar in shape, but they can vary widely in taste. Some can be eaten almost like an apple (the Vidalia, for example), whereas others are so pungent that they bring tears to your eyes. Three basic types are sold in American markets: the late crop or globe, the Bermuda-Granex globe, and the Spanish or Creole. Onions are high in vitamin C.

Look for well-shaped onions with skins dry enough to crackle. Onions with green sprouts are old and have lost their crispness and flavor.

Do not store fresh onions in the refrigerator. Unlike most vegetables, onions should be stored where the humidity is low. This will retard decay or sprouting. Do not keep onions with potatoes because they will absorb moisture from the potatoes and decay more rapidly.

PEAS

Peas, one of the most popular of vegetables, are also subject to wide variations in quality because they are very sensitive to over-processing. There are two distinct varieties: the early June and the sweet. Peas are moderately high in dietary fiber and are a good source of vitamins A and C.

Look for bright green pods that are smooth to the touch and well filled. Pods that are limp, swollen, and light or grayish in color are overly mature, and the peas will be mealy and poorly flavored. Use this vegetable as soon as possible after harvesting, because the flavor deteriorates rapidly.

PEPPERS

Although peppers are categorized in only two types—the mild or sweet-fleshed and the hot—the variations in taste, color, texture, and pungency are almost unlimited. The paprika pepper, for example, is so mild as to be almost tasteless, and the Japanese or Indian dried chili pepper is hot enough to raise blisters on your lips. Peppers are an excellent source of vitamin C and contain moderate amounts of vitamins A and E.

The most popular sweet-fleshed pepper is the bell variety, an attractive, rich green or red depending upon the maturity of the pepper. Look for thick walls, a firm, uniform shape, and no sign of bruises or grayish spots. A pale color is typical of an immature pepper, and blistering is a sign of internal decay. Store peppers at temperatures between 45° and 50°F.

The hot varieties—the chili, pimento, and cayenne—range in pungency from mildly warm to fiery hot. The chili pepper, for example, comes in several varieties such as the Fresno, the yellow, the Serrano, the Parsilla, and the hot. It is difficult to determine which ones are extremely hot just by their appearance, so approach any chili pepper with caution.

POTATOES

The consumption of potatoes in the United States has been declining, partly because of the availability of so many alternative starch foods and also because of the misconception that potatoes are high in calories. Actually, a medium-sized potato has about the same amount of calories as an apple. It's the mounds of butter and gravy that we put on top of a potato that adds the calories. Nutritionally, too, the potato is a good source of vitamins B and C and several important minerals.

One of the primary reasons that potatoes have been so popular throughout the world is because they can be stored without refrigeration for long periods. Every farm once had its root cellar, where vegetables such as potatoes and carrots could be stored for use in the winter and spring.

The following is just a partial list of the varieties available:

Cobbler (Irish). Round with very smooth skin, the cobbler is light in color but darkens somewhat after cooking. It is basically a boiling potato.

Green mountain. Oblong and somewhat flattened, with a smooth skin and medium deep eyes, this potato can be baked or boiled.

Katahdin. Round with a smooth, light skin, this variety is used mostly for boiling.

Kennebec. Oblong with a smooth skin, whitish color, and shallow eyes, this potato is best for boiling and frying.

Keswick. This variety is oblong, with a dark skin color and white flesh that does not discolor after cooking. It is good for boiling as well as baking.

Norgold russet. This is an oblong potato with heavy, netted russet skin. It is used for boiling or frying.

Red Pontiac. This variety is round to oblong, with deep red skin, and is used mostly for boiling or steaming.

Russet Burbank. Also known as the Idaho, this is a popular all-purpose potato. It is long and cylindrical, with the typical speckled, rough skin of a russet.

Sebago. A round potato with a smooth, light skin, this type can be boiled or baked.

White rose. Large and long with a smooth white skin, this potato darkens after cooking and is good for either boiling or baking.

Regardless of the variety, potatoes in bulk or bags should be firm, smooth, clean, and show no signs of greening. Greening is not a sign that the potato is young or "new" but that it was exposed to excessive natural or artificial light. This makes the potato bitter. Greening also produces toxins within the potato itself—a health risk if such potatoes are consumed in large quantities.

The surface of the potato should not be bruised, decayed, or cracked, nor should the "eyes" be sprouting small white shoots. Always store potatoes in a cool dark place, away from onions.

Cook the potato with the skin on to preserve the nutritional elements. Puncture the skin of any potato before baking in a conventional, convection, or microwave oven. (Once you've had to clean up after a baked potato has exploded, you will never forget this rule.)

Potatoes have other uses: Use a raw potato to reduce the amount of salt in a soup or stew—just add the potato and simmer until the flavor is right.

RADISHES

Only available fresh, a high-quality radish is identified by the root, not the condition of its leaves. Look for firm, crisp, fresh-looking roots, and avoid those with spongy and rubbery texture and feel. The long, white *icicle* radish has a very mild flavor, whereas the *red button* variety can be quite fiery in taste.

Radishes store best without the tops. Most supermarkets sell them already topped and packed in plastic bags, but you can still find fresh radishes in many stores with the tops intact. Remove the tops as soon as possible and store the radishes in plastic bags in the coolest section of the refrigerator. Radishes that have become dehydrated or wilted can be improved considerably by soaking them in slightly salted water with ice cubes. Do this for about 15 minutes before serving. Radishes are low in calories, have a trace of iron, and are relatively high in potassium.

SPINACH

Spinach has been a favored cooked vegetable for many years, but its popularity as a fresh salad green has increased dramatically over the past two decades. Spinach is a good source of vitamin A, iron, and other minerals.

The curly- and flat-leaf varieties are equally good for cooking and for salads. Look for crisp, well-developed leaves without brown edges and with a dark green color. The stalks should be small and crisp. Avoid spinach leaves that are wilted or turning yellow. Store spinach in very cool temperatures, and use as soon as possible. For crisp salad greens, place the spinach in a plastic bag with a few ice cubes, or sprinkle water on the leaves before refrigerating them.

SQUASH

"Summer" and "winter" are terms applied to different types of squash, but they actually mean very little. The best method of classifying squash is to sort the varieties according to the texture of the shell. The *soft-shell* varieties are almost 100 percent edible, including shells, pulp, and seeds, and are actually harvested before maturity. The zucchini, for example, is picked when it is 5 to 8 inches long, but as gardeners know only too well, if left to continue to grow, a mature zucchini will stretch halfway across the garden. The soft-shell kinds are perishable and should be stored at about 50° to 55°F. The *hard-shell* varieties are only about 60 percent edible, because only the pulp is consumed.

Squash is low in calories and contains vitamins A and C.

Soft-shell squashes

- *Yellow crookneck and straightneck.* These are the same squash, but with different-shaped necks. They should be harvested when the skin is a pale yellow, because the deeper the yellow, the more mature and tough the squash. The skin should be bumpy and tender. Watch out for brown spots, because these types of squashes decay rapidly.

- *Scallop.* This is a round, light green squash shaped like a flying saucer. As it matures, the skin will turn white, so look for the pale green color. It's an excellent squash for frying.
- *Zucchini.* A cylindrical green squash harvested when very young, the zucchini has a ribbed skin and should be very tender. As for very large, mature zucchini, only the pulp should be eaten.

Hard-shell squashes

- *Acorn.* Deep, dark green and shaped like its namesake, the acorn is yellow-fleshed and ideal for baking. It can be stored for four to six months, so long as there are no ruptures or cuts in the skin.
- *Banana.* A large squash often sold in sections, the banana variety has orange-tinted flesh and the skin is slightly wrinkled. It is pale green to creamy pink when mature.
- *Buttercup.* Shaped like the acorn variety, but with a bumpy ring around the stem, the buttercup is yellow-fleshed and ideal for baking.
- *Hubbard.* A large, dark green squash with bumpy skin and yellow flesh, hubbard can be successfully stored for long periods of time.
- *Spaghetti.* This variety is a large, light-skinned squash sold either whole or in sections. The interior flesh is light yellow when cooked and forms spaghettilike strands, hence the name.

SWEET POTATOES

One of the most complete foods, sweet potatoes are rich in vitamins A and C and also contain many of the minerals essential to good health. The principal types are the dry-meated and the moist-meated, popularly known as a yam.

WHEN IS A TOMATO REALLY RIPE?

A mature tomato and a ripe tomato are not the same thing. The term *mature* means that the fruit has reached the stage in its development when it can begin the ripening process. In fact, the tomato matures several days before it begins to change color from green to pink and, ultimately, to deep red. In order to ship the product to all parts of the country, the grower must determine when the crop has matured enough to begin the ripening stage. This is usually accomplished by cutting up samples of the crop and examining the stage of seed growth. These samples may be representative of most of the crop, but some immature tomatoes will still reach the supermarkets. Obviously, it would be better if tomatoes were not harvested until they began the color change, but the cost of spoilage in long-distance hauls would be prohibitive.

Since tomatoes are grown in every state for the fresh market, there are a few weeks during the year when the large, red, unblemished and vine-ripened fruit is available. During the rest of the year, you may have to abstain from fresh tomatoes, or follow these tips:

- Buy only those tomatoes that have begun the color change, which means those that are at least pink. Tomatoes that are still green will probably not ripen.
- Plan ahead. If you use tomatoes frequently, buy a few several days in advance so that you will always have some fully ripe ones on hand. If you use tomatoes only occasionally, try to buy them three to four days before you need them.
- Do not refrigerate tomatoes until they are fully ripe. A fully ripened tomato feels tender and has a deep red color.
- An unripe tomato will continue to ripen at room temperature. You can accelerate the ripening by placing the tomatoes in a paper bag along with a ripe apple.
- Always serve tomatoes at room temperature: Cold inhibits the flavor.

The dry type of sweet potato is very light or yellowish-tan in color, whereas yams are darker, ranging from tan to brownish-red. High-quality sweet potatoes should be firm and unblemished, without any signs of dehydration or decay. Store for short periods of time in low humidity at about 55°F.

TOMATOES

Not really a vegetable, the tomato is actually a fruit of the berry family. Tomatoes are low in calories and rich in vitamin A, and contain a moderate amount of vitamins C and E.

Fresh tomatoes are usually one of three basic market types: the typical field-grown or hothouse red type, the cherry, and the Italian or plum tomato. The red is truly all-purpose—it's used in salads, sandwiches, and casseroles. It can be sliced, baked, or used as a garnish. The small cherry tomato is used mostly in salads and for garnish. The Italian or plum can be used for all purposes, but because of its high flesh or pulp content, it is particularly good for making sauces.

Avoid tomatoes that are completely green, bruised, or over-ripe. An overripe tomato will be spongy and show signs of surface collapse or flat areas under the skin. Blemishes and deep growth cracks will decrease the yield, because these sections will have to be removed and discarded.

TURNIPS AND RUTABAGAS

Members of the same family, turnips and rutabagas are usually available only fresh and are generally prepared in the same manner. The turnip is round, white-fleshed, and small to medium-size, whereas the rutabaga is a larger, distinctly yellow-fleshed root. It is usually coated with a thin film of paraffin to prevent wilting and to enhance its appearance. Since both turnips and rutabagas are usually peeled before cooking, the paraffin presents no problems. Store turnips and rutabagas at very cool temperatures. Signs of quality are firm, smooth roots with no softness or shriveling. Avoid those that have been cut or punctured during shipment. Turnips are low in calories and provide a small amount of vitamin C.

WATERCRESS

A leafy green vegetable, watercress is used in soups, sandwiches, and salads. The leaves are delicate and tender, with a tangy taste. Handle watercress like leaf lettuce, and store a bunch at low temperatures. Look for crisp, bright, springy leaves, and avoid those that appear to be wilting or turning yellow.

SPECIALTY VEGETABLES

Numerous other vegetables are used in ethnic dishes or in salads. The following are generally available in supermarkets.

- *Bamboo shoots.* Tender young stalks from the bamboo plant, shoots are used in salads and stir-fry cookery.
- *Bean sprouts.* Very young bean shoots, these are excellent for salads, sandwiches, and oriental dishes. They should be tender and crisp when purchased. Many chefs recommend that they be chilled in ice water before serving.
- *Bok choy.* A leafy green vegetable with very prominent edible stalks, bok choy has a flavor that is a combination of celery and Chinese cabbage. Use it for soups and stir-fry cookery.
- *Snow peas.* A flat, edible pod with very tiny peas, snow peas are cooked and eaten like a green bean. They are used extensively in oriental cookery.
- *Soybeans.* Both the bean and sprout are used. Soybeans are very high in vitamin B and protein.
- *Swiss chard.* This is a leafy green vegetable with large ribs. Use it as a salad green or cook it like spinach.
- *Water chestnuts.* These are edible tubers used extensively in oriental cookery.

6

The Produce Section: Fruits

Not so many years ago, fresh fruit was a delicacy to be enjoyed only when in season. Now, as you walk through the produce section of your local supermarket, past the overflowing displays of numerous kinds of fruits, it's hard to believe that many of these items have been shipped thousands of miles to arrive practically at your doorstep.

That's not to say that a portion of the fresh fruit on sale doesn't show signs of improper handling on the way. Fruit is much more delicate than most vegetables, so there are many challenges in both the harvesting and the transportation process. Since bruised fruit will spoil or decay rapidly, special methods of handling and packaging have been developed to protect the product every step of the way from the fields to your home. Perhaps the most important technical advance is the concept of controlled atmosphere. By maintaining the right storage and transportation environment, the shelf life of many types of fruit can be prolonged.

Some may argue that a controlled atmosphere does not make for a superior apple or peach, for example. And, indeed, an apple or peach picked ripe from the tree is incomparable in taste. Nevertheless, if the storage process is properly handled, with the exact ratio of gases and humidity supplied, these fruits can be more than acceptable in both taste and texture.

How Fruits Ripen

"Respiration" refers to the way in which fruits absorb oxygen and release carbon dioxide during the ripening process. All fruits continue to respire after harvesting, and many actually ripen after they have been picked.

Although cold storage retards the ripening process somewhat, it is the reduction of oxygen in the controlled atmosphere that slows down the fruit's metabolism and decreases the rate of ripening even further. When a fruit is eventually allowed to ripen, the condition and flavor should be normal.

Continued refrigeration in your home will retard the ripening process. When fruits are kept at room temperature, the rate of respiration and ripening increases four to six times, thus increasing the chance of spoilage before the fruit is consumed.

Some fruits are more affected by cold storage than others, though. For example, improper cold storage with low humidity can affect many supermarket peaches, resulting in a dry, mealy texture and bland taste.

Sometimes you may buy citrus fruit that appears wholesome and ripe, only to find that the flesh is dried out and stringy. This phenomenon is usually the result of a less than adequate amount of rainfall in the growing region. Unfortunately, it is difficult to pinpoint these unsatisfactory products; one clue is that these fruits are generally undersized.

Fruit Packaging

Although some consumers have reacted negatively to prepackaged fruit, there is no doubt that prepacking is the most efficient way to avoid bruising and eventual spoilage. Tender varieties of apples and pears, for example, can be severely damaged when shipped in bulk. Packed in a paper pulp tray with a plastic overwrap, the fruit is protected, thus reducing the chance of spoilage. Prepacked fruit is more expensive, but it is an alternative when the bulk fruit is in poor condition—especially if appearance is important to you.

The U.S. Department of Agriculture has also established quality standards to be used in grading fruits. These grades must take into consideration both the natural quality—the maturity, color, surface blemishes, and size—and also the amount of damage from handling and processing. As with vegetables, the grading service is voluntary and must be paid for by those companies requesting the service. Consequently, less than 50 percent of fresh produce is graded by the USDA.

Canned and frozen fruits are also graded by the USDA on a voluntary fee basis. The grades for canned fruit are U.S. Grade A or Fancy, U.S. Grade B or Choice, and U.S. Grade C or Standard. Often fruits, like vegetables, are labeled "Grade A" but do not have the typical USDA shield. These products must also meet USDA Grade A standards, but were not processed under the continuous inspection of USDA inspectors. Most canned and frozen fruits are not officially graded because most processors rely on brand identification as the most important factor in consumer selection.

Types of Fresh Fruits

APPLES

Over 7,000 varieties of apples are recorded in horticultural literature, and no one knows how many other kinds have been developed and then discarded. Why so many? Because a tree grown from seed does not bear fruit of the same variety as the parent apple. In fact, if you planted several seeds from the same apple, each resulting tree would bear different fruit—not only from the parent, but also from one another. Desired varieties are regenerated by grafting buds or branches from the parent tree onto special rootstock. The resulting fruit-bearing trees are then continually inspected to determine which are best for the next grafting process.

Nutritionally, apples are high in vitamins and minerals and contain about 80 calories each. They also provide the necessary bulk or fiber to aid digestion.

Each of the many varieties of apples differs in texture and taste. Some are more suitable for eating raw, others are better for cooking or baking, whereas still others are considered to be all-purpose apples. There are, however, some general rules to follow when buying any variety.

CANNED FRUIT GRADINGS

The standards for the USDA grades are as follows:

USDA Grade A or Fancy fruits should be at the peak of their quality, with excellent color and uniform size. There should be no blemishes or spots, and the texture should be firm and show no evidence of deterioration from overprocessing. Both the flavor and the appearance should be excellent.

USDA Grade B or Choice fruits should have a very good color and only slight variations in size and texture. There should be almost no blemishes and no broken pieces. There may be some indication of overmaturity or overprocessing, but not enough to change the characteristic shape. The flavor and appearance should be very good.

USDA Grade C or Standard fruits may have variations in size and color. Some of the pieces may be broken or blemished. There may be signs of over- or undermaturity as well as overprocessing. The texture of the fruit may be too firm or too soft, and the appearance not pleasing.

- Look for evidence of severe bruising. An apple bruise is a flat, round spot that may or may not be softer than the surrounding surface. Bruises accelerate decay, and the flesh under the bruise will turn brown.
- Look for good color (the shade of color depends upon the variety) and an absence of cuts, indentations, and flat sections. The apples should be firm and the skin unwrinkled. If you are planning to use the apples for cooking, surface blemishes will not affect the taste and are therefore unimportant. In fact, you can sometimes buy blemished apples for considerably less than those that may be more perfect in appearance.
- Many varieties are multicolored or have one color overlaying another. The background color is the most important in determining the maturity or the stage of ripening. In

the red varieties, the background should be yellowish green: The deeper the green, the less mature the apple; the deeper the yellow, the more mature the apple. Larger apples mature faster than small ones.

- Don't believe the old tale that red apples are for eating and green for cooking or baking. To eat raw or to cook is strictly a matter of the variety, not the color (see below).

VARIETIES OF APPLES

Cortland. These apples have red stripes on a green-yellow background. They are excellent for eating, and good to excellent for cooking.

Golden delicious. Golden yellow, with some greening, this variety is the most versatile. It is a good eating apple, and good to excellent for cooking.

Granny Smith. Medium green with a slight speckle, this variety is a good all-purpose apple. Slightly tart in taste, it is one of the best choices for the classic apple pie.

Gravenstein. Red with a prominent yellowish-green background, this apple is tart but a good all-purpose apple.

Jonathan. Deep red in color, this variety is good for salads, eating, and garnishing, but is very poor for baking.

McIntosh. This apple ranges in color from red over green to completely red. An excellent eating apple, it is not very good for cooking or baking.

Red delicious. Deep red in color, this apple is excellent for eating but not for cooking.

Stayman. Red with a slight yellowish background, this variety is tart and quite soft.

Winesap. Deep red in color, this is an excellent apple for eating. It is also fairly good baked.

APRICOTS

A delicate fruit of the drupe family, which includes plums, peaches, and nectarines, the apricot is high in vitamin A and low in calories.

Look for firm and plump fruit, golden in color. Watch for bruises or discoloration, and don't buy apricots that are soft and mushy. Apricots deteriorate rapidly and should be refrigerated when ripe.

AVOCADOS

The avocado is another example of a product that was once highly seasonal but is now available throughout the year. Although California currently produces over 75 percent of the avocados consumed in the United States, Florida's crop is significant

---

WHEN IS AN AVOCADO RIPE?

The difference in taste and texture between an underripe and a ripe avocado is so extreme that many people avoid buying the fruit because they are not sure when it is ripe for eating.

There are several methods of determining when an avocado is ready to eat. The skin of the Hass variety, for example, turns from green to black as it ripens. Test other varieties by touch: The skin of a ripe avocado will yield to the touch because the ripening process changes the texture of the flesh from firm and almost hard to a soft, spreadable consistency. By exerting a slight pressure on the skin, you can feel the flesh give a bit. You may also push a toothpick into the stem area; if it moves in and out easily, then the fruit is ripe.

Unless you intend to use an avocado immediately, it is usually best to buy the fruit slightly underripe and let it ripen at home.

and continues to increase. There are over 700 varieties, but the leaders are the Hass, Fuerte, Bacon, and Zutano from California and the Booth, Lula, and Waldin from Florida. These varieties differ more in the shape, color, and the thickness of the skin than they do in taste and texture.

The flesh of an avocado turns brown very rapidly after it has been exposed to air. You can retard this color change by covering the exposed area with lemon or lime juice. Avoid buying avocados that are bruised or have dark, sunken surfaces. The flesh darkens when bruised even before the fruit is ripe.

Because of the delicate nature of its flesh, the avocado is not available canned, frozen, or dried.

The uses of the avocado are many: in salads, as a spread, stuffed, in soups, or whipped as the principal ingredient of guacamole. Avocados are high in calories but are an excellent source of vitamins A and E as well as potassium.

BANANAS

One of the few fruits that should never ripen on the tree, the banana is best when purchased slightly green and allowed to ripen at home. A ripe banana, which has about 100 calories, contains numerous vitamins and minerals, particularly potassium. Bananas are an easily digested food, so they are often baby's first dessert.

Despite a popular misconception, ripe bananas do well in the refrigerator: The skin will darken, but the flesh will retain its natural color, taste, and texture for several days. Like avocados, the flesh of a cut banana darkens rapidly when exposed to air; a coating of lemon or lime juice will retard the change.

BERRIES

Berries have continued to be an important part of our diet since colonial times.

A good source of vitamin C, all berries should be refrigerated upon purchase. In fact, they will keep their quality and freshness best if you sprinkle water over them just before refrigerating. Moisten them daily thereafter.

- **Blackberries.** Conical-shaped clusters of tiny black globes, these berries are slightly tart with a distinctive flavor. Clusters should be fully developed and firm, with no sign of deterioration around the stem.
- **Blueberries.** These are the most popular berries in the United States, but they have a limited fresh season (usually from May to September). They are single-globe berries with smooth skin. A blueberry is blue with a silvery bloom when it is at its flavor peak. Although available in several sizes, the larger berries have the most flavor. They are usually marketed in square containers with a plastic overwrap. Check the contents for soft berries with shriveled skin, an indication that the fruit is overripe.

  Note: Blueberries can be easily frozen at home. Spread them on a shallow pan in thin layers, and place the pan in the freezer. Move the berries around when half-frozen to keep them separated, and store them in plastic bags. In this way, you can always take out just the amount that you need.
- **Boysenberries.** A member of the bramble family, this berry is grown mostly in California. It is a cluster berry, larger than the blackberry, and becomes a dark reddish-black when ripe. Watch for fully developed clusters with plump globes. Boysenberries have a slightly acidic taste.
- **Cranberries.** A single bright red, globe-type berry with a longer shelf life than most, the cranberry is grown in marshy areas called bogs. Although there are some minor differences between varieties, look for firm, plump, red berries with a glossy surface. Signs of overmaturity are skins that are dull and shriveled and beginning to soften.

  You can easily freeze your own during the harvesting season by using the same freezing techniques suggested for blueberries.
- **Raspberries.** Most raspberries marketed today are either the black or red varieties, although there are numerous other less popular varieties with different colorations. The raspberry is a cluster-type berry, and is more round than conical. The flavor is more delicate than that of the blackberry.

  Look for brightly colored red or black berries with firm,

well-developed clusters. Shriveled sections of the clusters are a sign of overmature fruit, and they will have a decidedly sour or rancid taste. Raspberries can be frozen at home using the techniques described previously.

- **Strawberries.** This fruit has a built-in feature that signals maturity: When the berry is mature enough to ripen, the stem breaks before the cap will separate. There are numerous varieties that differ in sweetness and size, but the larger-sized berries are preferred for snacking.

  The Douglas variety seems to be increasing in popularity. A large berry, often fan-shaped with multiple points, the Douglas is both sweet and firm and is excellent for garnishing salads or cakes. With all varieties, look for plump, firm berries that show little or no green around the points. Avoid strawberries with any indication of shriveled skin, mold, or bruise spots.

  You can freeze strawberries at home, but leave the caps on to reduce dehydration.

CHERRIES

The Bing or Lambert is a sweet, dark cherry that is marketed throughout the country. One or more local varieties that cannot be shipped outside the growing area may also be available. Cherries are high in vitamin A and several essential minerals.

Although there are both dark red and light or white varieties of this fruit, the light-colored are such poor shippers that usually only the reds can be found in your local markets. Look for a large size, plump with a dark red, uniform color. Again, look for bruises, because cherries are very delicate and must be handled properly during shipping. They should be stored at 33° to 36°F in high humidity.

GRAPEFRUIT

The grapefruit is harvested when mature but not fully ripe. Often, shoppers mistakenly shy away from buying grapefruit that has a greenish tint, believing that the green is a sign of immaturity. Actually, the greening of mature fruit takes place during

THE GRAPEFRUIT: WHEN BEAUTY IS NOT SKIN-DEEP

A tart-sweet taste and abundant juice are the traits of high-quality, mature grapefruit. The best clue to look for when selecting the fruit is weight. The heavier the fruit, the more the juice. *The outside appearance is meaningless.* In fact, grapefruit that is allowed to fully ripen on the tree often develops blemishes, so slightly blemished fruit is the best. Signs of an overmature grapefruit are puffiness, light weight, and a shriveled and soft skin.

Grapefruit is grown in Arizona, California, Florida, and Texas and shipped throughout the world. Some of the sweetest varieties are also subject to more scarring and blemishing as they mature, especially those grown in Texas. Again, despite the fact that advertisements always show perfect unblemished fruit, blemished grapefruits are often the best.

---

the spring, when excess chlorophyll is produced during the new bloom. The actual color transition from green to yellow happens very early in the growth process, and therefore green immature fruit never gets to market.

Fresh grapefruit is very low in calories and is one of the best sources of vitamin C. The membrane separating the segments contains most of the nutritional elements.

GRAPES

Grape growing is the largest fruit industry in the world. The wine industry alone consumes tremendous quantities, and there are table grapes, raisins, grape juice, and canning grapes, the latter destined for fruit cocktail or salad.

The marketing of seedless varieties has steadily increased over the past four decades, especially the flame and the Thompson Seedless, but seeded grapes are still popular. Colors range from the deep purple of the Concord to the white of the muscat, and flavors range from very sweet to tangy, almost tart. Grapes contain 35 to 40 calories per portion (approximately 10 grapes) and vitamin A.

The greenish-yellow varieties often seen in the markets are the Thompson Seedless, the Calmiera, the elongated ladyfingers, and the round perlettes. Red varieties are the cardinal, the Flame Tokay, and the emperor. The purples are the Concord and the almost black Ribier.

Fresh grapes do not continue to ripen after they are picked, so select only ripe grapes at the supermarket. Pick the cluster with the most well-formed and mature grapes. The green varieties should have an amber shade, whereas the reds should have a yellow background, not green.

The Concord, an eastern grape, is full-fleshed and thick-skinned. It's excellent for wine, juice, or jelly. The Concord is also an excellent table grape, with a distinct tart flavor.

Grapes should be stored in the refrigerator.

LEMONS

The lemon is more of a flavoring ingredient than a table fruit. Unfortunately, unless you have access to a lemon tree, you'll never have the opportunity to taste a tree-ripened, fully mature lemon. Again, advertising has created the picture of the ideal lemon in the minds of the consumer: a relatively small, firm, symmetrical fruit without blemishes. In reality, lemons meet these criteria only during the early stages of maturing. As they become fully mature, the skin becomes rough, with some ribbing and blemishes. Although the look is less attractive, the taste of a fully ripened lemon is more concentrated and much less tart and acidic.

Look for a deep yellow color and heavy weight for its size. Don't be concerned if some are misshapen or have some blemishes. Do check the surfaces carefully, however, for bruises or perforations in the skin caused by the thorns of the lemon tree. Lemons are high in vitamin C and are best stored at temperatures in the low fifties.

LIMES

Another fruit used principally for flavoring, the familiar green lime turns to a light orange if allowed to fully ripen. Most are of the Persian variety and are harvested at the green, mature stage.

The Florida key lime, also known as the Mexican lime, is marketed when it matures to a light lemon color. The juice is strong in flavor and very acidic. Both varieties are an excellent source of vitamin C.

MELONS

The melon is known as "nature's dessert." The sweet taste of a fully ripe cantaloupe or honeydew melon will satisfy anyone's sweet tooth, and yet the melon is relatively low in calories and rich in vitamin C. Most varieties are only available fresh, although there is some demand for frozen melon balls.

- **Cantaloupe/muskmelon.** Unfortunately, there are no infallible ways to determine maturity, but look for the following signs to increase the odds of finding these melons at their peak of flavor: The mature cantaloupe/muskmelon breaks cleanly from the vine, leaving a small cavity. If any part of the stem is still attached, the melon was picked too soon and will not ripen at home. The netting of the skin should be very pronounced over a deep yellow background, with just a tint of green. (A dark green background is a sign of immaturity.) Softening around the stem cavity can mean that the melon is overripe and off-flavored. Hold the melon at room temperature for two or three days to soften the flesh of the fruit. Cantaloupes and muskmelons are particularly rich in vitamin A.
- **Casaba.** Look for the golden yellow skin color of a ripe melon. Light or white casabas are underripe.
- **Crenshaw.** The rind should be gold and green and, like the honeydews, the larger melons have the best flavor.
- **Honeydew.** Select a large melon for the best flavor. Look for a creamy white skin on all sides and a pleasant, sweet

aroma. Since honeydews are shipped underripe to lessen damage, a melon will often have the color and the size but will still be hard. Keep a honeydew at room temperature for several days until it begins to soften around the ends.

- **Persian.** This melon has the netting of a cantaloupe, but the color should be yellow. Watch for bruises, because it is very delicate.
- **Santa Claus.** Also known as the Christmas melon, this melon looks somewhat like a watermelon but has a greenish-yellow flesh.
- **Watermelons.** Regardless of the depth of the green on the top side, the underside should be at least turning from light green to yellow. The melon is often sold in cut sections in supermarkets, giving you a chance to check the color of the seeds. The melon is ripe when the seeds are very dark in color.

ORANGES

Every part of the orange has a commercial use—the flowers for citrus honey, the leaves for perfume and oils, the pulp and peel (by-products of the juice industry) for cattle feed, the seeds for oils and fertilizer, and of course the flesh itself. Although orange juice is high in vitamin C, many nutrients are contained within the membrane separating the segments, so eating a whole peeled orange provides a much more complete nutritional package.

The numerous varieties of oranges divide into two classifications: the sour and the sweet. The sour varieties are used primarily for rootstock and for decorative trees, although some people use the sour orange for a type of marmalade. The four major varieties of the sweet are the common orange (such as the Valencia), the pigmented, the navel, and the Mediterranean acidless. Another variety, actually a botanical classification of the orange, is the mandarin orange. It is available in many varieties, including the tangerine. The most dominant characteristic of the mandarin orange is the easy removal of the skin and the complete separation of the sections.

The clues to a high-quality, fresh orange do *not* include the color—much of the orange crop from Florida and Texas is artificially colored. Look instead for heavy fruit that is firm, with tender skin. Avoid bruised oranges or those that feel puffy and light. The Valencia is also subject to greening, much like grapefruit, when fully mature and ripe. The greenish tint around the stem has no effect upon the quality of the orange.

Twenty-five to 30 percent of a fresh orange is waste, but when comparing the cost to canned orange segments, you will find a 16-ounce can contains only about 11 ounces of solids.

PEACHES AND NECTARINES

Peaches. Two major types of peaches are grown in the United States: the clingstone and the freestone. As the names imply, the major difference is the degree of difficulty in separating the pit from the flesh. Varieties of clingstone are the first to ripen, but there are so many now that any general rules about peaches will include exceptions.

The flesh of a clingstone is usually much firmer and better suited to processing and canning, but the flavor is not as sweet as the freestone. The freestone has flesh that will "melt in your mouth," and can be identified by the reddish tint to the flesh near the pit. Both types are low in calories and contain vitamin A and several minerals.

Harvesting peaches takes a sense of timing that comes only from experience. They must be harvested mature but not fully ripe, with the hope that they will fully ripen by the time they reach the market. Unfortunately, not every grower is good at this guessing game, and peaches picked too early will not ripen properly. Improper cold storage of peaches—without sufficient humidity, for example—can also result in a dry, mealy, or "woolly" texture and little flavor.

Look at that important background color beneath the red. If it is a creamy white or yellow and the peach is turning from firm to soft, the fruit is at its peak of flavor. If the fruit is hard and the background is green, it is as ripe as it will ever be—which isn't much. Mature peaches approaching the fully ripe stage can be further ripened at home by placing them in a container that allows some air circulation but keeps them at room temperature.

Nectarines. As new varieties are shipped throughout the country, these sweet, juicy fruits are rapidly growing in popularity. Early nectarines were small and white-fleshed but so perishable that only certain local areas had supplies. With some of the characteristics of the peach bred into the strain, the newer nectarines are much larger, with firm yellow flesh.

The nectarine must be mature before it is picked, and its typical red-gold color develops before maturity. Consequently, the color cannot be used as an indication of ripeness. Look instead for fruit that is plump, fully rounded, and firm but not hard. If the skin is punctured or cracked, or the fruit is bruised, it probably will decay before it becomes fully ripe. Store nectarines at room temperature until ripe, and then refrigerate.

Nectarines contain considerable amounts of vitamins A and C, and they are low in calories and sodium.

PEARS

Whereas sales of canned pears seem to be decreasing, the popularity of fresh pears is on the upswing. The change in demand is probably part of the overall consumer move from the sweetened and artificially colored product to the natural and fresh version. Pears contain fair amounts of vitamins A and C, as well as most of the B vitamins.

Pears are shipped green because they ripen better off the tree, although they too must be mature before being picked. Since most are still not ripe when displayed for sale, two or three days at room temperature are usually necessary to bring them to their peak of flavor.

The popular varieties differ considerably in taste, texture, and use.

Anjou. This is a squat pear shaped like a teardrop. The color may range from yellow to green. When ripe, the Anjou begins to soften around the stem end.

Bartlett. Shaped like a bell and yellow when ripe, the Bartlett is eaten fresh and is the most popular canned pear.

Bosc. An excellent pear for baking, the ripe Bosc should have a deep yellow background color behind a brown russet.

Comice. A dessert pear with a granular, greenish-yellow skin. Because of its shape and coloring, the comice is often used in fruit baskets.

Seckel. This is a late-maturing pear with a sweet, rich flavor. The skin of the seckel is granular and russetted.

PINEAPPLES

Most of the fresh pineapple consumed in the United States comes from Hawaii or is imported from Honduras, Mexico, or the Caribbean. Canned pineapple comes mostly from the Philippines, Taiwan, and Malaysia. Pineapple is a tropical fruit containing vitamins A and C and some minerals.

Pineapples are picked when fully ripe, and no further ripening takes place after they are harvested. The larger fruits are the best buy because of a higher yield. Look for deep green leaves and a sweet, nonacidic fragrance. Do not buy bruised fruit.

PLUMS

Plums were discovered by the early colonists and were an important part of their diet. The source of over 75 percent of the world's production is now centered in California.

There are two principal types of plums—the Japanese and the European. The Japanese type, known for its juiciness, is grown in many shapes, sizes, and colors (except blue and purple). The European types are always blue or purple and generally are smaller in size. Both types are high in vitamin C and low in calories and sodium.

The peak of the plum season runs from May to September. Because some varieties store very well, supplies are usually available most of the year. Look for good color, and the texture or feel should be "on the turn"—that is, going from firm to slightly soft. The fruit does bruise easily, but proper packing will reduce bruising to a minimum.

FRUIT JUICES, MIXED JUICES, AND DRINKS

Despite all the provocative names—nectars, punches, and ades—the only important difference in all canned, refrigerated, and frozen juices and drinks sold in the supermarket is the amount of natural fruit juice contained in the product. Considering that the price differential between a 46-ounce can of 100 percent fruit juice and an identical can of 10 percent fruit juice (90 percent sugar water) is often less than 30 cents, it is well worth your time to read the label before you buy.

The FDA has issued very specific regulations on the information that must be on labels of fruit beverages. A can labeled "grapefruit juice," for example, must contain mostly juice from the mature grapefruit, extracted by an acceptable mechanical process. Some grapefruit concentrate can be added to adjust the amount of solids. If a sweetener is added, the label must state that fact. If the juice is prepared from concentrate, the label must state that it is "reconstituted" or "made from concentrate."

The term *nectar* refers to the juice and liquid pulp of fruits such as guava, papaya, and apples, in any combination. Again, the regulation requires that the amount of each variety be listed on the label.

A drink or a punch must state plainly on the label the actual percentage of fruit juice contained in the product, as well as all other ingredients. Most fruit drinks on the shelves today contain 10 percent juice, although some may go as high as 50 percent.

A money-saving tip: Buy 100 percent fruit juices and blend them at home. You'll have a thirst-quenching drink of much better nutritional quality for less money.

Orange Juice

The best orange juice comes packaged inside the orange, but most Americans choose the convenience and lower price of the juice in other packages. Such packages are legion: A typical supermarket offers plastic bottles of recently squeezed juice on ice in the produce section; cans of concentrate in the frozen food case; glass bottles, paperboard cartons, and plastic jugs of chilled juice in the dairy case; and cans and juice-pack boxes along the juice aisle.

Beyond ordinary O.J., there are pulp-free and extra pulp varieties; calcium-enriched orange juice; acid-reduced orange juice, with less "bite"; and "lite" orange drink, with less sugar and with aspartame added, for dieters.

FROM GROVE TO GLASS

The taste of freshly squeezed juice varies with the type of orange and from month to month in the growing season. Indeed, the fruit's flavor can vary from branch to branch on the same tree. Oranges high on the tree and those facing south are generally sweeter—and richer in vitamin C.

Packaged orange juice varies less. It's usually a mixture of orange varieties harvested at different times and in different places. Florida's growing season generally stretches from October through June. Early oranges, like the Hamlin, yield a pale, tart juice. The juice of the Valencia, the last and most prized orange of the season, is sweet and bright. Blending the varieties "averages" the oranges' natural characteristics and results in a product that tastes pretty much the same year-round.

Most of the production of orange juice is turned into concentrate, using an evaporation process. For many years, frozen concentrate was king of the supermarket. But if adding water to concentrate is more convenient than squeezing a few oranges, pouring juice directly from a container is more convenient still. Ready-to-serve, chilled juice, usually made from concentrate, now outsells frozen. Newer "premium" chilled juices, though, are not made from concentrate; the oranges are simply squeezed and their juice pasteurized, packed, and shipped. Fresh-frozen juice, yet another variant, is juice squeezed in Florida, packaged in an expandable plastic bottle, and flash frozen.

The main enemy of fresh-juice flavor is heat. Concentrates are heated during evaporation. Chilled juices made from concentrate may get a double heat treatment—once when the concentrate is produced and again when it's diluted back to full strength and packaged. Chilled premium juices are always pasteurized (without pasteurization, their shelf life would be around two weeks—not enough time to ship, sell, and use before fermentation sets in).

Nothing, however, compares with fresh-squeezed orange juice. To squeeze your own, buy juice oranges that are thin-skinned and heavy with liquid, a result of Florida's moist, subtropical growing climate. ("Eating" oranges, typically from arid climes of Arizona and California, are thicker-skinned, drier, and easier to peel and section.) Squeeze juice oranges gently—if you break the peel, you'll get bitter-tasting oil in the juice.

The best frozen concentrates just hint at the elusive fresh quality most processed juice lacks. The concentrates are a better bargain, too—sometimes a nickel a glass cheaper than chilled juices.

NUTRITION

Orange juice is the largest source of vitamin C in the American diet. Adults should consume 60 milligrams of the vitamin a day, according to government recommendations, and one 6-ounce glass of orange juice supplies that amount or a bit more.

To see whether the vitamin C content suffers as juice sits in the refrigerator, *Consumer Reports* food technicians tested a variety of brands right after opening them, then tested them again after two days and five days in the refrigerator. (The ready-to-serve juices were stored in their containers, and the reconstituted frozen concentrates in covered containers. Air can rob juice of both flavor and vitamin C.) The technicians found no appreciable drop in vitamin C. Even after five days, a glass of juice still supplied a day's quota.

But in one respect, orange juice makes you pay for the vitamin C: Ounce for ounce, it has as many calories as soda pop—about 85 calories in a 6-ounce glass. And though virtually all orange juice is "unsweetened"—no sugar is added—nearly every calorie comes from sugars: A serving contains the caloric equivalent of about five teaspoons of sugar.

Other fruit juices offer vitamin C with less sugar and fewer calories. And some have other strong points. For instance, grapefruit juice offers nearly a day's worth of vitamin C and 70 calories a serving. Tomato juice, with only 30 calories, supplies about half the quota of vitamin C and one-quarter that of the requirement for vitamin A. Pineapple juice and prune juice are higher in calories than orange juice (105 and 140 calories, respectively). Pineapple juice packs about one-third the daily vitamin C quota. Prune juice has far less but offers a fair amount of iron.

Orange juice hasn't got much to offer beyond vitamin C and some folic acid—unless you buy calcium-fortified juice. The calcium-fortified product provided as much calcium as milk, with a 6-ounce glass supplying more than one-fifth of a woman's daily quota. Calcium-enriched juice may be worthwhile for people who can't tolerate or don't consume enough dairy products.

7

The Dairy Case

Very few of us go through even one day without using at least one dairy product, whether it's milk, cream, yogurt, sour cream, butter, or cheese. One of the most complete natural foods, milk has been an important part of the human diet for thousands of years.

Milk is an excellent source of complete protein, calcium, phosphorus, thiamine, niacin, and riboflavin and has, in fact, some amount of all the elements necessary for good health.

The U.S. Department of Agriculture has set certain minimum standards for both the quality and the labeling of milk and many of the products derived from milk. The states themselves have the option of making the labeling requirements even stricter than the federal standards. For example, USDA standards require that whole milk must have at lease 3.25 percent butterfat, yet many individual states have increased the required amount to 3.4 or 3.5 percent to meet their requirements.

Milk Products

A typical supermarket will offer the following types of milk products:

- *Whole milk.* Whole milk has a minimum butterfat content of 3.25 percent (or the state's minimum requirement). The milk has been processed to break up the fat particles so they remain in suspension throughout the liquid. Federal regulations allow milk producers to fortify the product by adding vitamin D, or both vitamin A and D, to aid in the assimilation of calcium and phosphorus.

- *Low-fat 2% milk.* This is the same as whole milk except that the butterfat content has been reduced to 2%. It is usually also fortified with vitamin D or both A and D.
- *Low-fat 1% milk.* This is also the same as whole milk except that the butterfat has been reduced to 1 percent.
- *Skim milk.* The butterfat has been entirely eliminated from this milk, but all other nutrients and characteristics are the same.
- *Lactose-reduced milk.* In lactose-reduced milk, the lactose is broken down into simple sugars by the addition of the enzyme lactase, thus enabling lactose-intolerant people to drink it. The milk's taste is slightly sweeter than regular milk.
- *Buttermilk.* A fermented milk, buttermilk actually has less fat than whole milk: One cup of whole milk contains 8 grams of fat and 150 calories, whereas a cup of buttermilk contains 2 grams of fat and 100 calories.
- *Yogurt.* Another fermented milk product that is available in regular, low-fat forms and no-fat, yogurt is often mixed with various types of fruit. Read the labels, because a wide range of ingredients can be added.
- *Cream.* This is defined on the basis of butterfat content:
  Light or coffee cream—18 to 30 percent butterfat
  Light whipping cream—30 to 35.9 percent butterfat
  Heavy or whipping cream—36 percent butterfat or more
- *Sour cream.* This is a cultured cream usually mixed with nonfat milk solids and sometimes numerous other ingredients. (Check the label to be sure.) Sour cream is high in fat, although there are some low-fat types available.
- *Crème fraîche.* This product is an extra-rich sour cream made with cultured and matured pasteurized cream treated with certain enzymes. The flavor is similar to, but more intense than, sour cream, and is excellent with fruits and berries. Unfortunately, crème fraîche has a high fat content: A 1-ounce serving contains approximately 100 calories and 11 grams of fat.

- *Dry or powdered milk.* This is whole or nonfat milk with the water removed. Dry or powdered milk can be reconstituted and used as regular milk, or mixed with regular milk.
- *Evaporated milk.* This product contains whole milk from which about 60 percent of the water has been removed. The end product contains about 25 to 30 percent milk solids and about 8 percent butterfat. It can be easily diluted to approximate the consistency of whole milk.
- *Condensed milk.* This can be either whole or skim milk with part of the water removed. Sugar is then added so the final product contains about 40 percent sugar, 30 percent water, and 30 percent milk solids.

BUTTER

Made by churning pasteurized cream, preferably sweet cream, butter contains not less than 80 percent milk fat. Much of the butter sold is graded by the USDA, which allocates a certain number of points for flavor, body, texture, color, salt, and packaging. A few years ago, butter was labeled by the total score received (93 being the highest), but now only letter-grade designations are used. The grades are U.S. Grade AA, U.S. Grade A, U.S. Grade B, and U.S. Grade C.

MARGARINE

Margarine, a water-in-oil emulsion, is a popular substitute for butter. To be labeled as margarine, the emulsion must contain at least 80 percent fat. This amount of fat is considered too high by many health-conscious consumers, so supermarkets now offer a variety of margarinelike substitutes called "spreads," with substantially less fat content and, in some cases, reduced sodium levels as well. Most of these spreads and margarines also have no cholesterol.

ICE CREAM AND FROZEN DAIRY PRODUCTS

Ice cream is made from sweet cream, milk solids, sugar, and a number of other ingredients. The overall quality depends not only on the quality of the ingredients but also on the amount of air that is whipped into the product. To qualify as ice cream, the product must contain at least 10 percent butterfat.

All frozen dairy products should be stored at 0°F, which may be a problem for some household freezers. Automatic-defrosting refrigerators have a tendency to draw moisture from frozen dairy products during the defrost cycle, leaving them crystallized and spongy in texture. Once the package is open, cover the exposed surface with plastic film to reduce evaporation.

Cheeses

The world of cheese is divided neatly into two varieties—natural cheese and process cheese.

Natural cheeses—Brie, cheddar, Colby, cottage, jack, mozzarella, Muenster, Swiss, to name a few—always begin life as milk. To transform milk into cheese, milk solids must be concentrated and water removed: Milk is coagulated into curds and solidified through the action of enzymes, mild heat, selected microbes, salts, acidifiers, and physical "pressing." Some cheeses are ripened as well. Along the way, the milk undergoes chemical changes that lend natural cheese a rich and diverse palette of flavors, aromas, and textures.

Process cheese, on the other hand, begins life not as milk but as natural cheese—sometimes leftover natural cheese—to be further manipulated in a food-processing plant. In Europe, surplus Emmentaler and Swiss are used to make process cheeses such as *Swiss Knight* and *Laughing Cow*. In the United States, however, process cheese usually means so-called American cheese. It is generally made from cheddar, Colby, or nondescript varieties that consumers never see.

PROCESS AMERICAN CHEESE

To make process American, the cheese is ground finely, mixed with water, heated with emulsifiers (to improve its consistency), stirred, and cooked in giant vats, with seasonings and sometimes orange vegetable color added. Preservatives such as sorbates and propionates may also be folded in. What results, in the words of one federal standard, is a "homogeneous plastic mass," which is extruded in long ribbons, cut into slices, and packaged.

Because government standards specify a minimum fat content for products labeled as process American cheese, lots of cheese necessarily goes into the recipe. American cheese is about 90 percent cheese. The rest is water, additives, and ingredients such as cream or milk fat, which are added in processing.

If process American cheese is one step removed from natural cheese, its look-alikes are two steps or more removed. Here's a rundown on the other kinds of process slices in the supermarkets.

Cheese food. This is the product most often used in place of regular process American cheese. Government standards require that it contain at least 51 percent cheese, but it often contains more—about 65 percent, usually. Taking up the slack: water, milk, skim milk, buttermilk, powdered milk, and whey (the liquid that remains after the milk solids coagulate), among other ingredients.

Cheese product. No standards cover this light (or "lite") product. It contains less cheese (up to 40 to 50 percent, but perhaps none) and more water than other cheese slices. Some makers charge more for this cheesoid than for cheese food or cheese spread. And some consumers are apparently willing to pay more for added water because water has no calories or fat.

Cheese spread. This is cheese food with extra water to make it soft enough to spread at room temperature. It can come in slices, tubs, or blocks. Gums and gelatin thickeners are often added, as are sweeteners.

TASTE

You'd never mistake American cheese for cheddar. Still, American can have a pleasingly full and blended dairy flavor, some cheese character, and a moderate cheddar taste.

Fullness is key: It refers to a robust and complex taste of many notes that come across distinctly and yet are woven into a harmonious overall flavor. Tasting such a flavor is akin to listening to a choir singing harmony rather than a single, monotonic melody line. The opposite of a full flavor is one that's flat, singular, even monotonous.

An excellent American cheese can also have a moderate amount of saltiness, very slight sweetness and bitterness, and a little "bite," the tongue prickle that sharp natural cheeses often induce. It should not have off-tastes: plastic or chemical notes and the spoiled-milk or fruity flavors that betray improper processing, cheap ingredients, or old product.

In appearance and texture, an excellent American cheese should not be too glossy. Nor should it be pockmarked, unevenly colored, or rubbery. As it's chewed, it should dissolve smoothly and evenly in the mouth; it should not disintegrate into bits that never seem to melt.

Many sliced products are individually wrapped for convenience and better storage. Plastic wrapping may not only impart a plastic taste; it adds to the nation's load of solid waste. *Consumer Reports* food specialists estimated that some three square feet of wrap is used in a 16-slice pack of cheese food "singles." If only the outer package were wrapped, a fraction of the plastic would be needed.

CHEESE NUTRITION

Process American cheese, made from cheese that's made from milk, possesses milk's nutritional pluses and minuses. It contains high-quality protein in good quantity. A 1-ounce slice has about the same amount of protein as a large egg. Since process cheese food and cheese spread are made with a little less cheese, there tends to be a little less protein.

Perhaps a more important nutritional plus than the protein, which is in abundant supply in the American diet, is cheese's good supply of calcium, vitamin A, and riboflavin. A 1-ounce slice of process American cheese or cheese food would supply about 160 milligrams of calcium, about 20 percent of the day's quota for an adult.

On the minus side, a 1-ounce slice of process American cheese supplies 9 grams of fat, slightly more than that in two pats of butter. Since the fat is milk fat, its profile is identical to butter's: Two-thirds is saturated. By eating just 2 ounces of cheese in a sandwich, a woman trying to keep her fat intake down to 30 percent of the day's calories would exhaust about 25 percent of the day's limit for fat. She'd also consume about one-sixth the recommended daily limit for dietary cholesterol. Process American cheese tends to be sodium laden, too, with 200 to 300 milligrams or more per slice from salt and other additives.

All that should spell moderation. Or you might instead eat imitation cheese, made with vegetable oil. It contains about as much sodium and fat but less saturated fat and cholesterol. Then again, if you want to avoid sodium and saturated fat, it might be more enjoyable to eat fruits and vegetables, which taste like fruits and vegetables, rather than imitation cheese, which tastes like nothing much.

Another alternative is cheddar cheese. The flavor runs from mild to mellow to sharp and extra sharp, depending largely on how long the cheese has been aged. The sharpest cheddars may have been ripened for a year or longer. Unless it's made from pasteurized milk, cheddar must be aged at least 60 days.

An excellent cheddar tastes robust, with some nutlike notes. The flavor is partly sharp, partly sour, with a tang called "cheese bite." The cheese is firm but a bit dry and crumbly. It dissolves smoothly and evenly in the mouth, leaving a coating of fine particles, especially if it's aged cheddar.

Ounce for ounce, cheddar packs about 10 percent more protein and 15 percent more calcium than does process American cheese, and has only about half the sodium. It does have a few more calories and a little more fat. But it can taste a lot better than process cheese.

NATURAL CHEESES

Natural cheeses depend upon many factors—the type and temperature of the milk, the climate, the grass the animals eat, the size of the curds and how they are pressed and dried, the way the cheese is turned, the salting process, and the aging factor—all of which help to develop the characteristic taste and texture of individual types of cheese. Each step of the process makes use of nature's little peculiarities to produce the desired results.

How to buy natural cheeses. All natural cheeses are perishable, to different degrees. Some, such as the French Brie, are at their peak for only a day or two, whereas others can be stored for weeks at peak quality. Because natural cheeses are a dairy product, they absorb odors easily and should not be stored close to other foods that have pungent, dominant aromas. Similarly, strong and mild cheeses should not be stored or displayed together.

The most important criterion when selecting a good cheese store is to find a retailer who knows how to handle the product correctly and who trains its staff in all aspects of cheese retailing, from receiving to selling. A well-trained salesperson can be an excellent source of information and can tell you what cheese currently in stock is in the best condition to serve your purpose.

The rate of turnover of the stock is another important factor. A busy cheese shop or supermarket deli counter will have fewer cheeses that have passed their prime *if the owner or supermarket manager knows how to buy right.* The best clue is the appearance of cut cheeses on display. Each piece should be carefully rewrapped in plastic film, and the face of each piece should be fresh, bright, and show no signs of discoloration or drying out. A careful manager will also ensure that the cut cheeses are refaced or trimmed periodically.

Most cheese retailers will have both bulk (large wheels, rounds, or loaves sold sliced to order or in chunks) and prepacks or prewraps (wrapped either by the producer or the retailer). Appearance is important when selecting cheeses, so buying from bulk, which lets you see what you are getting, is recommended.

Eggs

Eggs are an important source of high-quality protein as well as one of the few sources of vitamin D. They also contain vitamin A, iron, and riboflavin in significant amounts, plus small amounts of other nutrients. Eggs are high in cholesterol—213 milligrams.

VARIETIES OF NATURAL CHEESES

All of the following can usually be found in the cheese section of your supermarket:

Bel Paese. This is a round, creamy, soft-textured cheese from Italy. A dessert cheese, it's often served with fruit.

Blue. A semisoft, flavorful cheese with veins of blue mold running through it, this type is popular for cheese trays, for salads, and as a spread.

Boursin. A French triple creme (high in butterfat) sold in packages, this cheese is mixed with either herbs or black pepper. It's an excellent spreading cheese for hors d'oeuvres or for the cheese tray.

Brie. A classic cheese, the fully ripened Brie has a taste that knows no equal. Unfortunately, finding one at its peak is difficult. If the Brie is still unripe when the first cut is made, it will never reach its potential. (A chalky center means the Brie was cut too soon.) Brie at its peak is soft enough to run when at room temperature, and the odor is sweet and fresh, never ammoniated.

Camembert. A soft cheese from France, Camembert is a first cousin to the Brie. Because Camembert is sold in packages or containers, it's difficult to check for ripeness. Press the cheese in several places—it should be uniformly firm and yielding, but not hard. Check also for the smell of ammonia. Camembert is excellent on a cheese tray or after dinner.

Cheddar. Fine cheddar is sharp and penetrating, but should never be bitter. It is excellent for cooking, the table, the cheese tray, and for just plain nibbling.

Colby. Similar to an American cheddar but softer, this cheese also has a more open texture and a mild flavor.

Edam. A cheese with a mild flavor and a crumbly but firm texture, Edam makes an excellent breakfast or sandwich cheese but is not adaptable to cooking.

Feta. A white pickled or brined cheese first produced in Greece and now made domestically, this one is good for salads.

Goat cheese. Gaining rapidly in popularity, goat cheese is now produced all over the world, from the chèvres of France and the Gjetost of Norway to domestic types from California and Washington State. The taste develops rapidly and varies from mildly tart to strong and full-bodied.

Gorgonzola. The king of the softer blue-veined cheeses, Gorgonzola is creamy, rich, and pungent.

Gouda. This cheese from Holland is similar to the Edam but less firm. A newer version is the smoked gouda.

Monterey Jack. Originally produced in California, the whole-milk Monterey is a mild semisoft cheese.

Muenster. Made first in Germany, Muenster is now produced in the United States. It's a semisoft cheese with a mild yet distinctive taste.

Parmesan. This pungent cheese begins to lose its flavor soon after it has been grated, so grate it only just before you plan to use it.

Pecorino Romano. A fine, hard sheep's-milk cheese from Italy, Pecorino is often mixed with the grated domestic Parmesan to improve its flavor.

Despite the way the shell appears, it is important to realize that an eggshell is actually porous—it's a thin layer of gelatinous material that hardens as it is exposed to air. This covering helps seal the egg and reduces the amount of dehydration through the shell. Underneath the shell is a double membrane that gradually separates as moisture evaporates, forming an air pocket at the large end. The size of this air pocket is an accurate measure of the age and quality of the egg.

GRADING

The USDA has three standards for measuring the quality of eggs:

- *Exterior*. This standard involves the soundness, size, and shape of the eggs (the color, either brown or white, has no bearing on quality).
- *Interior*. This standard concerns size and position of the air space, mobility and visibility of the yolk, and condition of the white. (These criteria are determined by turning the egg in front of a lighting device, a process called candling.)
- *Weight*. Eggs are sized by weight of the individual unit.

Although eggs are separated into four grades, only the top three—Grade AA, Grade A, and Grade B—are usually found in supermarkets. Of these three grades, Grade A is most often seen on the shelves.

Grade A eggs must have a firm, sound shell and a regular-shaped air cell not exceeding a quarter inch in depth. The yolk should be well centered and slightly mobile.

The choice of what size egg to buy is basically a matter of use. If you usually serve eggs sunny-side up and you are satisfied to use two medium eggs, why pay more money for extra-large or jumbo? If you are serving scrambled eggs to a number of people

TESTING FOR FRESHNESS AND QUALITY

The white of a fresh Grade AA or Grade A egg is formed in two distinct layers: The first is somewhat thin and watery and the second, nearest the yolk, is thick and viscous. As the egg ages, the thick inner layer surrounding the yolk begins to break down, changing in viscosity until it disappears almost completely. (There are also some fresh eggs in which the thick layer of the white has not developed because of the condition of the hen, but these should be eliminated during the candling process.) Unfortunately, the only part of the egg that the shopper can see is the shell, and there is little about its appearance that can give any clues about what's inside. There is, however, a test that you can perform in your own kitchen, using an ordinary dinner plate: Take the egg, and break it gently. Carefully empty the contents onto the center of the plate. The yolk of a Grade AA egg will be centered in the thick layer of white, and there will be a very defined difference between the two layers of white. Although the thin, watery layer will spread and flatten, the thick layer will hold together and mound, with the yolk sitting centered on top. In a Grade A egg, the difference between the two layers of white is still well defined. However, the yolk will not be as centered, and the thick, white layer will spread more, not mounding as high. In the Grade B egg, the difference between the two layers of white virtually disappears and the thin, watery white will spread over almost the entire plate.

or using them as an ingredient based on weight, then comparing the prices among the various sizes becomes worthwhile.

The following table supplies the USDA terms for the various egg sizes, the required weights for each size, and cost comparison method. (Assume a base price of $1.08 a dozen for large eggs, or 4½ cents per ounce.)

Table 7.1
Comparison of Egg Sizes and Values

USDA Label	Weight per Dozen	Price per Dozen (Price at Base)
Jumbo	30 oz.	$1.35
Extra large	27	1.22
Large	24	1.08
Medium	21	.95
Small	18	.81
Peewee	15	.68

Egg prices vary according to size and grade but not always in direct proportion to the weight. If the difference between one size and the next largest size is less than 13 or 14 cents, then the next largest size will be the best buy. However, as noted before, if you are going to serve the eggs in units—one or two eggs per person—buy the smallest egg that will provide an adequate serving.

EGG TIPS

- Check the carton for cracked or broken eggs before you buy.
- A small amount of soil on an egg is not harmful. Do not wash the eggs until just before you are ready to use them.

WHOLE-EGG ALTERNATIVES: THE FACTS

Recent research by the USDA has resulted in the reduction of estimates of cholesterol found in a single whole egg, but even the revised amount—213 milligrams—represents more than two-thirds of the 300 daily milligrams recommended by the American Heart Association. Consequently, many health-conscious consumers have turned to egg substitutes to satisfy their cooking and menu needs.

Since the yolk is the cholesterol culprit in whole eggs, many egg substitutes use only the whites, which are essentially cholesterol- and fat-free but still contain about half of the protein of a normal egg. To make these substitutes suitable for use in cooking, other ingredients such as oil, sodium, and coloring are added. People on low-sodium diets or with other food or additive sensitivities should read the label before purchasing the product.

One alternative to using egg substitutes is to choose just the whites or, if the appearance is important, use two or three whites to one yolk. The cholesterol level is significantly reduced and yet the dish has at least some color.

- Keep eggs refrigerated. They lose as much quality and freshness in one day at room temperature as they will in a week when refrigerated.
- It is often said that the twisted strands of concentrated white near the yolk are signs that the egg is fertile. This is not true. The strands are called chalazae and are present to some degree in every egg because they help anchor the yolk in place.
- Two general rules about hard-cooked eggs: First, the older the egg, the easier it is to peel. Second, the greenish color between the white and the yolk is the result of a chemical reaction caused by cooking the eggs at a high temperature or by overcooking. The discoloration is harmless but can be reduced by cooking eggs at a low heat.

8

Shopping the Aisles: Food Staples

Rows of shelves in a supermarket are devoted to those food staples that make up the bulk of a shopper's grocery list and fill up the shopping cart. Boxes of cereals and pasta; bags of coffee and flour; bottles of oils and assorted beverages are the nucleus of any supermarket shopping expedition.

Whole Grain Cereals

Natural whole grain cereals are an important source of concentrated nutrients and fiber, and there's no doubt that a daily dose of fiber is good for you. According to research at a Minnesota veterans hospital, a breakfast of high-fiber cereal may increase satiety later in the day. People who had breakfasted on high-fiber cereal took significantly less food from a lunchtime buffet than those who had eaten low-fiber cereal.

All cereal grains, including rice, wheat, oats, corn, barley, and rye, consist of three parts: the bran, the endosperm, and the germ. Often the processing method removes the bran and the germ, the source of much of the nutritional elements. Many of these lost vitamins and minerals are returned to the cereal product through *enrichment*, a method used in the production of both cereals and breads. A look at the ingredients list of most cereals will tell you just what nutrients have been replaced. Obviously, a product that is labeled "100% whole wheat" will contain more of the cereal grain per ounce than a product that lists sugar as its second-highest ingredient.

In both cooked and ready-to-eat cereals, an ounce is considered to be an adequate serving. In an informal 1991 survey, the costs of various types of cereals on a cost-per-ounce basis were compared, with the following results:

Table 8.1
Comparison of Cereals, Cost per Ounce

Type of Cereal	*Price Range per Ounce*
100% whole grain, cooked	\$.071 to \$.088
Natural cereal, instant	.204 to .252
Processed, ready to eat (sugar added)	.193 to .223
Sugar-coated, ready to eat	.156 to .175
100% whole grain (may have some sugar)	.147 to .172

The most expensive ready-to-eat cereals were the processed types, and in practically every case sugar was the second or third ingredient listed. Although many of the "100% natural" whole grain cereals had sugar listed as the fourth- or fifth-highest ingredient, they cost significantly less per ounce. The least expensive were the cooked cereals, and no sugar or sodium is added to these products.

WHY DOES CEREAL COST SO MUCH?

If you think the price of cereal has escalated in recent years, you're right. Kellogg and General Mills, which together sell about two-thirds of the ready-to-eat cereal Americans eat, say they have to hike prices to cover higher expenses.

Perhaps those new fruit- and fiber-filled cereals are indeed more expensive to produce, but business publications and analysts who study cereal companies say that the increases went in good part to underwrite intensified promotion—advertising, marketing to retailers, and "couponing."

Why are those advertising and promotion budgets so high? For one, although the cereal business is lucrative—nearly $8 billion worth is sold a year—it's also highly competitive. Makers of the big brands worry increasingly about losing sales to supermarket brands and competitors. Rather than cut prices to compete, they turn up the advertising. Another factor: There are now more cereals to be advertised. Six years ago, about two dozen cereals accounted for two-thirds of total sales; now 40 cereals do, and each must be marketed all the more aggressively.

Coupons play an increasingly important role in selling cereal, and their cost must also be factored in. Six years ago, less than a fifth of the nation's cereal was bought with a coupon; today, about half of all cereal—a higher percentage than for any other grocery item—is bought that way. In 1991 some 31 billion cereal coupons were distributed nationwide. That works out to about 325 for each household.

The face value of coupons has also inched up. There are more $1 coupons, and there's even an occasional $2 coupon. All that sounds as if cereal companies are giving with one hand while taking back with the other, in higher prices. In the end, a dedicated coupon-clipper *might* pay the price a cereal maker would have charged without all this couponing. The way matters stand, as one marketing analyst said, "You have to be nuts to buy cereal without a coupon."

The primary question to ask when shopping for cereals is not "Am I getting what I paid for?" but "What am I paying for?" Granted, the cost per serving is low and the difference in dollars and cents between products is not extreme, but the difference in quality and nutritional content is striking. (See Appendix for Ratings of brand-name cereals.)

Flours

Those same grains used for breakfast cereals are also used in the production of flours for making bread and bakery products and for general kitchen use. These flours have a high starch content—about 75 percent—and contain from 7 to 16 percent protein. Many of the fats, minerals, and vitamins are lost during the milling process, and now most states require that the flours be enriched to partially replace those missing nutrients.

Most flours are available in supermarkets, and each has its own characteristics when used for breads, pastries, and general cookery.

Although there are government grades for some types of flour, it is virtually impossible for consumers to check quality. You will have to depend upon the integrity of the manufacturer and the knowledge of the retailer to ensure that flour stock is stored and rotated properly.

TYPES

Wheat flour. Used more than any other type of flour because of its unique qualities, wheat flour contains gluten, an element needed in dough to hold the gases and allow for aeration. The terms *hard* and *soft* wheat refer to the differences in gluten-to-starch ratios. *Bread* flours, for example, are blended hard wheat flours with a high gluten content. *Cake* or *pastry* flours are made from soft wheat, with a smaller amount of gluten, which allows for a much finer texture. *Family* or *all-purpose* flours are a mixture of hard and soft wheats and, as the name implies, can be used for both bread making and cakes. By adding salt and a leavening, usually bicarbonate of soda and calcium phosphate, *self-rising* flour is created.

Two other terms used in the description of flours are *bleached* and *unbleached*. It was necessary, at one time, to store flours for months to develop the strength and elasticity of the gluten. Millers found that by bleaching the flour, they could reduce the conditioning and storage time and produce a more uniform product. However, bleaching destroys the small amount of vitamin E in flour, so the unbleached variety is more popular with many health-conscious cooks.

Buckwheat flour. Not a cereal flour, buckwheat makes a good mixing flour and is often used for pancakes.

Corn flour. Actually a cornmeal ground very fine, corn flour can be mixed with other flours for making breads.

Graham flour. Actually a variation of wheat flour, graham flour contains all of the wheat berry.

Oat flour. A flour made of finely ground hulled oats, oat flour is used in combination with wheat flour because of its lack of gluten.

Potato flour (starch). Another noncereal flour used for thickening, potato flour is often mixed with other flours to make moist breads and rolls.

Rice flour. Made from both white and brown rice, rice flour is used in combination with other flours and as a thickener. It is also used as a substitute for wheat flour by those who are allergic to cereal grains.

Rye flour. Rye flour is used in making breads, mostly in combination with wheat flour. There are a few breads—pumpernickel, for example—that are made solely from rye flour. The gluten in rye, which is very unstable, produces a dark, dense bread.

Soy flour. Not really a cereal grain flour, soy flour is gaining in popularity because it contains many essential nutrients. Soy flour has no gluten but can be substituted for part of the gluten flour in many recipes.

Whole wheat flour. Whole wheat flour is milled from the entire wheat kernel, including the bran and the germ. It is often mixed with unbleached flour in making bread at home.

Rice

In the United States, meat and potatoes may be king, but rice is at least a pretender to the throne. The newfound fondness for the grain has little to do with nutrition and much more to do with its low calorie, sodium, and fat content (assuming you forgo seasoning with salt and butter).

Worldwide, there are more than 40,000 varieties of rice in three basic sizes and a rainbow of colors—red, blue, and purple in addition to the usual hues of white and brown. Only about 20 strains are grown commercially in the United States, mostly in California and the rice-belt states of Arkansas, Louisiana, Mississippi, Missouri, and Texas. Because distinctions in grain size, milling, and processing techniques can prove confusing, a few definitions of terms are in order.

LONG-, MEDIUM-, AND SHORT-GRAIN RICE

Long-grain rice is four or five times as long as it is wide. Because it has a high proportion of the starch amylose, long-grain rice tends to cook up dry and fluffy, with separate grains. That makes it useful in curries, pilafs, and salads. Long-grain is the size grown—and sold—most often in the United States.

Medium-grain rice is slightly plumper than long-grain, and short-grain is nearly round. Both cook up tender and moist, and are laden with the sticky starch amylopectin. They're better than long-grain rice for desserts, meat loaf, croquettes, sushi, and other dishes in which "cling" is advantageous.

BROWN RICE

After rice has been harvested, the inedible outer hull is removed at the mill, but layers of bran are left behind. Those layers, which give brown rice its color and slight crunch, contain most of the grain's fat, vitamins, and minerals. Brown rice may have ardent devotees, but they are few in number; it accounts for just 4 percent of total rice sales.

WHITE RICE

Further milling removes the bran layers to leave white, or polished, rice. That processing also removes nutrients. But in virtually all rice grown or processed in the United States, some nutrients are replaced when a solution of iron, niacin, and thiamine is sprayed on the rice in amounts specified by federal standards. Rinsing rice before cooking washes away the added nutrients, defeating the purpose of enrichment.

White and brown rice can be treated in two additional ways:

Parboiled. Parboiled rice has been subjected to a steam-pressure process before milling. The grain is soaked, steamed, and dried; then the hull is removed. The rice is not actually cooked, but its starch is gelatinized and its nutrients penetrate the grain. The procedure results in an extra-fluffy rice whose grains stay separate. Another word for parboiled is "converted," a trademark associated with *Uncle Ben's*, a leading brand.

Precooked (Instant). Precooked rice has been completely cooked and dehydrated after milling. You need only add it to boiling water and let the pot stand for a few minutes. It is available in boxes or in premeasured servings contained in plastic pouches, which you boil.

Some less common varieties of rice include:

AROMATIC RICE

Indigenous to the cool highland regions of Asia, aromatics smell and taste different from the rice most Westerners are used to.

These have distinct nutty, floral, popcornlike, or sweet flavors. Their grains don't get wider when cooked; they elongate and curl. Aromatic varieties like basmati, wehani, and jasmine find the hot, humid climate of America's rice belt hostile. Breeders have, however, crossed long-grain types found here with true basmati.

The Hindi word *basmati* means "queen of fragrance," and two crosses developed in Texas retain much of the bouquet of their Asian cousins. Texmati brown and Texmati white rice contain almost 10 times more of the natural compound responsible for an intense nutty or popcornlike scent than does regular rice. The unique flavor of the aromatics may not be to everyone's liking, but the rice is certainly worth trying as a change from the routine.

WILD RICE

Wild rice isn't a rice at all, but the brown seed of an aquatic grass native to North America. It has more protein and lysine, an essential amino acid, than brown or white rice but carries a hefty price tag—$8 a pound or more.

COST

Rice is not likely to be a strain on your budget. A half-cup serving of most regular white or brown rice costs about a nickel; for parboiled varieties you'll spend a few cents more. Avoid pre-cooked rice—it comes to almost $.19 per serving and is not very tasty, although it is convenient to use and hard to ruin.

It pays to buy the larger sizes of rice. The 1-pound long-grain enriched is about $.55 a pound, whereas the 5-pound size is only $.44 a pound.

HOW TO COOK RICE RIGHT

Regular and parboiled rice intimidate many cooks. The proliferation of "foolproof," precooked varieties is testimony to that. But those products can be bland and rubbery. You can pass them up and produce first-rate long-cooking rice by following a few general rules:

IS BROWN RICE BETTER FOR YOU?

Many people believe brown rice is more nutritious than white because of its bran coating. It's true that white rice has lost some vitamins and minerals during milling, but with enrichment the varieties are similar in nutrients. Analyses show that brown rice does contain 50 percent more fiber (1.5 grams per half-cup serving versus 1 gram for white rice), but that's still not much. You would have to eat nearly six servings of brown rice (nine of white) to get the fiber in a single bowl of *Kellogg's All-Bran*.

- Use 1¾ cups (not the commonly suggested 2 cups) of very hot or boiling water per cup of uncooked rice. A cup of raw rice will yield about 4 cups of cooked rice. A cup of uncooked instant rice will yield 2 cups.
- Never allow rice to go into a full, rolling boil; this will rupture the grains and produce a starchy mass.
- Rice is best cooked at a very low simmer—higher heat can cause the grains to stick to the pan. Use package instructions as a guide to cooking times.
- Let the finished product absorb residual moisture by keeping it tightly covered and off the heat for five minutes. If it's still too damp, fluff it with a fork, replace the lid, and leave the pan over very low heat for another couple of minutes.

In an unopened box, white rice will keep on the shelf for one or two years. Refrigerate white rice once opened and brown rice as soon as you buy it. Use an airtight container. Cooked rice will keep for a week when refrigerated and about four months when frozen.

Pasta

Almost all pastas, also classified as macaroni products, are made from hard durum wheat that has been repeatedly milled and sifted until the bran, germ, and flour have been removed, leaving the amber crystals called "middlings" or "semolina." Some pasta products are made from semolina in combination with other hard-wheat flours, whereas others use only hard-wheat flours. The quality of the pasta is determined by the quality of the hard wheat, which, in turn, affects both the flavor and, more important, the cooking characteristics. Top-quality pasta will cook up firm without being gummy or sticky, whereas lower-quality products tend to cook in clumps despite frequent stirring. Most of the nationally advertised brands are of good quality, as are some house brands. The problem with the house brands, however, is that you don't know who is manufacturing the product. It may be a national brand with a house label or it may be from a poor-quality manufacturer who produces only for private labels or house brands. You have two choices: Pay a little more for the national brand, or experiment with the house brand.

Pasta or macaroni products are high in nutrition, providing protein, amino acids, vitamin B, and iron. They are a low-fat and low-sodium food and contain about 105 calories per ounce of uncooked product. Those who are allergic to wheat can turn to several other types of noodle products including cellophane noodles, made from mung bean flour, or rice noodles.

HOW TO COOK PASTA

Cooking pasta incorrectly can result in a gummy mass. The secret is plenty of water and a rapid boil. Using a large pot, add about 2 teaspoons of salt and a tablespoon of cooking oil to every 5 quarts of water. Bring the water to a rapid boil before adding the pasta. Add the pasta slowly to keep the boil moving and then cook, uncovered, stirring occasionally. When done, the pasta should be tender but firm—*al dente*, according to the Italians. The only true test is to taste, because cooking time will differ according to the shape. The color will give you a clue, however: Uncooked pasta is an amber color. When the color changes from amber to an off-white during cooking, check the tenderness. If done, drain the pasta immediately to avoid overcooking. (See Appendix for Ratings of brand-name spaghettis.)

Nuts

Many shoppers compare the price of chickens, top round roasts, and lettuce but just grab that small package of walnuts on the way to the checkout counter.

Consequently, packaged nuts are a high-profit item for a supermarket, and the prices for the same product may vary by as much as 20 to 30 percent from one store to another. Despite the variations in packaging and pricing, there are a few general facts to know about buying both packaged nuts and nuts in the shell.

- Buy what you need for your purposes. Most nuts are packaged in a variety of forms: whole, halves, pieces, chips, sliced, slivered, and diced. The prices for each form can differ by as much as 40 percent. There is little sense in paying a premium for whole nuts and then chopping them up.
- Buy the larger size. As a general rule, the larger the net weight of the package, the lower the cost per ounce.
- Convenience costs. Nuts in the shell (based on the cost of the nut meat alone) cost less than packaged, shelled nuts.
- Check the mixtures. Mixed nuts vary in price because of the percentage of each type of nut in the package. Peanuts are usually the cheapest, so packers can lower the price or increase the profits by loading a bag of mixed nuts with peanuts. If the mixture is in clear plastic, check the mix visually. If you buy a can of mixed nuts, then note its contents after you open the can. If you find too many peanuts, try another brand next time.

CHECKING FOR QUALITY

Although the USDA has an inspection and grading service for nuts, the service is voluntary and provided for a fee to the packer. Consequently, most nuts are not inspected. If you do see the typical USDA shield on the package, you can be assured that the product is of a very good quality. If the nuts are not inspected, look for the following clues: In-shell nuts should have clean, bright, and well-shaped shells; avoid nuts with dull, cracked, or broken shells. Nuts that have well-developed kernels will be heavy for their size. Packaged nuts should have brightly colored meat with no sign of mold or dark discoloration. A yellowish, oily appearance can mean that the nut meats are turning rancid. Check also for an excessive amount of chaff, because this condition is the result of poor screening.

Several types of nuts are available dry-roasted, which means they were roasted without oil. These are for nibbling, not for cooking. Nutritionally, nuts are good for you—they have an adequate amount of protein, calcium, iron, and phosphorus. Unfortunately, they are also high in fat and calories.

Peanut Butter

Peanuts alone are a good source of protein, but that protein is incomplete because some essential amino acids (ones the body can't make itself) are lacking. Add peanut butter to a slice of bread, however, and you improve the quality of the protein. Peanut butter also contains dietary fiber and B vitamins. It has a lot of fat, but most of the fat is monounsaturated. Like olive oil, peanut oil tends to lower blood cholesterol levels. (Because peanuts are plant seeds, they contain virtually no cholesterol.)

Most peanut butters contain more than ground peanuts. Hydrogenated vegetable oil is added as a stabilizer to maintain the mix of ground peanut solids and peanut oil. Most products contain a little salt and sweetener (sucrose, dextrose, and/or corn syrup).

"Natural" peanut butters may have salt but no sweeteners or stabilizers. Without a stabilizer, the peanut oil in natural brands separates from the solids, so you have to stir arduously to blend oil and peanuts when you first open the jar. It's messy, but you shouldn't have to remix it if you refrigerate the jar after that first stirring.

Peanut butter is a nutritious, tasty, inexpensive food with wide appeal for adults and children alike. Whether you prefer creamy or chunky styles, there are a number of very good products from which to choose.

Most of the peanut butter in the United States is sold under only three brand names—*Jif, Skippy,* and *Peter Pan*—but you can also find smaller regional manufacturers and supermarket labels. You can do your own taste tests by experimenting with small jars of various brands. The differences in peanut flavor, sweetness, and saltiness may surprise you. The fats in peanut butter turn stale faster at room temperature, so refrigerate peanut butter as soon as you get it home from the store. If it takes you a while to go through a jar, buy smaller jars.

BETWEEN THE BREAD

Peanuts aren't really nuts but legumes, like peas and beans. Like those vegetables, peanuts (and their butter) are a good source of protein and dietary fiber. A 3-tablespoon serving of peanut butter provides about a third of an adult's daily protein requirement and as much fiber as a bowl of raisin bran.

The government requires all brands to be at least 90 percent peanuts, so any difference in the lesser ingredients doesn't add up to much. (Salt is an exception. Some brands leave it out.) The stabilizer in regular peanut butter contributes saturated fat but not enough to worry about. Generally, the fat in peanut butter is unsaturated.

In a 1990 report, *Consumer Reports* food scientists compared a peanut butter sandwich with three other popular sandwiches—process American cheese, beef bologna, and chunk light tuna packed in water.

The only one of the sandwich fillers with fiber, peanut butter is also the only one that contains virtually no cholesterol. It has the least sodium of the four, and less saturated fat than the cheese and bologna sandwiches. It's also likely to cost the least.

On the other hand, a peanut butter sandwich contains much more total fat and calories than the tuna sandwich. And it has less calcium than the cheese sandwich. The moral, as usual: Eat a varied diet.

Snack Foods: Potato Chips

Dining in a Saratoga, New York, restaurant in 1853, Cornelius Vanderbilt complained that his fried potatoes were "too thick" and sent them back to the kitchen. The cook scornfully cut paper-thin potato slices and deep-fried them to a turn. Vanderbilt thought they were sensational. Soon, people couldn't get enough "Saratoga chips."

More than a century later, the potato chip is king of the salty snacks, outselling popcorn, pretzels, and corn chips.

Buying potato chips used to be as easy as eating them. You had only to choose between smooth ones and the ridged kind preferred for dips. Nowadays, things have become more complicated. You can pick from bags of low-salt potato chips, "lite" chips made with less fat, and flavored chips, including mesquite barbecue, dill, and jalapeño.

You can still find regular chips, with and without ridges. But more recently, manufacturers have been promoting two other subspecies: kettle-style and fabricated chips. Kettle chips are cut somewhat thicker than regular chips and slowly fried by hand in small batches "the old-fashioned way," as companies love to say. Fabricated chips are made not from sliced raw potatoes but from a dough of dehydrated potato flakes and other ingredients.

TASTE AND FLAVOR

Many potato chip products are regional. Only a handful of brands are sold nationwide, among them *Eagle, Ruffles, Lay's,* and *Pringles.* Because of the difficulty of shipping over great distances, even the national brands are made in regional factories. And local tastes fuel the local markets.

Regional preferences aside, an excellent chip has good color and few if any blotches; just the right crispiness (regular chips) or crunchiness (kettle chips); distinct potato taste, coupled perhaps with some "earthy" and "browned" notes from potato skins and from frying; some saltiness; and no hint of stale or overworked cooking oil.

Flavored chips have been coming on strong in recent years: jalapeño, dill, ranch, barbecue, taco, bacon, and salt-and-vinegar chips, to name a few. Barbecue (including mesquite) and sour cream and onion chips are the most popular.

CHIP NUTRITION?

It's a stretch to speak of potato chips and nutrition in the same breath. The potato chip, made with fat and salt, has a big image problem. In the 1970s, entrepreneurs countered by adding vitamins, but the fortified chips flopped. More recently, others have tried adding oat bran, with the same results.

HOW SALTY SNACKS STACK UP

With fat and salt as key ingredients, potato chips aren't exactly health food. Pretzels or plain air-popped popcorn, by contrast, are lowest in fat. Corn chips and microwave popcorn are almost as fatty, peanuts even more so. Potato chips are middling in sodium content—they have more than peanuts, less than pretzels.

TABLE 8.2
Nutritional Comparisons of Snack Foods
(1 oz. serving)

	Potato Chips	Pretzels	Popcorn*	Corn Chips	Peanuts
Calories	152	111	76	153	170
Fat	10 g.	1 g.	1 g.	9 g.	14 g.
Calories from fat	60% of calories	8% of calories	12% of calories	53% of calories	74% of calories
Sodium	160 mg.	451 mg.	1 mg.	218 mg.	138 mg.

*Air-popped corn. The regular microwave type has about twice the calories. It contains 9 grams of fat (or 55 percent of its calories) and 196 milligrams of sodium.

Perhaps the best the chip trade can do is to accentuate the positive. Many bags now proclaim "no preservatives." Most brands tested carry nutrition labeling, maybe hoping that the chart of vitamins will impress, no matter how scant the supply.

Potato chips, like potatoes, do supply some vitamins and minerals. In one ounce (about as many chips as in a vending-machine bag), there's a fair amount of vitamin C—perhaps as much as 10 percent of a day's quota. There's some potassium and phosphorus, too. Mostly, though, there's fat. One ounce of chips has about 10 grams of fat, which accounts for 90 of the snack's 150 calories. That's the amount of fat in 2½ pats of margarine or butter. But how many people can eat just one ounce?

Very little of the fat in chips is saturated, however. And there's no cholesterol, as many bags spell out in big letters.

As for salt, you might think potato chips are loaded with it. That's because all the salt is on the surface. Actually, a one-ounce serving averaged only 160 milligrams of sodium, about one-fifteenth of a teaspoon of salt. Ounce for ounce, even some breakfast cereals contain more sodium. Often the potato chips had less sodium than stated on the bag's nutrition chart. Some salt undoubtedly ends up coating the inside of the bag.

Still, if you're watching your sodium, you may want to write off potato chips—or try the unsalted variety. But for most folks, potato chips without salt just aren't potato chips.

Compared with plain potato chips, flavored chips deliver about the same amount of fat and calories. But they typically pack more sodium—from added salt and monosodium glutamate. Barbecue chips supply about 25 percent more sodium than plain salted potato chips; sour cream and onion, close to 40 percent more.

Potato chips are a tasty snack, provided you can muster enough self-restraint not to overdo it. Thinking of 2½ pats of margarine for each ounce of chips you put away may bolster your self-control. Substituting pretzels or air-popped corn can cut fat and calorie consumption. But beware pretzels' salt content.

Fats and Oils

There are few areas of food purchasing as confusing to the consumer as the selection of the right fat or oil for a specific cooking need. Many products are advertised as all-purpose, but this is simply not true. You would not use an all-purpose vegetable shortening to make salad dressing, nor would you use it for stir-frying. To complicate matters further, increased concern about calories has prompted oil producers to develop methods of altering or eliminating some of the more undesirable elements of their products. As in most areas of foods selection, your best weapon is an understanding of the properties and the quality factors of fats and oils as well as a knowledge of how each one is used.

In every case, the form and chemical properties determine which fat or oil will be most appropriate. For example, an oil for frying should have a high smoking point, an oil for baking cakes should be colorless and odorless, and a fat for flavoring should resist turning rancid. The method of production can have considerable impact upon the level of saturated fats and calories.

TYPES

Shortenings. Shortenings are edible fats used in the production of baked goods. Originally, lard—a product resulting from the rendering of hog fats—was the only solid fat used for this purpose. The cotton industry, however, developed cottonseed oil, and it was discovered that hog fat and cottonseed oil could be combined into a compound that was then sold as a pure lard substitute. In the early twentieth century, the process of hydrogenation was developed, enabling manufacturers to produce a solid plastic fat from liquid vegetable oil without having to add the hog fat.

Shortenings actually tenderize baked goods by surrounding the particles of starch and the strands of wheat gluten with fat, thus keeping them relatively isolated during the baking process. Although liquid oils, butter, and margarine can also be used as shortenings, the semisolid types made from hydrogenated oils and fat that are soft, pliable, and creamy are still the most popular.

For those concerned about saturated fats, a word about the hydrogenation process may be helpful: Liquid vegetable oils are composed primarily of unsaturated fatty acids, either monounsaturated or polyunsaturated (referring to the number of hydrogen atoms missing). The hydrogenation process adds hydrogen to the unsaturated fatty acids and, depending upon the extent of the process, changes them from unsaturated to saturated. The texture is also changed from liquid to semisolid. By further adding mono- and diglycerides, the dispersion qualities of these fats are improved.

Shortenings, both vegetable and vegetable-animal combinations, will keep at room temperatures for a short period of time. If you do not use these products often, keep them under refrigeration.

Liquid oils. Liquid oils are made from several vegetable sources, including cottonseed, olives, safflower and sunflower seeds, soybeans, and peanuts. Although they can be used as shortenings, most often they are used for salad dressings and for frying. Most are partially hydrogenated but with no cholesterol. Those who wish to limit their intake of saturated fats should check the label for information concerning the amount of unsaturated versus saturated fats. If the term *liquid vegetable oil* precedes *hydrogenated oil* on the label, then you know that the oil is predominantly unsaturated.

Since these oils are used extensively for frying, most have a high smoking point. Stir-frying demands an oil with a very high smoking point, and peanut oil is best for this purpose.

Some oils will cloud when kept in the refrigerator. Although this clouding can be prevented by additional filtration, it is not an indication of low quality and does not result in any difference in taste or smoking point. In fact, all oils should be refrigerated after being opened, including olive oil, which may develop an off-taste if kept at room temperature.

Butter. Butter produces a characteristic taste in baked goods when used as a shortening—a taste that is often superior to that of other oils. But it's not worth the extra cost if you plan to use the baked product as a base for other flavors. Butter also has a low smoking point because of the presence of some milk solids. You can raise the smoking point by adding some vegetable oil, but this point will never be as high as it would be with pure oil. There are some combination products available but, again, the smoking point of pure oil is still higher.

CAN OLIVE OIL HELP THE HEART?

Olive oil has been promoted in the popular press and in advertisements as if it were a magic bullet against heart disease. It isn't. But health authorities like the American Heart Association and the National Research Council do agree that monounsaturated fats, found in the highest concentrations in olive oil and canola (rapeseed) oil, may offer some benefit, particularly to the extent that they take the place of saturated fat in the diet. In other words, as one medical researcher says, "Don't think you can erase that steak you just ate by adding olive oil to the salad. You've got to balance what you eat and not overdo it."

Margarine. Because standard margarines must have a fat content of 80 percent, some type of vegetable oil—often more than one— is the predominant ingredient. The fat content of most margarines is usually about 11 grams per tablespoon. Because of the high oil content and relatively low water content, most margarines can be used for frying and some types of baking. But margarine containing skim milk has a lower smoking point and therefore is less suitable for frying.

- *Margarine spreads.* These products vary in the percentage and types of vegetable oils used. Most so-called fat-free or low-fat types have water as the dominant ingredient and therefore are not good for frying or baking. Others may have fat levels as high as 70 percent and can be used for sautéing or browning. Most spreads contain from 0 to 7 grams of fat per serving; the higher the number of grams of fat, the higher the percentage of oil.

- *Butter-flavored spreads.* Gaining rapidly in popularity are margarines or spreads that contain an addition of sweet-cream butter to improve the flavor. The amount of butterfat or butter can range from just a trace to as high as 40 percent. Again, products using skim milk as an ingredient are not suitable for sautéing or frying.

Mayonnaise and salad dressing. Many fat- or oil-based products are oil-in-water emulsions. Mayonnaise is an example of a permanent emulsion, whereas some salad dressings are examples of temporary emulsions—some, very temporary. Mayonnaise must have at least 65 percent oil and is usually stabilized by adding egg yolks. One mixture that is similar to mayonnaise, usually known as salad dressing, contains between 30 and 45 percent oil. As a general rule, the higher the oil content, the more expensive the product. Lower-priced salad dressings also have some cooked cornstarch paste substituted for part of the egg yolks. Again, read the labels.

PRICE

If you compare the prices of the various forms of fats and oils on the market, you will note the usual 10 to 20 percent difference between national and house brands. Whether or not the price differential is justified can be answered only by experimentation. Some house brands are almost chalky in color, even at room temperature, while others are identical to the national brands. You will also notice that the competition between national brands of oil is fierce, and there are always sales or specials resulting in significant savings on both margarine and liquid oils. As noted before, there are also price differences according to the type of basic oil, and any product using a compound of vegetable oils usually costs less than the pure product.

Ground Coffee

The typical American coffee is a blend. It consists mostly of arabica beans from Brazil and Colombia, generally regarded as the best beans. The coffee may also include some Central American arabicas, which can also be high-quality beans. Robusta beans from Africa, generally of a lower quality than arabicas, may round out the mixture.

Coffee companies blend the beans as a way of maintaining a brand's familiar flavor consistently, despite changes in crop conditions or commodity prices. Coffee companies have been known to try enhancing the image of a run-of-the-mill product by blending in a soupçon of a classic coffee such as Arabian mocha, Jamaican Blue Mountain, or Hawaiian Kona, then advertising that fact. But, no matter how clever the blender may be, using the cheapest available beans needed to maintain flavor inevitably compromises a brand's potential for excellence.

"Mountain grown," "premium," "gourmet supreme," and other such phrases on a coffee label mean little or nothing. A term such as "100% Colombian" tells you where the beans originated, but it's no more illuminating than a wine label that says "made from 100% French grapes."

IT'S ALL IN THE ROAST

Beneath the skin of each berry on a coffee tree lies a layer of sweet pulp enclosing two coffee beans. The pulp and inner skin surrounding the two beans must be removed before the beans can be dried and roasted. The roasting develops a volatile oil called caffeol, which is responsible for much of the taste and aroma of the finished product.

Beans roasted to a dark chestnut brown make the familiar American coffee; the same beans, roasted until black, produce an espresso-flavored coffee.

Coffee roasts are distinguished by color, ranging from Cinnamon (the lightest) through American, Full City, Vienna, French, and Italian. Different coffee beans reach their peak flavor at different roasting times and temperatures, so the art of roasting is in knowing when to stop.

In this country, commercial coffees tend to be roasted on the lighter side, falling somewhere between American and Full City roast. Some people consider any dark, European-style roast to be "gourmet" coffee, but within limits it's the quality of the bean rather than its roast color that piques a true gourmet's interest.

The grind—drip, automatic, all-purpose—refers to the size of the ground coffee particles. These particles range from coarse and granular to a pulverized powder. Finer grinds are best for coffeemakers that pass the water through the grounds once; coarser grinds are best for percolators that circulate water through the grounds.

DECAFFEINATED GROUND COFFEE

Modern decaffeination methods use organic solvents, carbon dioxide, or charcoal filters. Solvents are most widely used, giving rise to fears that solvent residues may pose a cancer risk for coffee drinkers. But there's little evidence to support that fear.

Classic decaffeination uses a solvent such as methylene chloride. Unroasted coffee beans soak in hot water containing the solvent, which dissolves the caffeine. The solvent is separated, then the caffeine is precipitated out and generally sold to soft-drink and pharmaceutical companies. The beans go back in the soaking water to help restore some of their flavor; then they are rinsed. Any surviving residue is apt to be vaporized when the beans are roasted. These days, decaffeination often involves the "indirect" method: The beans are soaked in plain water, which is drained off and decaffeinated separately.

The proprietary Swiss Water Process decaffeination system involves soaking the coffee in plain water, then using charcoal filters to remove the caffeine from the water. Since Swiss Water Process lends cachet to the decaf, some commercial roasters try to borrow the image by saying their solvent-processed coffee is "water processed." But any decaffeinated coffee can be called "water processed."

Some roasters use ethyl acetate as a solvent and term the process "natural decaffeination." Ethyl acetate does occur naturally in fruits, but decaffeinated coffee doesn't occur in nature. Coffee is always decaffeinated artificially.

HOW TO BUY AND STORE COFFEE

Most of the flavor and aroma of coffee comes from the oils, and these oils begin to evaporate as soon as they are exposed to air.

Oxidation can also cause disagreeable odors and tastes to develop that will, within a relatively short period of time, completely change the character of the coffee. The most severe evaporation and oxidation begins as soon as the coffee is ground, so unless you can use the ground beans immediately, some of the flavor and aroma will always be lost. There are, however, a few things that you can do to retard or reduce this loss.

- After opening a can of coffee, always replace the lid securely and refrigerate the can. Cold temperatures retard evaporation and oxidation.
- Never buy more than you would normally use in a few days. Buying several weeks' supply in a 3-pound tin may save you a few pennies, but it is hardly worth it when you have to drink the stuff after the flavor changes.
- Always make sure your coffee-making equipment is sparkling clean. Residual oils from the previous batch will turn rancid and affect the flavor of the new brew.
- To enjoy the best flavors, find a market where you can buy the whole beans ground to order or, better yet, buy a grinder and grind the beans just before you use them.

Cost. Comparing prices of tinned blended coffees and whole coffee beans is like comparing apples and oranges: The two products are too dissimilar in taste and aroma for a true comparison to be made.

Flavors. Certain countries produce coffees with dominant characteristics. The African Kenya, for example, has a rich, distinctive taste that can be blended with an acidic mild for more of a bite. The Colombian Aged has a unique flavor, almost woody, that does not blend well, yet most Brazilian coffees are best when they are blended. As you become familiar with the flavors of the pure-strain coffees, you may want to experiment with your own blends. Make sure that the beans are thoroughly mixed before they go into the grinder.

If you wish to buy pure-strain coffee beans, find a source that has competent, knowledgeable personnel. Like cheeses, coffees differ widely in both taste and use. Considering the price that you will have to pay, you should receive both good coffee and good advice.

Instant Coffee

Instant coffee can't compare with ground coffee because instant suffers many more travails in its transformation from whole beans to brew to powder.

COFFEE AND CHOLESTEROL

First it was the bacon, eggs, cream, buttered toast, and dough-nuts—all under indictment for hiking your cholesterol count. Now it's the coffee.

But don't retire your coffee mug yet. Coffee has been in the lineup of breakfast suspects off and on for years. Numerous researchers have investigated whether it raises blood cholesterol. Often, just as one group implicates it as a potential culprit, another exonerates it. Since the mid-1960s, dozens of studies have produced a wide range of conflicting results. Some suggested that blood-cholesterol levels rise with increasing coffee consumption; others found no such association.

Studies among Norwegians show a more consistent link between coffee drinking and cholesterol levels than do studies in the United States, and recent findings point to a possible explanation: People in the two countries make coffee differently. Unlike Americans, Norwegians prepare coffee by boiling it, and the resulting brew appears to have a kick of its own.

Why should the brewing method make any difference? In 1989, a group of Scandinavian researchers hit on a possible answer. They found that boiled coffee contains up to 200 times more coffee oil than filtered coffee. The researchers then extracted such oils from boiled coffee, whipped them in with a custard, and served the preparation to 10 men and women regularly. After six weeks, the subjects' blood-cholesterol levels rose an average of 23 percent.

Although the findings still need to be confirmed by a larger, better-controlled study, they offer a potential explanation for the effect of boiled coffee.

Meanwhile, the inconsistency of results in the U.S. studies probably amounts to good news for the average American coffee drinker. With so much research already weighing in on the coffee-cholesterol connection, any significant effect of coffee should have emerged by now. The inconsistency in the findings suggests that any effect that might exist is likely to be small.

Nevertheless, there are still gaps in scientific knowledge of coffee's possible role. The effects of percolated coffee, for example, are unknown. And other factors that might influence coffee's effect on blood cholesterol have yet to be studied, such as the variety of coffee beans, the method of roasting and grinding, the amount used per cup or pot, and the like.

Accordingly, if your cholesterol count is above 240 and your HDL ("good") cholesterol is below 40 (50 for premenopausal women), consider drinking less coffee or using drip-filtered only. Consider these steps particularly if you drink five or more cups of coffee a day or if you have other risk factors for coronary disease, such as diabetes, high blood pressure, smoking, or a family history of heart attack before age 55.

In addition, instant coffee often contains a high proportion of robusta beans. Those beans, generally of lower quality, are said to hold up to processing better than high-quality arabicas do. Robusta beans also yield more caffeine.

Once roasted and ground, the coffee moves into high-pressure retorts, a series of 20-foot-long "percolators" ganged together. Hot water surges through the retorts at pressures that can be high enough to extract almost half the beans' weight as liquid. The process liquefies the beans' cell membranes and other structures, detritus that the processors would otherwise have to discard as spent grounds.

The brew is then either spray-dried or freeze-dried. Spray-drying, the older method, atomizes the coffee with hot air. The resulting powder is often agglomerated—moistened, heated, and pressed into little chunks that superficially resemble ground coffee. Freeze-drying, a slightly gentler process, subjects frozen brewed coffee to a vacuum and low heat. The ice evaporates without passing through a liquid state, leaving granules of coffee behind.

In both of these drying methods, some of the flavor essences are recaptured from the retorts and cycled back into the powder, a process called aromatization.

Instant coffee, the epitome of modernity when it became popular after World War II, has lost favor steadily in recent years. Still, instant accounts for about one-third of coffee sales at the supermarket.

TASTE

In tests conducted by *Consumer Reports*, the best instants were all freeze-dried, but that doesn't mean freeze-drying is always superior. One freeze-dried brand was judged only fair.

As a group, the instants were thin-bodied and had a cooked flavor. The better ones had hints of woodiness; the worst often tasted grainy or exhibited signs of overheating, with resinous, tarry, burned, or slightly harsh notes. On the positive side, most instant *decafs* tasted about as good as their regular counterparts. Instant coffee undergoes such intense processing that the added step of decaffeination doesn't seem to have much effect on the flavor.

COST

Instant coffee, a processed food, has always been a potentially costly product. *G. Washington*, an instant sold in the 1920s, cost $5 a pound and was promoted as a luxury item seen in the finest homes.

Nestlé's *Nescafé*, a brand name synonymous to some with instant coffee, was the first instant aimed at the masses. It originally consisted of half coffee and half cornstarch. Only in the 1950s, when Borden's countered with an instant trumpeted as "100% pure coffee," did Nestlé drop the cornstarch. The race was on to find ever-cheaper ways to make instant coffee.

Today, instant coffee costs barely more than fresh-brewed, averaging about 6 cents a serving for spray-dried brands and about 8 cents for freeze-dried. Ground coffees themselves range from 3 to 10 cents a cup.

Teas

All the world's tea comes from a single species of evergreen shrub, *Camellia sinensis*, a relative of the flowering camellia. The taste differences among the 3,000 or so varieties of tea arise from the varied growing conditions and processing methods.

There are three basic methods of processing teas.

- *Green tea* is made by steaming, rolling, and then drying the leaves of varying qualities.
- *Black tea*, also made from various qualities, is first dried, allowed to oxidize or ferment, and then fired—resulting in a leaf with a dark, coppery red color.
- *Oolong tea*, which is processed mostly in Taiwan, is made by allowing the leaf to semiferment before drying.

The quality of the tea depends upon the size of the leaves. The finest are leaves from the bud and the next two on the stem. Medium grades include the next two leaves, and lower-grade teas include the fourth and fifth leaves. Smaller leaves are better because they have not yet developed the tannic acid that can give tea a bitter taste. The term *orange pekoe* is used to identify the most perfect black leaves, and *pekoe souchong* the next-lower quality. Other variations in taste and aroma are produced either by smoking the leaves or by adding various blossoms that result in the scented teas. Tea-leaf quality is also affected by the soil and the weather.

Most of the varieties consumed in the United States are the fermented black teas blended from several different types and grades. Green and oolong teas are most commonly found in Chinese and Japanese groceries and some specialty shops.

Instant tea is often mixed with carriers, or substances used to stabilize the mixture. Probably half the shelves in the supermarket devoted to instant teas are occupied by iced tea mixes or lemon and sugar–flavored iced tea. A look at the ingredients list of these mixtures clearly shows that tea is only the second or third ingredient. Sugar leads the list. The unsweetened lemon-flavored variety will usually have tea as the first ingredient, followed by citric acid. (See Appendix for Ratings of brand-name tea products.)

COST

Loose or bulk teas are not a popular item in most supermarkets, so any discussion of costs should focus on the big tea seller—tea bags.

The "100% natural" tea in bags costs between 2.9 and 10 cents per bag, depending upon the brand and the number of bags in the package. Buying the bigger size of tea bags does pay off. One national brand cost .045 for the 16 count, .035 for the 48 count, and .028 for the 100 count.

Decaffeinated tea is more expensive. One national brand flavored with orange and spice costs 9 cents per bag.

Prices for tea bags triple when you change from the recognized standard brands to the specialty brands—from .028 cents to almost 10 cents per bag.

THE PERFECT CUP OF TEA

Start with fresh cold water, and get it boiling furiously. Warm the teapot by rinsing it out with some hot water from the kettle. Set the kettle to boil again, and add the tea—one bag or one teaspoonful per cup—to the warmed pot. Pour in the boiling water, and let the tea steep for about three to five minutes for bags, or up to seven minutes for large-leafed loose tea.

If you use tea bags or a tea ball, remove the tea after the steeping is done to keep the tea from growing bitter. With loose tea, don't make more than you plan to serve within 10 minutes or so. For a stronger brew, use more tea rather than a longer brewing time. If the result is too strong, it's better to dilute it in the cup with additional hot water.

HERBAL TEAS

For centuries, people have made beverages from herbs submerged in boiling water to release their aromatic oils. Most of these brews have been used for medicinal purposes. Chamomile tea was taken for digestive problems, horehound tea as a cough remedy, and sassafras tea was used as a spring tonic.

The natural-foods movement of the sixties and the desire of many to avoid caffeine created a whole new market—herbal teas. Now, every supermarket has a section that includes 10 to 30 types of herbal teas, most of them blends of several different herbs and spices.

With so many variations available, it is impossible to determine comparative quality, especially since most are now sold as prepacks and bags. As far as cost is concerned, expect to pay from 5 to 15 cents a cup for prepacked herbal teas.

Soft Drinks

More space in supermarkets is devoted to the sale of various types and brands of soft drinks than any other product. Although no one really knows why, colas dominate the soft drink market, amounting to approximately 75 percent of total sales. Two companies, Coca-Cola and Pepsi, control 70 percent of the sales of cola-flavored products. The amount of advertising by these two companies (and others) in the soft drink market is enormous, but its focus has long been recognition and not quality or ingredients.

When buying soft drinks, quality is seldom the issue, since there are no established quality standards. Two factors, taste and price, should control your selection. Obviously, taste is a matter of individual preference, but you may be interested in the results of blind taste tests conducted by *Consumer Reports* (see Appendix for Ratings of brand-name colas). One test was designed to determine whether or not veteran cola drinkers could tell the difference between the two major brands. The second test involved rating all of the national brands of colas plus some store brands. Both tests included regular and diet colas; the second test also included caffeine-free and diet caffeine-free colas.

Slightly more than a third of the panel could identify the brand of regular cola, and less than a third could identify the brand of diet cola. The second test rated all brands in the good-to-very-good range (for regular and caffeine-free colas) and rated diet colas in the fair-to-good range. Prices were far less consistent: The least expensive brand was slightly more than half the price of the most expensive brand. Based on the results of these tests, it is safe to say that price should be either the sole reason for buying soft drinks or, at the least, an important consideration.

Fortunately for the consumer, the major brands are used by many supermarket chains as weapons in their price wars, and at any given time you usually can find at least one chain with a soft drink "special." Most soft drinks have a long shelf life if stored in a cool dark place, so stocking up when the price is right can save you a significant amount of money.

Bottled Water

Almost all supermarkets now carry a selection of bottled water, including drinking, distilled, purified, spring, natural, well, carbonated, and flavored. The choice of which brand or type to buy is largely a question of use and taste and, since prices vary, you will be in a better position to decide if you know the following facts about the bottled water industry.

The companies make a clear distinction between sparkling bottled water, which is normally used solely as a refreshment, and nonsparkling bottled water used for drinking and for cooking. There are over 700 different brands of domestic bottled water and 75 brands of imported waters, most of which are carbonated mineral waters.

WHAT'S WHAT IN BOTTLED WATERS

Many brands of sparkling water, seltzer, and mineral water are available in various flavors—lemon-lime, raspberry, strawberry, and orange.

Still water. Still water is water without gas bubbles. Examples include ordinary tap water and drinking water sold in large containers.

Sparkling water. Sparkling water originates from a tap or underground source and contains carbon dioxide gas. The gas can occur naturally in underground water or it can be man-made. "Naturally sparkling water" on a label means water from an underground source that already contained enough gas to make it bubbly. The gas escapes as the water surfaces, but it is captured at the spring and added back during bottling. Don't be confused by transposed adjectives: Spring water carbonated with carbon dioxide from another source is sold as "sparkling natural water," not "naturally sparkling water."

Seltzer. Seltzer is virtually the same as sparkling water, but the source is almost always tap water. The water used in seltzer is filtered and carbonated. No minerals or mineral salts are added, so seltzer has a lower mineral content than club soda does.

Mineral water. Water containing dissolved minerals will be labeled as such. (To a chemist, all water but distilled or deionized water is mineral water.) It can come from either underground or surface water. "Natural mineral water" is usually taken from a spring and contains only the minerals present in the water as it flows from the ground. It may be sparkling or still. If mineral water is not labeled "natural," some minerals may have been added or removed.

Club soda. Club soda is carbonated water to which the manufacturer has added mineral salts—bicarbonates, citrates, and phosphates of sodium, for instance. It typically has more sodium than seltzers and sparkling waters, and carries the same risk of chlorination by-products as do seltzers and other products made with tap water.

COST

Bottled water is not cheap. The average price for the gallon bottle (128 ounces) is 90 cents, and the price for a domestic or imported

HERBS, SPICES, SEEDS, AND FLAVORINGS

Herbs are the leaves, stems, or flowers of plants. Spices are the products of the buds, bark, or roots, whereas the seeds are the fruits or seeds. All impart a special flavor and aroma to foods, and are essential to many dishes.

Those herbs and spices that owe their flavor and aroma to the presence of aromatic oils have a much shorter shelf life than do spices of the astringent type. This is especially true if they are ground, because the essential oils evaporate much faster from the ground spice than from whole spice. To retard evaporation, keep herbs and spices in airtight containers in a cool, dry location. The worst possible place is over the stove.

If stored properly, whole spices and seeds keep their potency for several years. Replace leaf herbs every year, and ground spices after six months.

Flavoring extracts. Extracts are the concentrated essential oils or parts of a plant that have been dissolved in alcohol. The extract tastes and smells somewhat like the original plant and imparts that flavor and taste to cakes, pies, and other prepared foods. Vanilla, lemon, peppermint, and almond are the most common extracts available in the supermarket. You will also find less expensive "imitation" extracts next to the real thing. This is not the place to economize, so check the labels before buying.

50.7-ounce bottle of mineral water is two to three times the cost per ounce of the gallon sizes. Since the cost of tap water in most U.S. municipalities ranges from .002 to .008 cents per gallon, those who buy bottled water because of a fear of contamination may find it worthwhile to have their tap water tested and analyzed.

Many bottled water products are sold in supermarkets, so they are increasingly used as specials or even loss leaders. These waters also have a long storage life and, like soft drinks, they can be purchased in volume when the price is right. (See Appendix for information on contamination in bottled water and for Ratings of brand-name products.)

Convenience Foods

Convenience foods include such products as frozen dinners and entrées, frozen desserts, canned soups and stews, canned entrées, dehydrated or dried products, and entrées in a bag or pouch.

When comparing convenience foods with similar foods prepared at home, keep the following points in mind:

- Any type of processing necessary to prepare and preserve food also alters the food's taste, texture, and aroma.
- Often, the choice of ingredients in a prepared entrée, for example, is limited because of the preservation method, either because it does not freeze well or because it does not reconstitute properly. Ingredients are also left out to lower the cost.
- To save money, the manufacturer may use the cheapest ingredients available.
- The question of additives is always a consideration. A look at the ingredient list on most convenience food labels may convince you that the product is nothing but a chemical stew.

The question of whether or not it makes economic sense to buy convenience foods must be based on:

- *Time.* Because the cost of the products will be two to four times what it would be to prepare the item at home, time should be the deciding factor. Obviously, few of the products are better than similar foods you prepare at home, particularly since you are able to control the ingredients.
- *Taste.* The quality of many of the products, particularly frozen ones, has improved over the past 10 years. There is still, however, a wide range in quality, and only experimentation can identify what you consider to be an acceptable product.

COOKING CONVENIENTLY

If you are using prepared products because of tight time schedules but would prefer not to use them so often, here are some suggestions to diversify and improve your meals at home.

Never cook a meal for just one person. When you plan your menus and your shopping list, always buy enough to prepare three to five meals. For example, buy a whole chicken and cut it up according to the types of dishes you want to prepare. You might make two meals of broiled chicken breast and use the legs and thighs for chicken à la king, sweet-and-sour chicken, or chicken stew. The carcass can be used for chicken soup. These various dishes can then be frozen in individual containers. By cooking one to two hours twice a week, you can have a variety of meals available at a moment's notice.

Or have a cooking morning every weekend. Shop for sales and then prepare several dishes for the following week. For example, you can prepare meat dishes one week, poultry dishes the next week, and so forth. Every three or four weeks, make a large pan of lasagna or some other casserole and freeze it in individual portions. If fish is on sale, buy two or three pounds and then cut them up into portions to be frozen. This way, you have about a dozen frozen entrées to choose from when it's time to prepare dinner.

9

How to Prepare and Store Food Safely

by Lisa Y. Lefferts

Eating is one of the true pleasures of life. Yet headlines about dangerous bacteria in chicken and burgers, animal drugs in milk, pesticides in produce, contaminants in fish, and artificial sweeteners in soda may have left you wondering: Is anything safe to eat?

Yes, but shopping for food today does require some knowledge and an awareness of how food is produced. Choosing good-tasting, nutritious food need not mean more bacteria, pesticides, toxins, metals, drugs, or questionable additives in your diet. Knowing the risks can help you choose products that are both safe and good to eat.

Contaminants in Our Food

The typical supermarket presents an array of tempting, wholesome foods—fruits, vegetables, meats, and other items. Unfortunately, some of these products, because of contamination by bacteria, pesticides, or other additives, may be harmful to your health.

BACTERIA

Each year in the United States, food-borne microorganisms cause from 6 to 80 million cases of illness, and thousands of deaths. While any type of food can harbor undesirable microbes, foods derived from animals and fish are the most likely to be contaminated. As many as 90 percent of raw chickens leaving some processing plants for the supermarket are reported to contain salmonella and other bacteria. And one out of every 10,000 eggs—even uncracked, Grade A eggs—is likely to be contaminated with salmonella. If you're like many people and eat 200 eggs per year, your chances of consuming an egg contaminated with salmonella are about one in 50.

Although salmonella may be the most talked-about bacterium, it may not be the most common. Campylobacter bacteria, for example, are probably the most frequent cause of food poisoning. *Listeria, E. coli*, staphylococcus, and yersinia are other bacteria that can contaminate food. Viruses and parasites, particularly those in raw and undercooked seafood, can also cause food-borne illness.

Some experts estimate that most of us get one or more illnesses from food every year or two. Usually the symptoms include bloating, cramps, nausea, vomiting, fever, diarrhea, or flulike symptoms. In some cases, food poisoning can cause kidney or heart disease, certain kinds of arthritis, malnutrition, a weakened immune system, or even death.

If you do get sick, seek treatment if the symptoms are severe, or if the victim is a child, a pregnant woman, an elderly person, or someone with a chronic illness. Drink plenty of liquids, such as water, tea, apple juice, and bouillon, to replace fluids lost through vomiting and diarrhea. If you think the food that made you sick was a commercial product or came from a commercial establishment (restaurant, deli, grocery store), save the remaining suspect food and its packaging, and report the incident to your local health department. Other people may also have been affected by the same food, and it's important that the source of the contamination—especially a food supplier—be pinpointed and corrected.

To avoid infection, take these precautions:

- Avoid raw or undercooked foods derived from animals or fish. These include raw and undercooked fish or shellfish, raw or undercooked meat and poultry, eggs, and raw (unpasteurized) milk and cheese.
- Treat all raw meat, poultry, fish, and eggs as if they were contaminated with disease-causing bacteria. Don't allow raw juices to touch other food. Put packages of raw meat, poultry, or seafood in a plastic bag before putting them in your shopping cart. Anything that has touched raw meat, poultry, or fish should be thoroughly washed with soapy water to prevent any bacteria from spreading. This includes hands, utensils, or kitchen surfaces such as countertops and cutting boards.
- Marinate food in the refrigerator, not at room temperature. If you plan to use the marinade for dipping or basting on the grill, reserve some in the refrigerator before applying it to food. Do not reuse a marinade from the raw meat, fish, or poultry, since it may contain bacteria. If you do, you must boil it first.
- When the food is cooked, transfer it to a clean platter—never to the dish that held the raw product.
- When you are reheating broths, soups, or gravies, boil for several minutes to remove any possible bacteria that might be present.
- Do not taste suspicious or bad-smelling food.
- Use a separate cutting board for raw meat and poultry. Wash it thoroughly afterward with hot, soapy water.
- When handling meat, poultry, or fish, wear rubber gloves if you have a cut on your hands, and be sure to wash the gloves thoroughly.
- Don't wash eggs, since washing removes the protective oil that is found naturally on eggshells.
- Keep cold foods cold and hot foods hot—don't leave foods sitting out on the counter for more than two hours.
- Thaw frozen meat, poultry, and fish in the refrigerator or in cold water (changed at least every half hour), not on the counter. The following chart shows how long it takes to thaw turkey:

Turkey Weight	In Refrigerator	In Cold Water
8–12 pounds	1–2 days	4–6 hours
12–16 pounds	2–3 days	6–9 hours
16–20 pounds	3–4 days	9–11 hours
20–24 pounds	4–5 days	11–12 hours

- Stuff raw poultry just before cooking it, and remove all stuffing after cooking. Don't store leftover chicken or turkey with the stuffing still in it (it takes longer to cool, which gives bacteria more opportunity to multiply).
- Transfer leftovers from hot cooking pots to small, cool storage containers to be refrigerated.
- For other questions about safe handling of meat and poultry, call the USDA Meat and Poultry Hotline at 1-800-535-4555. Call the FDA Seafood Hotline at 1-800-FDA-4010 for information on seafood safety.

PEOPLE AT RISK

Pregnant women, people over age 60, and people with liver disease, diabetes mellitus, cancer, AIDS, ulcerative colitis or other gastrointestinal disorders, or those taking immunosuppressive drugs need to be particularly scrupulous in following safe handling, storage, and cooking guidelines. In addition, they should:

- *Never* eat raw shellfish (such as oysters and clams). They may contain *Vibrio* or other bacteria that can be life-threatening. Bite for bite, raw shellfish is the riskiest commercially available food you can eat. Mussels, clams, and oysters should be thoroughly cooked (four to nine minutes).
- Do not eat raw fish (including sushi, sashimi, and ceviche), dishes made with raw eggs (including homemade eggnog, Caesar salad dressing, or uncooked cookie dough), and any other raw or undercooked food derived from an animal (including partially cooked hamburgers, "pink" chicken,

rare roast beef, or eggs cooked sunny-side up). Eggs
should be cooked until the yolk and white are firm, not
runny.

- Thoroughly reheat leftovers and ready-to-eat foods such
  as hot dogs until steaming hot (165°F).
- The *Listeria* bacteria can cause miscarriage and stillbirth in
  pregnant women, and other serious illnesses in high-risk
  individuals. These individuals should avoid soft cheeses
  such as feta, blue, Roquefort, Brie, Camembert, and
  Mexican-style cheeses (soft, white Latin American cheeses
  such as queso blanco and queso fresco). Hard cheeses, cottage cheese, yogurt, and processed cheese slices are fine.
  Although the risk from deli foods is low, it's a good idea
  to avoid or thoroughly reheat cold cuts before eating. *Listeria* are unusually tough and can resist heat, cold, salt, and
  acid much better than most bacteria.
- Beware of buying ready-to-eat food that is displayed next
  to raw food, since bacteria from the raw product may have
  contaminated it. For example, avoid cooked shrimp displayed on ice right next to raw shrimp.
- When traveling in foreign countries with different hy-
  gienic standards, avoid eating salads and uncooked fruits
  and vegetables, as well as food from street vendors. Drink
  water only if it's boiled (that goes for ice cubes, too) or
  carbonated in a bottle. Peel your fruit, and make sure
  cooked food is still hot.

PESTICIDES AND OTHER CHEMICALS

Do pesticide residues in food endanger your health? The answer
is uncertain. Outbreaks of poisoning linked to consuming pesticides in food are rare, although there have been a few. (Aldicarb
contamination of watermelon is one such case.)

Your risk of getting cancer from the low levels of pesticides in
food is very small. But when millions of people are repeatedly
exposed to pesticides in their diet, the risk of an increase in cancer
cases becomes a significant public health concern.

The extent to which pesticides in food may contribute to cancer or other long-term effects, such as damage to the immune or nervous systems, is impossible to determine accurately at this time. Children are considered to be at greatest risk, however, since they eat more food, relative to their size and weight, than adults do. In addition, their developing bodies are more susceptible to the toxic and cancer-causing effects of some pesticides.

But don't let worries about pesticides prevent you or your family from eating plenty of fresh fruits and vegetables, since that is one of the most important steps you can take to lower your risk of cancer. Washing and peeling produce will remove some of the residues on the surface—not to mention any dirt or bacteria that may be present—although such steps won't remove any pesticide residues absorbed into the growing fruit or vegetable.

Pesticides are most often applied to plants, but certain pesticides and other chemicals tend to accumulate in animal fat. Avoiding fat—something that's healthy to avoid anyway—will also reduce your exposure to these chemicals.

Fatty fish that swim near the coast or in freshwater—such as bluefish, wild (not farmed) catfish and carp, and salmon and lake trout from the Great Lakes—tend to have the highest levels of pesticides and other contaminants like polychlorinated biphenyls (PCBs), a potential carcinogen and reproductive hazard. In a report published in 1992, *Consumer Reports* found that 50 percent of lake whitefish and 43 percent of the salmon tested contained PCBs. Fish like flounder, sole, cod, haddock, and pollack tend to have the lowest levels (see chapter 4).

Here are some other ways to reduce your intake of pesticides.

- Wash and scrub all produce, preferably with a brush. Chop up broccoli, cauliflower, and spinach before washing it for best results. A drop of dish detergent in a large bowl of water will remove more pesticides than just water alone, but rinse produce thoroughly. Discard the outer leaves of cabbage and lettuce and the leaves and tips of celery to reduce your exposure to pesticides. Peel vegetables and fruits that have been waxed (pesticides may be mixed in with the wax).
- Trim away skin and fat from poultry, and fat from meat. Trim skin, the belly flap, and any dark meat on fresh fish

---

ORGANIC FOODS: ARE THEY WORTH THE MONEY?

Which foods you eat—steaks and potato chips, or steamed broccoli and brown rice—are far more important to your health than how those foods were grown.

But there's no doubt that foods grown organically, without the use of most synthetic pesticides and fertilizers, are easier on the health of farm workers and the environment, and may be better for your long-term health.

Organic foods may cost more, however. The price difference between organic and conventionally grown foods is likely to be greater for fresh produce than for grains, soups, and non-perishable food items. On the other hand, the cost of cleaning up contaminated groundwater, treating farm workers harmed by exposure to toxic chemicals, and developing new pesticides as pests become resistant to old ones is also expensive and makes the extra cost of organic foods seem much more reasonable.

Federal regulations to implement a 1990 law requiring national standards to define the term "organic" are long overdue. In the meantime, 26 states regulate or certify the production and marketing of organic food. In other states, farmers can pay to get their operations certified by independent certifying groups. Always look for a certified organic label on food before you buy it—don't just take someone's word for it.

---

before cooking. Don't eat the green-colored tomalley in lobster or the so-called mustard in blue crabs, since those organs concentrate pollutants. Don't prepare sauces, stews, and soups from liquid fish drippings, or dishes that call for the whole fish with internal organs intact.

NATURAL TOXINS

Some of the chemical contaminants found in food occur naturally, although most can be avoided by selecting, storing, handling, and cooking foods properly. For example, the nerve toxin solanine, found in green potatoes, can be avoided by storing potatoes in a cool, dark place (or cutting away any green spots). Improper storage and harvesting of some foods can cause them to become moldy, and some molds can produce toxic and cancer-causing chemicals. One such substance is aflatoxin, which occurs in peanut butter made from moldy peanuts. The big national brands have the lowest levels of aflatoxins, undoubtedly because they exercise strict quality control procedures to exclude moldy peanuts.

Food poisoning by ciguatoxin, a natural toxin produced by tiny organisms eaten by reef fish, occurs mainly in tropical areas such as Hawaii, Florida, and the Caribbean islands. To play it safe, avoid eating reef fish such as amberjack, grouper, goatfish, barracuda, and some species of snapper unless you have reliable information that they were caught from waters unaffected by ciguatoxin. Scombrotoxin is another natural toxin produced when certain fish (particularly bluefish, mahimahi, and tuna) begin to spoil. Illegally harvested shellfish can also contain a natural toxin that causes paralysis in people who eat the shellfish. The solution: Buy seafood only from reputable dealers.

Some people, even scientists, argue that it is a waste of time to worry about hazards from manufactured chemicals because so-called natural chemicals pose a greater risk. Whether the risk from natural chemicals is greater or not is debatable—and also completely beside the point. The fact that some toxins occur naturally in food should not excuse the presence of synthetic ones such as pollutants. Toxic or cancer-causing chemicals of whatever origin should be reduced or eliminated whenever possible.

CONTAMINANTS FROM COOKING

Certain ways of cooking can produce contaminants in food.

If you regularly eat grilled or smoked foods, you need to take precautions to avoid suspected cancer-causing chemicals known as polycyclic aromatic hydrocarbons (PAHs). These are formed when fat drips onto hot coals, or another heat source during the grilling and smoking process. PAHs also form when meat is charred. Avoid these suspected cancer causers when you grill by using a drip pan, wrapping food in foil, grilling food to one side of the coals (not directly over them), choosing foods with little or

DON'T OVERDO IT ... BUT DON'T UNDERDO IT

The secret to cooking meat, poultry, and fish is to cook it long enough to kill any disease-causing microbes but not to overcook it, because prolonged cooking can produce chemicals suspected of causing cancer. According to the National Cancer Institute, these chemicals (called heterocyclic amines, or HAs) may contribute up to 2,000 cases of cancer each year in the United States. Here's how to cut your risks:

- Try roasting, baking, poaching, and stewing, because these cooking procedures produce far fewer HAs than panfrying or broiling.
- If you do panfry or broil, precook meat, poultry, or fish in a microwave on high for about a minute, and discard any juice that collects. Then thoroughly cook the food immediately after, so bacteria don't have time to grow. Don't put the food too close to the broiler, and use a moderate temperature for panfrying.
- Cook a cut of beef until it reaches an internal temperature of 145°F (medium-rare), poultry until the juices run clear (170° to 180°F), boneless turkey roast to 170° to 175°F, and other meats to 170°F. Insert a cooking thermometer into the thickest part of the meat, without touching any bone or fat. If cooking in a microwave, test several spots to determine if the meat is cooked through.
- Avoid making gravy from meat drippings.
- Eat more vegetables, fruits, and grains—they don't contain any HAs, and they have less fat, too.

no fat for the grill (chicken breasts instead of hamburgers, for instance). You can also try using low- or no-fat marinades (try barbecue sauce) and cutting off any charred parts. Grill only properly thawed meat to minimize charring the outside and undercooking the inside. And use regular charcoal rather than mesquite, since mesquite forms more PAHs when it burns.

Other suspected cancer-causing chemicals form when meat, poultry, or fish is panfried or broiled until it is overdone (see box page 167).

METALS

One out of every six children in the United States under age six has a potentially harmful level of lead in the body. Lead is a toxic metal that can have a devastating effect on the brain and nervous system. Lead can affect a child's IQ, mental functioning, behavior, and hearing. The fetus is especially sensitive to lead. Although most children are poisoned by lead-based paint and dust in their homes, food (and water) can also be a source of lead. Low levels of lead also may increase blood pressure in adults. To minimize lead exposure from food sources:

- Don't store food (including brandy or other spirits) in leaded crystal. Don't use leaded crystal every day, and don't use it at all when serving children, or women who are pregnant or of child-bearing age.
- If you are or think you may be pregnant, avoid drinking or eating from lead-glazed dishware. Glass dishes and stoneware dishes (which are heavier and less glossy than glazed china) generally do not contain lead, unless they have painted or decal-type decorations on the surface. China dishes may also contain lead. The only way to tell for sure is to have the dishware tested (see below). For a list of china patterns known to meet California standards (which are far stricter than the FDA's), write or call the Environmental Defense Fund, 257 Park Avenue South, New York, NY 10001, telephone 212-505-2100.
- Don't store food in glazed china dishes, and don't allow children to routinely use china unless you know it is lead-free.
- Domestic dishware made before 1971, imported or hand-crafted dishware, or dishware that shows a dusty or chalky gray residue on the glaze after washing may contain very high amounts of lead. If in doubt, don't use it. And avoid serving food or drink on antique pewter or silver.

- Although most food cans no longer contain lead solder, some imported cans still may. Run your finger down the seam. If it feels uneven or bumpy, the can is possibly soldered with lead. Welded seams, by contrast, are very neat, and the metal around them is shiny. They don't contain lead. Some cans have no seam and no lead at all. Never heat food in cans or refrigerate food in opened cans.
- Serve children those foods that are high in iron, calcium, and vitamin C and low in fat, to help protect them against lead poisoning. Do not serve them clams, which may have high levels of lead.
- You can buy a lead-testing kit to make sure your dishes do not contain high levels of lead. The kits, which cost about

CUTTING BOARDS: WOOD OR PLASTIC?

For years, cooks have been advised to prepare food using plastic cutting boards, not those made of wood. That's because wood seemed more likely to harbor harmful bacteria from contaminated foods. In 1993, however, a study at the University of Wisconsin threw doubt on that advice.

The researchers contaminated several samples of both kinds of cutting boards with various bacteria linked to food poisoning. Three minutes later, virtually all the bacteria had disappeared from the wooden boards, while all the germs remained on the plastic surfaces. Even when the researchers used soap and water to clean sticky, contaminated chicken fat from both types of boards, some bacteria stubbornly clung to the plastic boards. None remained on the wooden cutting boards.

Researchers can only speculate that the wood may kill bacteria by depriving them of moisture (theoretically, water molecules seep into the wood fibers and so are unavailable to bacteria). Or the wood may draw the germs directly into the board's wooden core. Before you throw out your plastic cutting board, however, remember that this is only one study and further research is needed to confirm these results.

$24 to $30, are available from two companies. Contact Hybrivet Systems, Inc., at 1-800-262-LEAD, or write to P.O. Box 1210, Framingham, MA 01701. Another source is Frandon Enterprises at 1-800-359-9000, or 511 North 48th Street, Seattle, WA 98103.

Mercury is another metal that in large amounts can damage the brain and nervous system, and to which the fetus is extremely sensitive. If you're pregnant, avoid eating shark, swordfish, and tuna steaks, which frequently contain high levels of mercury. Tuna steaks have higher levels of this element than canned tuna does. Large tuna, which have had more time to accumulate mercury, are the ones used for steaks. To play it safe, also go easy on canned tuna when you're pregnant.

ANIMAL ANTIBIOTICS

Animal feed contains about half of the more than 31 million pounds of antibiotics produced annually in the United States. Drugs given to farm animals sometimes leave residues in milk and meat. According to 1990 tests by the USDA, almost 3 percent of bob veal carcasses (those used for processed and chopped veal products) contained illegal antibiotic drug residues—the highest overall rate for any type of meat. Dairy cows came in second—notably those older cows who can no longer give milk and whose meat is used for hamburger and other chopped meat products. Chicken and turkey rarely contain illegal drug residues.

The heavy use of antibiotics in animals used for human consumption can lead to the development of antibiotic-resistant bacteria. It may take longer or be more difficult to treat sick people with antibiotics if they have an antibiotic-resistant strain of bacteria in their systems.

Another animal drug now being used is the recombinant bovine growth hormone, or bGH, which increases the amount of milk produced by a dairy cow. Dairy farmers in the United States already produce more milk than Americans can consume, so it is questionable whether this drug will benefit the consumer. Moreover, the increase in milk production puts extra strain on the animal, so more antibiotics may have to be used to keep the cow healthy.

Steroid hormones, once used to promote growth in cattle, don't seem to pose a problem today. In 1979 the FDA banned the use of the carcinogenic hormone DES in cattle; potential problems in humans (such as premature sexual development) were linked to the misuse of this and other hormones in animal feed, but monitoring rarely detects a problem today.

If you eat meat, it may be difficult to totally avoid consuming animal drug residues, but the risks they pose are small. To avoid any risk, and also to support farmers who use animal-raising methods that are kinder to the environment, buy meats with "raising claim" labels. The labels explicitly state that the animal is raised without the use of antibiotics or other feed additives. You will have to pay more for this type of product, but it may be worth it to you.

Don't rely on products labeled "natural." The USDA allows meat and poultry containing drug and pesticide residues to be marketed as "natural," so long as the meat is minimally processed.

ADDITIVES

Most food additives are perfectly safe, but there are a few that call for caution.

Sulfites, for example, are harmless for most people but can be deadly for others. Found in wines, dried fruits, and fresh shrimp, sulfites are especially risky for those who suffer from asthma.

Some people are sensitive to the flavor enhancer monosodium glutamate, or MSG. Consuming foods with MSG can lead to "Chinese restaurant syndrome," with symptoms of headache, tightness in the chest, and/or a burning sensation in the upper body. Others report reactions to the artificial sweetener aspartame, including headaches, dizziness, and menstrual problems, although scientific studies have not confirmed these claims.

Certain additives are suspected of increasing the risk of cancer. The list includes the food dye Red No. 3, the artificial sweeteners saccharin and acesulfame K (also known as Sunette), and sodium nitrite, which is a preservative in bacon and other cured meats.

Although nitrite is not dangerous in itself, it can combine with other chemicals to form nitrosamines, which cause cancer in laboratory animals. Read the product label to find comparable foods that don't contain these additives, or use foods with these additives sparingly.

Caffeine doesn't cause cancer, but too much can give you the jitters and cause insomnia. Caffeine is also mildly addictive, which is why many coffee drinkers get headaches or feel lethargic after they stop the habit. Women who wish to become pregnant should avoid caffeine. In a 1988 study, the National Institute of Environmental Health Sciences reported that women who consumed more than a cup of coffee a day were about half as likely to become pregnant as women who abstained.

IRRADIATED FOOD

You won't find much irradiated food in your supermarket—at least not yet.

Although irradiation is allowed for spices, flour, fruits, vegetables, and poultry in the United States, very few foods (other than some spices) are in fact irradiated because of the controversy surrounding its safety.

Proponents correctly point out that irradiation could help curb food poisoning caused by salmonella and other microbes, and that it could replace the use of some fumigants and pesticides. Critics of irradiation argue that it can destroy nutrients and leave behind potentially risky chemicals. They also oppose it on the grounds that increasing the use of radioactive materials poses an increased risk to workers and the environment.

The FDA maintains that the changes in food caused by irradiation are minimal, and much like the changes typically caused by cooking.

There are better ways to deal with bacteria and microbes in food. Sweden, for example, has largely eliminated salmonella in poultry by using salmonella-free chicken feed, cleaner pens, and other safeguards. Carbon dioxide, hot vapor, or chilling can kill germs and pests in other foods.

Consumers have a right to choose whether or not they want to buy irradiated food. Currently, food that is treated with radiation must be labeled with a "radura" symbol and the words "treated with irradiation"—unless the food is an ingredient in a processed product or is served at a restaurant.

Food Storage

No one likes to throw money away, which is what happens when you have to discard stale or moldy food. Take these steps to prevent food spoilage.

- Keep bread in the freezer, particularly during warm weather. Storing bread in the refrigerator may retard mold, but it will still become stale, even faster than at room temperature.
- Place perishable groceries and leftovers in the refrigerator as soon as possible. You can safely store the following items in the refrigerator for the periods indicated:

Fresh poultry	One to two days
Ground meat	One to two days
Fresh meat	One to three days
Fresh fish	One to two days
Leftovers	Three to four days
Fresh eggs	Three weeks
Hard-boiled eggs	One week
Leftover egg whites and yolks	Two to four days

- If your refrigerator breaks down, or the electric power goes off for a long time, keep the door closed. Cook the food as soon as possible, or move it to a friend's refrigerator.

Despite all your efforts, mold will sometimes appear on refrigerated leftover foods. Here's what to do:

- Mold can be safely trimmed from hard cheeses, salami, and firm fruits and vegetables such as carrots and cabbage. Cut off an inch around and below the mold (to remove any invisible mold spores), taking care not to cut through the mold. Use the food immediately, or store it in fresh wrap or a clean container and use as soon as possible.

- If a jar of jelly or jam has a spot of mold, scoop it out. Remove some additional jelly or jam that was near the mold to eliminate any spores. If the product tastes fermented, discard it.
- Some moldy foods can't be used. Throw away moldy bread, yogurt, soft cheeses, and other soft-bodied foods. Don't eat moldy or discolored peanuts or nuts.

MICROWAVING: WHAT'S SAFE AND WHAT'S NOT

Today you don't have to worry about microwave ovens leaking radiation—unless your unit was made before 1971 or is obviously damaged. Current models have a door seal and at least two interlocks that keep them from operating if the door is not tightly closed. These units are well within the U.S. Bureau of Radiological Health's standard for radiation leakage.

Some safety precautions, however, should be observed when using a microwave:

- Don't allow plastic wrap to come into direct contact with food, and don't use foam containers, yogurt cups, or margarine tubs for heating foods in the microwave. At high temperatures, chemicals can migrate from plastic wrap and containers to the food.
- Avoid using the "brown and crisp" packaging that is included with most microwavable pizza, popcorn, waffles, and french fries. Although tests have not identified any particularly hazardous chemicals in the packaging that might contaminate the food, you're better off not eating traces of plastic or glue.
- Don't use brown paper bags in the microwave—they may contain flecks of metal that could damage the oven.
- Always puncture potatoes, tomatoes, and sausages (and similar foods with skins) before cooking them in the microwave. They might explode.

- After microwaving, open popcorn bags or other closed containers carefully to avoid steam burns. Other foods can also cause burns—jelly doughnuts, for example, may feel cool on the outside but the jelly inside may be boiling hot. Follow directions on the package and teach children how to avoid burns.
- To avoid food poisoning, cook and reheat foods *thoroughly*. Also cook food immediately after defrosting in the microwave. Debone large pieces of meat. Use a thermometer to make sure food is cooked to 165°F. Observe standing time directions. Stir soups or stews during cooking, and turn casseroles.
- Don't warm up baby bottles in the microwave. The milk may get too hot and cause burns.

Water: Bottled, Tap, or Treated?

Is bottled water worth paying 500 to 1,000 times as much as you pay for tap water? It depends. Bottled waters made from municipal tap water may contain risky chemicals called trihalomethanes, or THMs. THMs, which are by-products of chlorine disinfection, are suspected of increasing the risk of rectal and bladder cancer. They are frequently found in tap water unless it is derived from underground sources.

Bottled water is decidedly safer than tap water, however, if your tap water is contaminated with lead. (Most bottled waters are virtually lead-free.) Everyone should have his or her water tested for lead. If the test shows elevated lead levels in the water, and if your household includes persons at high risk—pregnant women, adults exposed to lead on the job, children under age six, children with high levels of lead in the blood, or infants who are fed formula made with tap water—it's recommended that you use bottled water. Otherwise, install a water-treatment device that will reduce lead.

The standard strategy for limiting the amount of lead in tap water is to let the water run for a minute or two until it is purged or good and cold. This method, however, is not always effective, so when you test for lead levels, test both first-drawn and purged water. Water utilities in New York City and some other municipalities have begun offering free tests for lead. Call the EPA Safe Drinking Water Hotline at 1-800-426-4791 to find a certified laboratory in your area. Never drink or cook using water from the hot-water tap, because lead is more soluble in hot water than cold.

If you drink water drawn from your own well, it's up to you to test it for bacteria and the microorganism *Giardia*. If you live in a farming area, also test for nitrates and pesticides. If you live near an industrial site, have your well water tested for organic chemicals such as trichloroethylene.

People with private wells and those whose water comes from small community water systems serving fewer than 500 people should consider testing their water for radon. Radon, a naturally occurring radioactive gas, poses a greater cancer risk than any other single environmental pollutant. But you need to test for radon in your water only if radon is already present in the air of your home.

Radon detectors are available in many hardware stores and even some supermarkets. If you can't find one, call your state department of environmental protection. The agency can provide you with a list of radon-testing companies that have passed the EPA's Radon Measurement Proficiency program. Or you may be able to get a radon test free—some utility companies offer one as part of an energy audit.

References

1. Articles appearing in *Consumer Reports* magazine.

   - "Too Much Fuss About Pesticides?" October 1989, pp. 655–658.
   - "Fit to Drink?" January 1990, pp. 27–40.
   - "Hold the Mold." September 1990, p. 591.
   - "Dioxin in Coffee Filters." January 1991, p. 47.
   - "Is Our Fish Fit to Eat?" February 1992, pp. 103–114.

- "Udder Insanity." May 1992, pp. 330–332.
- "Carbonated Waters." September 1992, pp. 569–571.
- "Is There Lead in Your Water?" February 1993, pp. 73–78.
- "Water-Treatment Devices." February 1993, pp. 79–82.

2. Books and periodicals

Jacobson, M. F., L. Y. Lefferts, and A. W. Garland. *Safe Food: Eating Wisely in a Risky World.* Los Angeles: Living Planet Press, 1991.

Todd, Ewen. "Epidemiology of Food-Borne Illness: North America." *The Lancet* 788 (September 29, 1990).

U.S. Department of Agriculture. "Preventing Food-Borne Illness: A Guide to Safe Food Handling." *Home & Garden Bulletin* 247 (1990).

U.S. Department of Agriculture and U.S. Department of Health and Human Services. *Preventing Food-Borne Listeriosis.* Background paper, April 1992 (revised).

APPENDIX
CONSUMER REPORTS RATINGS OF BRAND-NAME FOOD PRODUCTS

BARBECUE SAUCES

In a 1991 test, *Consumer Reports* found that most barbecue sauces fit into one of three distinct categories: sweet and dominated by the taste of smoke and molasses; spicy, with distinct tomato and vinegar flavors; and simply tomatolike, with perhaps a hint of spice. Those categories are included in the Ratings to help you find the type you like. Sauces listed without a type weren't distinctive enough to categorize.

An excellent barbecue sauce can vary in color from orange to light brown to brownish red. Translucence may indicate too much thickener. A sauce should taste balanced and well blended; none of its basic characteristics—tomato and spice flavors, vinegar taste, sweetness, or saltiness—should stand out excessively or be notably absent. A sauce can be smoky but shouldn't taste harsh or burned. The "burn" of its spices can range from mild to hot.

Consumer Reports scored each sauce on how close it came to those standards, which allowed for a wide range of flavor combinations. Although the scores are based on overall taste, the panelists' measurements of how smoky and how hot each sauce tasted are also noted in the Ratings.

Recommendations

Thirteen sauces, representing all three flavor categories and varying degrees of smokiness and heat, were rated very good.

Which you like best will depend on your taste buds. The tasters' descriptions, provided in the Ratings, should prove helpful.

Not that most barbecue fanatics would care, but nutritionally speaking, barbecue sauce is mostly calories and sodium. Based on manufacturers' information, a 2-tablespoon serving of the tested sauces averages 44 calories and 349 milligrams of sodium, with very little protein or fat. Sweeteners and tomato products supply most of the calories; most of the sodium comes from salt. Most readers don't have to bother about their sodium intake, but sodium values are listed in the Ratings for those who must.

Kraft Thick 'N Spicy Hickory Smoke had the most sodium, at 510 milligrams. *Bull's-Eye Original* and *Heinz Select*, both high in the Ratings, had lower sodium levels than other top sauces. For people on a low-sodium diet, there's *K.C. Masterpiece Original No Salt Added*, which substitutes potassium chloride for sodium chloride. For a low-salt product, it was pretty good.

These sauces contain enough corn syrup, sugar, molasses, and honey that people on a sugar-restricted diet should think twice about consuming them regularly.

CEREALS

Even a nutritionally savvy shopper can find it difficult to sort through the myriad claims that cereal makers put on boxes. There are the "fat-free" claims, although most cereals contain an insignificant amount of fat, and the "low-fat" claims for products to which fat (but not much fat) has been added. Some cereals still tout oat bran, hinting or promising that the ingredient will lower blood cholesterol—something oat bran can do to only a modest degree.

Yet the basic nutritional issues in choosing a cereal are simple. Most important, a cereal should provide a significant amount of dietary fiber. Cereal is one of the best sources of fiber in a typical diet, and most Americans don't get enough fiber from the rest of their foods. A cereal should also be relatively low in sugar and fat. You get less nutritional value than you should from brands that are high in sugar, and the few cereals (mainly granolas) that are high in fat just add calories without nutritional benefit. Although fortification with vitamins and minerals can be a plus, it's

(continued on page 184)

RATINGS

As published in the July 1991 issue of Consumer Reports

Barbecue sauces

Listed in order of overall sensory quality. Sauces within a few points of each other were very similar in quality. Those with equal scores are listed alphabetically.

1 Type. Most sauces fell into one of three categories: sweet, dominated by smoke and molasses flavors (**SM**); tasting mainly of toma- to, vinegar, and a blend of spices (**TS**); and less spicy, dominated by tomato flavor (**T**). A dash marks sauces whose flavor was not distinct enough to allow them to fit neatly into any category.

2 Price. Except as noted, these are estimated average prices, based on a nationwide survey of supermarkets.

3 Cost. For a two-tablespoon serving.

4 Sensory index. How close each product came to our criteria for excellence, based on taste tests by CU's trained panelists.

5 Heat. How much each sauce "burned" our panelists' mouths. The scale ranged from very mild to very hot. None of the brands was very hot, and none packed anywhere near the zing of mouth-melters like tabasco sauce or jalapeño peppers.

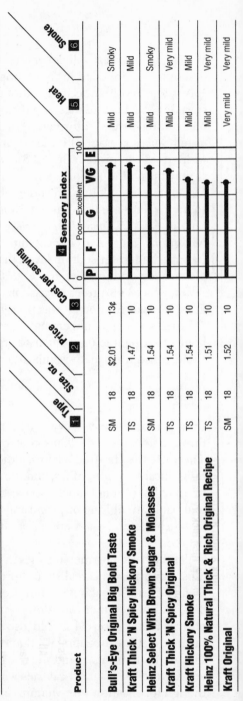

Product	1 Type	Size, oz.	2 Price	3 Cost per serving	4 Sensory index	5 Heat	6 Smoke
Bull's-Eye Original Big Bold Taste	SM	18	$2.01	13¢		Mild	Smoky
Kraft 'N Spicy Hickory Smoke	TS	18	1.47	10		Mild	Mild
Heinz Select With Brown Sugar & Molasses	SM	18	1.54	10		Mild	Smoky
Kraft Thick 'N Spicy Original	TS	18	1.54	10		Mild	Very mild
Kraft Hickory Smoke	TS	18	1.54	10		Mild	Mild
Heinz 100% Natural Thick & Rich Original Recipe	TS	18	1.51	10		Mild	Very mild
Kraft Original	SM	18	1.52	10		Very mild	Very mild

180

Product		Size	Price			
Heinz 100% Natural Thick & Rich Hickory Smoke	TS	18	1.49	10	Mild	Medium
Hunt's All Natural Thick & Rich Hickory Flavor	TS	18①	1.27	8	Mild	Medium
Chris' & Pitt's Original	T	14	1.60	13	Very mild	Very mild
French's Cattlemen's Smoky	T	18	1.74	11	Very mild	Mild
K.C. Masterpiece Hickory	SM	19	1.99	13	Medium	Medium
K.C. Masterpiece Original	SM	19	2.01	13	Medium	Medium
Bull's-Eye Hickory Smoke Big Bold Taste	SM	18	1.99	13	Mild	Very smoky
Maull's Smoky	T	24	2.59	13	Mild	Mild
French's Cattlemen's Hearty Original	T	18	1.77	11	Very mild	No smoke
Hunt's All Natural Thick & Rich Original Recipe	TS	18①	1.25	8	Mild	No smoke
K.C. Masterpiece Original No Salt Added	SM	19	2.69	17	Hot	Medium
Chicken 'N' Ribs Hickory Smoke	—	18	1.01②	7	Medium	Very mild
Kroger Thick & Rich Hickory Smoke Flavor	—	18	1.50	10	Very mild	Mild
A & P Hickory Smoked	—	18	.79	5	Very mild	Very mild
Open Pit Hickory Flavor	—	18	1.56	9	Medium	Medium
Kroger Thick & Rich Traditional	—	18	1.32	9	Very mild	Very mild
Open Pit Original Flavor	—	18	1.65	10	Hot	Very mild
Chicken 'N' Ribs Homestyle	—	22①	1.86②	11	Medium	Very mild
A & P Original	—	18	.79	5	Very mild	No smoke
Open Pit Special Recipe Original	SM	18	1.92	11	Medium	Very smoky

① Squeezable plastic bottle (all others packed in glass).　② Price is what was paid in 1990.

Ratings
Continued

⑥ **Smoke.** How smoky each sauce tasted, from no smoke to very smoky. A little smokiness can improve the flavor of baked or broiled foods. Too much can produce a harsh, burned taste.

⑦ **Sodium.** For a two-tablespoon serving, based on manufacturers' information.

⑧ **Calories.** Per two-tablespoon serving.

An average woman needs 2,000 calories per day, an average man, 2,700.

⑨ **Sensory comments.** Except as noted, sauces were brownish-red and had a slight to moderate tomato flavor, a slight to moderate vinegar flavor, a moderately intense blend of spices, a slight onion/garlic flavor, and moderate sweetness, sourness, and saltiness.

Product	⑦ Sodium per serving	⑧ Calories per serving	⑨ Sensory comments
Bull's-Eye Original Big Bold Taste	328 mg	50	Well-blended, robust flavor; hint of cumin.
Kraft Thick 'N Spicy Hickory Smoke	510	50	Well-blended, robust flavor; distinct black pepper; hint of lemon.
Heinz Select With Brown Sugar & Molasses	300	46	Well-blended, robust flavor.
Kraft Thick 'N Spicy Original	490	50	Well-blended, robust flavor; distinct black pepper; hint of lemon.
Kraft Hickory Smoke	490	40	Hint of lemon.
Heinz 100% Natural Thick & Rich Original Recipe	416	36	Slightly saltier than most.
Kraft Original	490	40	Hints of paprika and lemon.
Heinz 100% Natural Thick & Rich Hickory Smoke	428	36	Slightly saltier than most.
Hunt's All Natural Thick & Rich Hickory Flavor	380	50	Dehydrated onion and vegetable flavors.
Chris' & Pitt's Original	294	35	Mild.
French's Cattlemen's Smoky	436	38	—
K.C. Masterpiece Hickory	190	60	More tomato flavor than others of this type; a bit fruity; more sweet than sour; a bit less salty than most.

Product			Description
K.C. Masterpiece Original	190	60	More tomato flavor than others of this type; a bit fruity; more sweet than sour; a bit less salty than most.
Bull's-Eye Hickory Smoke Big Bold Taste	330	50	Slightly harsh smoke flavor.
Maull's Smoky	296	42	Slight flavor like that of Worcestershire sauce.
French's Cattlemen's Hearty Original	348	46	Vinegary.
Hunt's All Natural Thick & Rich Original Recipe	380	40	Translucent; distinct dehydrated onion and vegetable flavors.
K.C. Masterpiece Original No Salt Added	40	60	More tomato flavor than others of this type; much more sweet than sour; less salty than most.
Chicken 'N' Ribs Hickory Smoke	200	50	Translucent; slightly fruity, with little tomato flavor; distinct flavor of brown spices (such as cinnamon, clove, nutmeg, and allspice).
Kroger Thick & Rich Hickory Smoke Flavor	305	33	Orange color; vinegary; hints of paprika and brown spices; hint of lemon; hamlike smokiness; more sour than sweet.
A & P Hickory Smoked	400	32	Translucent orange; slight tomato flavor; vinegary; distinct paprika; more sour than sweet.
Open Pit Hickory Flavor	420	40	Dyes meat a rusty pink; vinegary; distinct brown spice flavor (clove especially noticeable).
Kroger Thick & Rich Traditional	305	33	Translucent orange; vinegary; hints of paprika and brown spices; hint of lemon; more sour than sweet.
Open Pit Original Flavor	420	40	Dyes meat a rusty pink; vinegary; distinct brown spice flavor (clove especially noticeable).
Chicken 'N' Ribs Homestyle	270	50	Translucent light brown; slightly fruity; little tomato flavor; distinct brown spice flavor; hint of gingerlike flavor; slight plastic flavor.
A & P Original	400	32	Translucent orange; "hollow" flavor; little tomato flavor; vinegary; distinct paprika; more sour than sweet.
Open Pit Special Recipe Original	360	60	Thick, pasty texture; molasses flavor; little tomato flavor; harsh, burned smoke flavor; bitter.

not a primary reason for choosing a cereal. You're buying a food, not a vitamin pill, and most nutrients are widely available in other foods.

In 1992, *Consumer Reports* food scientists analyzed the nutrient content in popular cereals.

Beyond Fiber

Although fiber is the key to a cereal's nutritional worth, other factors can add to or detract from the bottom line:

Micronutrients. Some cereals provide generous doses of vitamins and minerals that were never in the grain in the first place. Those include calcium; vitamins A, C, and D; folic acid (a B vitamin); and beta-carotene, a vitamin A relative present in *Total* but typically found in vegetables. As a rule, Americans can get the basic nutrients they need from other foods, though some people— women especially—may benefit from added folic acid, calcium, and iron.

Most of the tested cereals are fortified with at least three vitamins and minerals to supply 20 percent or more of the U.S. Recommended Daily Allowance (RDA). The products with the highest fortification provide 100 percent of the daily allowance for at least eight vitamins and minerals.

Sugars. The Sugars column in the Ratings includes sucrose (table sugar), glucose (from corn sweetener), and fructose (fruit sugar). Grain normally contains very little sugar, but manufacturers often add it along with other sweeteners (honey and fruit juice, for instance) and dried fruit, which packs sugar of its own. Companies may also sugarcoat the raisins in their raisin bran.

The natural sugar in a cereal's dried fruit (or in fresh fruit that you add) comes along with some fiber, vitamins, and minerals, but sugar added by the manufacturer or at the table means empty calories and less room in your bowl for a cereal's desirable nutrients.

How much sugar is in a cereal? Many of the presweetened children's brands contain 12 or more grams per cup, the equivalent of about 3 teaspoons. *Smacks* and *Oatmeal Raisin Crisp* supply the equivalent of about 5 and 6 teaspoons, respectively. That makes *Smacks* more than half sugar. *Oatmeal Raisin Crisp*, a heavier cereal, is about 30 percent sugar.

Even some cereals aimed at adults are approximately one-third sugar. Among them are many raisin brans, as well as other cereals with added fruit (the fruit supplies much of the sweetness). The Ratings give the grams of sugar per cup and the percentage of sugar by weight for all the cereals.

Fat and protein. Cereal grains normally don't contain much of either. Most brands supply 2 grams of fat per cup, or less. Especially fatty cereals are noted in the Ratings Comments.

As for protein, a cup of most cereals provides from 1 to 6 grams. At most, that's about a tenth of an adult's daily need. But most Americans already get more than enough protein from other foods during the day, so they needn't look for it in cereal.

Sodium. Most readers don't have to worry about their sodium intake, but sodium values are listed in the Ratings for those who must. Typical amounts in processed cereals are 200 to 300 milligrams per cup, though some brands have very little sodium or none at all. Most sodium is from added salt, also present in the flavored instant hot cereals.

Recommendations

Cereal with skim milk and fruit is a quick, healthful way to start the day. Despite steady hikes in cereal prices, a bowl of cereal and milk remains relatively inexpensive—less than 45 cents for a cup of most cereals with three-fourths of a cup of milk and sometimes far cheaper if you use coupons for cereal or buy store brands. *Consumer Reports* found some store cereals to be as good-tasting as national brands, with comparable nutritional value.

You can also save money if you think big. Large packages are generally less expensive than small ones. So are bulk containers of hot cereal, which yield a serving that can cost half as much as a single-serving packet.

The healthfulness of any particular cereal depends on its success in supplying the nutrients you expect in cereal—those you may not encounter often in the rest of your diet. Cereal should first and foremost offer an abundant supply of fiber (4 + g per

(*continued on page 192*)

RATINGS

As published in the November 1992 issue of Consumer Reports

Cereal

Listed by types. Within types, listed in groups by fiber content. High-fiber cereals supply at least 6 grams of dietary fiber per serving (generally one cup, or 30 percent of the daily need; moderate-fiber cereals supply 1½ to 5 grams; low-fiber, less than 1½ grams. Within groups, listed in order of fiber density (grams of fiber per hundred calories). Cereals with the same fiber density are in alphabetical order. Low-fiber cereals are listed in order of increasing calories; low-fiber cereals with the same number of calories are in alphabetical order.

1 Manufacturer. General Mills (**GM**), Kellogg (**K**), Nabisco (**N**), General Foods' Post brand (**P**), Quaker Oats (**Q**), Ralston Purina (**R**), American Home Food Products (**A**), Great Foods of America (**GFA**), Health Valley (**H**), Pillsbury (**PI**), Malt-O-Meal (**M**), New Morning (**NM**), and U.S. Mills (**U**).

2 Per serving. Serving size is one cup for nearly all the ready-to-eat cereals. For densest cereals, noted under Cost, serving is one-half cup; other data for those cereals are based on that portion. For hot cereals, serving is one cup of cooked cereal or one packet, which makes less than a cup. Cost is based on the estimated average price paid nationally in 1992. Typically, cereals were purchased in 15- to 20-ounce boxes. Weight and nutrition data have been rounded. Dashes indicate less than 1 gram of fiber or sugars, or less than 1 percent sugars.

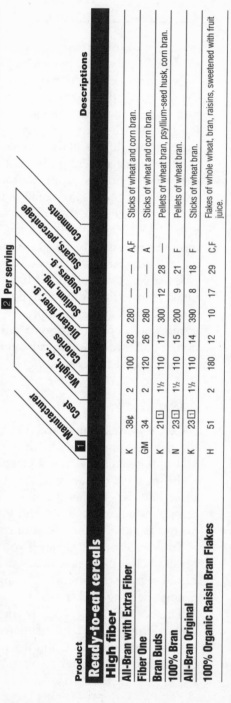

Product	Manufacturer 1	Cost	Weight, oz.	Calories	Dietary fiber, g.	Sodium, mg.	Sugars, g.	Sugars, percentage	Comments	Descriptions
Ready-to-eat cereals										
High fiber										
All-Bran with Extra Fiber	K	38¢	2	100	28	280	—	—	A,F	Sticks of wheat and corn bran.
Fiber One	GM	34	2	120	26	280	—	—	A	Sticks of wheat and corn bran.
Bran Buds	K	21 ⊡	1½	110	17	300	12	28	—	Pellets of wheat bran, psyllium-seed husk, corn bran.
100% Bran	N	23 ⊡	1½	110	15	200	9	21	F	Pellets of wheat bran.
All-Bran Original	K	23 ⊡	1½	110	14	390	8	18	F	Sticks of wheat bran.
100% Organic Raisin Bran Flakes	H	51	2	180	12	10	17	29	C,F	Flakes of whole wheat, bran, raisins, sweetened with fruit juice.

Cereal		g	cup	cal.					Comments	Description
Uncle Sam	U	28	2	220	14	130	—	—	F	Toasted whole wheat flakes, whole flaxseed.
Bran Flakes	K	23	1½	140	8	330	8	18	—	Flakes of wheat bran, other wheat parts.
Bran Flakes	P	21	1½	140	8	320	8	18	—	Flakes of whole wheat and wheat bran.
Crunchy Corn Bran	Q	28	1½	140	8	380	9	21	—	Puffed squares of corn, corn bran, oat flour.
Fiberwise	K	43	1½	140	8	210	8	18	—	Flakes of whole wheat, oat bran, psyllium-seed husk.
Raisin Bran	P	30	2	180	9	300	21	35	—	Flakes of whole wheat and bran, sugared raisins.
Multi Bran Chex	R	25	1½	140	6	300	9	21	—	Squares of corn, with oat, wheat, rice, corn bran.
Shredded Wheat 'N Bran	N	28	1½	140	6	0	—	—	C	Bite-size whole wheat biscuits, bran.
Fruit & Fibre Peaches, Raisins, Almonds & Oat Clusters	P	38	2	180	8	240	12	23	—	Flakes of whole wheat, bran, rolled oats, rice, dried fruit, almonds.
Fruitful Bran	K	43	2	180	8	360	18	30	—	Flakes of whole wheat and bran, raisins, dried fruit.
Raisin Bran	K	29	1¾	160	7	280	16	30	—	Flakes of wheat bran, other wheat parts, sugared raisins.
Shredded Wheat	N	29[2]	1⅓	160	6	0	—	—	C	Whole wheat biscuits.
Cracklin' Oat Bran	K	44	2	220	8	280	14	25	D,F	Cookielike rings of whole oats, oat and wheat bran, brown sugar.
Skinner's Raisin Bran	U	27	2	220	8	90	12	21	F	Rolled whole wheat flakes including bran, raisins.
Frosted Wheat Squares	N	40	2	200	6	0	12	21	F	Sugared bite-size shredded whole wheat biscuits.
Grape-Nuts	P	29[1]	2	220	6	340	6	11	F	Nuggets of whole wheat, malted barley.
Moderate fiber										
Shredded Wheat Spoon Size	N	28	1½	140	5	0	—	—	C	Bite-size whole-wheat biscuits.
Common Sense Oat Bran	K	27	1½	130	4	330	8	21	—	Flakes of oat bran, whole-grain wheat.

[1] Half-cup serving size (cereal denser than most).
[2] Two large biscuits.
[3] Five biscuits.
[4] In individual-serving packets.
[5] One packet makes slightly less than one-half cup.
[6] One packet makes less than three-fourths cup.

Features in Common
Except as noted, all supply: • Less than 6 g. of protein per serving. • Less than 3½ g. of fat per serving. • At least 20 percent of the U.S. RDA for 3 to 8 vitamins and minerals.

Key to Comments
A—Contains aspartame artificial sweetener.
B—Highly fortified (supplies 100 percent of U.S. RDA for at least eight vitamins and minerals).
C—Not fortified (although B vitamins may have been restored, with calcium and iron added for some brands).
D—About 6 g. fat per serving.
E—About 3½ to 4 g. fat per serving.
F—About 6 to 8 g. protein per serving.

Ratings continued

Ratings
Continued

Per serving

Product	Manufacturer [1]	Cost	Weight oz.	Calories	Dietary fiber, g.	Sodium, mg.	Sugars, g.	Sugars, percentage	Comments	Descriptions
Frosted Mini-Wheats	K	28[3]	1¼	130	4	0	8	21	—	Lightly sugared bite-size shredded-wheat biscuits.
Grape-Nuts Flakes	P	19	1¼	110	3	160	6	18	—	Flakes of whole wheat, malted barley.
Whole Grain Total	GM	23	1	100	3	200	3	11	B	Flakes of whole wheat.
Whole Grain Wheat Chex	R	24	1½	150	5	350	5	11	—	Whole wheat squares.
Whole Grain Wheaties	GM	16	1	100	3	200	3	11	—	Flakes of whole wheat.
Total Raisin Bran	GM	30	1½	140	4	190	14	33	B	Flakes of wheat bran, other wheat parts, raisins.
Raisin Nut Bran	GM	37	2	220	5	280	16	28	D,F	Flakes of wheat bran, other parts, nut-covered sugared raisins, almond slivers.
Raisin Squares	K	38	2	180	4	0	12	21	—	Raisin-filled shredded whole wheat biscuits.
Oates with Extra Oat Bran	NM	27	1	110	2	0	6	6	C	Rings of toasted oats and brown-rice flour, oat bran, unsweetened fruit juice.
Nutri-Grain Almond Raisin	K	47	2	210	5	330	11	18	—	Flakes of brown rice and whole corn, with raisins, almonds.
Crispy Wheats 'N Raisins	GM	24	1⅓	130	3	180	13	35	—	Sweetened whole wheat flakes, raisins.
Life	Q	26	1½	150	3	230	9	21	F	Squares of whole oat, oat bran, corn, and whole wheat flours.
Multi Grain Cheerios	GM	24	1	100	2	220	6	21	—	Rings of whole grain corn, oats, barley, rice, wheat.
Oat Squares	Q	34	2	200	4	270	12	21	F	Squares of whole oat with oat bran, whole wheat flours, brown sugar.
Mueslix Crispy Blend	K	50	2¼	240	5	220	19	31	—	Blend of whole barley, brown rice, wheat, oats, raisins, dates, brown sugar, almonds, corn, rice.
Cheerios	GM	15	⅓	90	2	230	—	4	—	Rings of whole oat flour.
Cinnamon Oat Squares	Q	35	2	220	4	250	14	25	F	Puffed squares of whole oat with oat bran and whole wheat flours, brown sugar, cinnamon.
Clusters	GM	44	2	220	4	280	25	14	—	Flakes of wheat bran and other wheat parts, rice, clusters of nuts and sugar/honey.
100% Natural Wholegrain with Raisins (Low Fat)	Q	39[1]	2	220	4	30	14	24	C,E,F	Blend of whole grain rolled oats, wheat, brown sugar, raisins, almonds, coconut, honey.

Cereal	Mfr									Description
Honey Bunches of Oats with Almonds	P	29	1½	180	3	240	9	—	21	Flakes of corn, whole wheat, cluster of rolled oats, almonds, brown sugar, rice, honey, cinnamon.
Low-Fat Granola with Raisins	K	36☐	1⅓	180	3	90	14	E	29	Blend of whole grain oats and wheat, brown sugar, raisins, rice, coconut, almonds.
Basic 4	GM	38	1¼	170	3	310	11	—	22	Blend of corn, wheat, barley, oats, rice, dried fruit, nut pieces.
Just Right with Fruit & Nuts	K	42	1¾	190	3	250	12	B	24	Flakes of whole wheat, corn, oats, rice, with dried fruit, almonds, brown sugar.
Apple Cinnamon Cheerios	GM	25	1⅓	150	2	240	13	—	35	Sugar-sweetened whole oat flour rings with apple pieces.
Honey Nut Cheerios	GM	26	1⅓	150	2	330	13	—	35	Sugar/honey-sweetened whole oat rings with tiny almond pieces.
Oatmeal Raisin Crisp	GM	47	2½	260	3	340	20	F	29	Flakes of rolled oats and rice with raisins, almond pieces, sugar, honey.
Nut & Honey Crunch	K	29	1½	170	2	300	12	—	28	Corn flakes covered with sugar, peanuts, honey.
Low fiber										
Puffed Rice	Q	13	½	50	—	0	—	C	—	Puffed rice.
Puffed Wheat	Q	15	½	50	1	0	—	C	—	Puffed wheat.
Kix	GM	16	⅔	70	—	170	2	—	11	Puffs of cornmeal and oat flour.
Honey-Comb	P	17	¾	80	—	140	8	—	39	Sugar/honey-sweetened "honeycombs" of corn and whole grain oat flours.
Corn Flakes	K	10	1	100	1	290	2	—	7	Flakes of corn.
Product 19	K	23	1	100	1	320	3	B	11	Flakes of corn, oat, wheat flour, rice.
Rice Chex	R	17	1	100	—	250	2	—	7	Squares of rice.
Apple Jacks	K	23	1	110	1	130	14	—	49	Sugar-sweetened multigrain rings, dried apples, apple juice concentrate, cinnamon.
Cocoa Puffs	GM	21	1	110	—	180	13	—	46	Sugar-sweetened corn puffs with cocoa.
Cookie-Crisp Chocolate Chip	R	25	1	110	—	140	13	—	46	Sugar-sweetened chocolate-chip "cookies" of corn, rice, wheat, oat flours.
Corn Chex	R	19	1	110	—	310	3	—	11	Squares of milled yellow corn.
Corn Pops	K	22	1	110	1	90	12	—	42	Sugar-sweetened puffed corn.
Crispix	K	21	1	110	1	220	3	—	11	Hexagonal "Chex" of corn and rice.
Froot Loops	K	21	1	110	1	130	13	—	46	Sugar-sweetened fruit-flavored rings of corn, wheat, oat flours.
Lucky Charms	GM	22	1	110	—	180	12	—	42	Sugar-sweetened shapes of whole oat flour with colored marshmallow shapes.

Ratings
Continued

190

Product	Manufacturer [1]	Cost	Weight, oz.	Calories	Dietary fiber, g.	Sodium, mg.	Sugars, g.	Sugars, percentage	Comments	Descriptions
Marshmallow Alpha-Bits	P	23	1	110	1	150	14	49	—	Letters of sugar-sweetened whole grain oat and corn flours and colored marshmallow.
Rice Krispies	K	18	1	110	—	290	3	11	—	Crisped rice.
Special K	K	22	1	110	1	230	3	11	F	Flakes of rice and wheat.
Teenage Mutant Ninja Turtles	R	23	1	110	—	190	11	39	F	Sugar-sweetened squares of rice, marshmallow bits.
Total Corn Flakes	GM	28	1	110	—	200	3	11	B	Flakes of corn and wheat.
Trix	GM	24	1	110	—	140	12	42	—	Sugar-sweetened fruit-flavored puffs of cornmeal, oat flour, in fruit shapes.
Fruity Pebbles	P	24	1¼	130	—	150	14	42	—	Sugar-sweetened, fruit-flavored puffed-rice flakes.
Wheaties Honey Gold	GM	20	1⅓	130	1	270	13	35	—	Sugar/honey-sweetened flakes of whole wheat, corn.
Cocoa Krispies	K	28	1⅓	150	—	250	15	39	—	Sugar-sweetened crisped rice with cocoa.
Cocoa Pebbles	P	28	1⅓	150	—	200	17	46	—	Sugar-sweetened crisped rice with cocoa.
Frosted Flakes	K	20	1⅓	150	1	270	15	39	—	Sugar-coated corn flakes.
Golden Grahams	GM	27	1⅓	150	—	370	12	32	—	Sugar/honey-sweetened squares of corn and whole wheat.
Kenmei Rice Bran	K	22	1⅓	150	1	310	5	14	—	Flakes of brown rice and rice bran.
Smacks	K	24	1⅓	150	1	90	20	53	—	Sugar/honey-sweetened puffed wheat.
Triples	GM	22	1⅓	150	—	330	4	11	—	Crisped puffs of wheat flour, rice flour, cornmeal, oat flour.
Cap'n Crunch	Q	22	1⅓	160	—	290	16	42	—	Sugar-sweetened puffed rectangles of corn, oat flours.
Cap'n Crunch's Crunch Berries	Q	23	1⅓	160	1	280	16	42	—	Sugar-sweetened puffed rectangles of corn, oat flours, fruit-flavored puffs.
Cinnamon Toast Crunch	GM	26	1⅓	160	1	280	12	32	—	Sugar-sweetened squares of whole wheat and rice flour, cinnamon.

[2] Per serving

High fiber

Product										Description
Wheatena	A	14	1½	160	6	0	—	1	C	Toasted crushed wheat, wheat bran, wheat germ.

Moderate fiber

Product										Description
Quaker Oat Bran	Q	13	1	100	4	0	—	—	C,F	Oat bran.
Instant Quaker Oatmeal Regular Flavor	Q	20 4	5	90	3	160	—	—	—	Rolled oats, oat bran.
H-O Quick Oats	GFA	12	1⅓	130	4	0	—	1	C,F	Rolled oasts.
Old Fashioned Quaker Oats	Q	14	1½	150	4	0	—	—	C,F	Rolled oats.
Quick Quaker Oats	Q	13	1½	140	4	0	—	—	C,F	Rolled oats.
Instant Quaker Oatmeal Apples & Cinnamon	Q	24 4	6	120	3	100	10	29	—	Instant oatmeal, dried apples, cinnamon.
Instant Quaker Oatmeal Maple & Brown Sugar	Q	24 4	6	140	3	240	14	33	—	Sugar-sweetened instant oatmeal with maple, brown-sugar flavors.
Maypo (Instant)	A	22	1¾	170	3	0	5	11	F	Instant oatmeal and rye flour, artificial maple flavor, maple syrup.
Instant Quaker Oatmeal Cinnamon & Spice	Q	25 4	6	160	3	260	16	35	—	Sugar-sweetened instant oatmeal, cinnamon, other spices.
Instant Quaker Oatmeal Peaches & Cream	Q	25 4	5	130	2	150	12	34	—	Sugar-sweetened instant oatmeal, artificial creamer, dried apples, peaches.
Instant Quaker Oatmeal Strawberries & Cream	Q	25 4	5	130	2	160	13	35	—	Sugar-sweetened instant oatmeal, artificial creamer, dried apples, strawberry solids.
Instant Cream of Wheat	N	14	1½	150	2	0	—	—	C	Wheat farina (the grain's starchy center) and germ.

Low fiber

Product										Description
Farina	PI	9	1¼	100	1	0	—	—	C	Wheat farina.
Instant Cream of Wheat Original	N	24 4	6	100	1	170	—	—	—	Wheat farina and germ.
Quick Cream of Wheat	N	12	1	110	1	90	—	—	C	Wheat farina and germ.
Cream of Rice	N	14	1¼	120	—	0	—	—	C	Granulated rice.
H-O Quick Cream Farina	GFA	7	1¼	120	1	0	—	—	C	Wheat farina.
Quick Malt-O-Meal	M	9	1¼	120	1	0	—	—	—	Wheat farina, toasted malt.
Regular Cream of Wheat	N	12	1½	120	1	0	—	—	C	Wheat farina and germ.
Instant Cream of Wheat Apple 'N Cinnamon	N	29 4	6	130	1	250	13	37	—	Sugar-sweetened wheat farina, dried apples, cinnamon.

serving). You need fiber to stay healthy, and you should expect it in cereal. Yet about one-third of the cereals tested have just a token amount, if any.

As you scan the Ratings, concentrate on brands from high- and moderate-fiber groups. If you pick an ultra-high-fiber cereal, increase your overall fiber intake gradually, giving your system time to get accustomed to the roughage. Boosting your fiber intake too fast can cause diarrhea, bloating, gas, or other digestive problems.

COLAS

Colas account for about three-quarters of all soft drinks sold. Why cola, of all things, should utterly dominate all other soft-drink flavors is a mystery no one has satisfactorily explained. Flavors like orange or cherry show up in a wide variety of food and drink, but they've never attained the popularity of the cola flavor.

Obviously, heavy advertising, wide availability, and decades of familiarity all contribute to cola's phenomenal popularity. Some have speculated that mild addiction plays a role as well. Regular colas contain an abundance of sugars and, often, a good deal of caffeine (an average of 40 milligrams of caffeine per 12-ounce can of caffeinated cola, compared with about 100 milligrams in a cup of brewed coffee). And caffeine, at least, is mildly habit-forming.

The Tests

Back in 1991, *Consumer Reports* tested 28 colas, covering four types: regular and diet in both caffeinated and caffeine-free versions. The roster includes the giants *Coca-Cola* and *Pepsi*, the smaller *Royal Crown, C&C,* and *Shasta*, and the store brands *Big K* (Kroger), *Cragmont* (Safeway), *A&P*, and *Chek* (Winn Dixie).

The primary sensory tests by *Consumer Reports* measured quality rather than taste preference. A taste panel, trained to identify and score each sensory nuance, evaluated the colas for 18 attributes, from fizziness to "cola impact" to individual spice notes.

An excellent cola should be quite fizzy, with moderate cola impact. The constituent flavors should be well blended, and there should be no off-flavors or defects. These can arise from the product's formulation. An artificial sweetener might leave a lingering aftertaste, for example. Or a cherry flavor might be too prominent for a cola. Off-flavors can also result from mishandling. When cola sits around too long or is stored in too warm a place, the flavor oils start to deteriorate, creating a telltale piney note, somewhat like pine-scented cleaner.

Several individual samples had the piney off-flavor, but they were isolated cases. Such samples didn't turn up consistently enough for the brand to be downrated.

No cola was judged excellent, but nearly all the regular colas—both caffeinated and caffeine-free—were judged very good (*Big K* and *Cragmont* were the only exceptions).

The best diet colas were judged only good. Their artificial sweeteners lack the fullness of a natural sugar and leave a lingering aftertaste. The saccharin-sweetened colas fared worse than the aspartame varieties because saccharin's impact—especially its bitterness—comes through very clearly in a cola drink.

Leaving out the caffeine doesn't seem to harm a cola's flavor: The caffeine-free products did as well as and sometimes better than their caffeinated brandmates. In fact, with some brands of cola it was hard to tell the difference between the two versions.

In a separate taste test, die-hard *Coca-Cola* and *Pepsi* fans were challenged to find their brand in a blind tasting. They were fed four unidentified samples of cola one at a time, regular colas for regular cola drinkers, diet versions for diet drinkers.

Getting all four samples right was a tough test, but not too tough for 7 out of 19 regular-cola drinkers who correctly identified their brand of choice in all four trials. The diet-cola drinkers did a little worse—only 7 out of 27 identified all four samples correctly.

Whereas both groups did better than chance would predict, nearly half the participants in each group made the wrong choice two or more times. Two people got all four samples wrong. Over-

(*continued on page 196*)

RATINGS

As published in the August 1991 issue of Consumer Reports

Colas

Listed by types; within types, listed in order of sensory quality. Closely ranked colas were essentially similar in overall quality.

1 Sensory index. Overall sensory quality, based on tests by *Consumer Reports* trained panel.

2 Price. Per six-pack, average price paid nationally in 1991.

3 Calories. Calories per 12-ounce can, according to manufacturer. Diet varieties should have less than one calorie per can.

4 Caffeine. Per can, according to manufacturer. Caffeine-free colas should have less than one milligram per can.

5 Sodium. According to manufacturer.

6 Sensory comments. An excellent cola should be moderately sweet, slightly sour, very slightly bitter. Cola impact—a blend of citrus, vanilla, brown-spice, and caramel flavors—should range from low moderate to moderate. Flavors should blend well. Hints of cherry, chocolate/coffee, or wintergreen are allowable, but the cola shouldn't taste too much like root beer or cherry cola. All the diet colas had some "artificial sweetener impact"—a sweet taste that lacks the fullness of sugar; that sweet taste and a bitterness builds and then lingers in the mouth. Defects noted: a taste reminiscent of baking soda; a vegetable/earthy taste like aging celery.

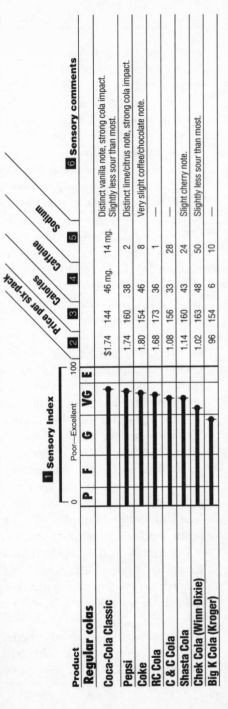

Product	1 Sensory Index (Poor—Excellent)	2 Price per six-pack	3 Calories	4 Caffeine	5 Sodium	6 Sensory comments
Regular colas						
Coca-Cola Classic		$1.74	144	46 mg.	14 mg.	Distinct vanilla note, strong cola impact.
Pepsi		1.74	160	38	2	Slightly less sour than most.
Coke		1.80	154	46	8	Distinct lime/citrus note, strong cola impact.
RC Cola		1.68	173	36	1	Very slight coffee/chocolate note.
C & C Cola		1.08	156	33	28	—
Shasta Cola		1.14	160	43	24	Slight cherry note.
Chek Cola (Winn Dixie)		1.02	163	48	50	Slightly less sour than most.
Big K Cola (Kroger)		96	154	6	10	—

Regular caffeine-free colas

Cola					Comments
Pepsi Caffeine Free	1.86	160	—	2	Distinct lime/citrus note, strong cola impact.
Coca-Cola Classic Caffeine Free	1.86	144	—	14	Distinct vanilla note, strong cola impact, slightly less sour than most.
C & C Free Cola	1.08	162	—	28	—
Coke Caffeine Free	2.16	154	—	8	—
A & P Cola[1]	1.14	180	—	0	Distinct citrus note.
Shasta Cola Caffeine Free	1.26	160	—	24	Distinct fruity note.
Cragmont Cola (Safeway)[1]	1.02	160	—	70	Vegetable/earthy off-note; slight coffee/chocolate note; more bitter than most.

Diet colas

Cola					Comments
Diet Pepsi	1.80	—	36	2	Distinct lime/citrus note.
Big K Diet Cola (Kroger)	1.02	—	6	30	—
Diet Coke	1.80	—	46	8	—
Diet Shasta Cola[2]	1.20	—	43	79	Distinct cherry note.
Diet RC Cola	1.68	—	48	1	Less cola impact than most.
Chek Diet Cola (Winn Dixie)[2]	1.02	—	48	50	Notable artificial-sweetener impact; fruity and very slight wintergreen (root-beer) notes.
Tab Sugar Free[2]	2.04	—	46	8	Big artificial-sweetener impact; strong cola impact; distinct vanilla note.
C & C Diet Cola[2]	1.20	—	34	70	Big artificial-sweetener impact; distinct citrus flavor with artificial orange off-note.

Diet caffeine-free colas

Cola					Comments
Diet Pepsi Caffeine Free	1.86	—	—	2	Distinct lime/citrus note.
Diet Coke Caffeine Free	1.86	—	—	8	—
Diet Rite Low Calorie Caffeine Free	1.92	—	—	1	—
Shasta Diet Cola Caffeine Free[2]	1.32	—	—	51	Notable artificial-sweetener impact; slight cherry note.
Cragmont Diet Cola (Safeway)[1][2]	1.02	—	—	70	Big artificial-sweetener impact; medicinal cherry note.

[1] Not labeled caffeine-free.   [2] Sweetened partially or wholly with saccharin.

all, half the participants did about as well on the last round of tasting as on the first, so fatigue, or taste burnout, was not a factor.

The preference-test results suggest that only a few *Pepsi* partisans and *Coke* fanatics may really be able to tell their favorite brand based on taste alone. So perhaps you should ignore the TV commercials and the rest of the marketing hype, and choose your brand by taste and price.

Recommendations

Consumer Reports thinks you should buy cola by price. Sometimes that will mean choosing *Coke* or *Pepsi* products that are deeply discounted. The big two have special arrangements with retailers, which are known as calendar marketing agreements. In exchange for quarterly payments or substantial rebates on the soft drinks sold, many stores agree to "feature" a brand for specific weeks of the year. That means giving it the best ads, the best displays, and, in some cases, ensuring it the lowest price in the store. *Pepsi* and *Coke* bottlers like to characterize calendar marketing agreements as a marketing tool that ensures the best price for their product. To other bottlers, it's a device that shrinks the shelf space allocated to them and impairs their ability to stay competitive and, as a result, restricts the choices available to consumers.

Despite such agreements, finding the best cola prices usually means choosing one of the smaller brands that tasted about as good as the megabrands. Among regular colas, look for *RC Cola*, *C&C*, or *Shasta*. Among caffeinated diet colas, check out Kroger's *Big K* or *Diet Shasta*: among caffeine-free diet colas, look for *Diet Rite* or *Shasta*.

LOW-FAT FROZEN DESSERTS

Although nutrition-conscious Americans have given up other rich foods in recent years—switching from whole to low-fat milk and from beef to chicken—they've been reluctant to part with their mocha fudge and rum raisin. Ice-cream sales have held steady over the past decade.

Now an array of reduced-fat frozen desserts has begun to challenge ice cream's supremacy. They promise the taste of ice cream with a much lower burden of calories and fat.

Frozen yogurt, a sluggish product for most of the last two decades, is tripling in sales every year, and manufacturers have recently brought out "frozen dairy desserts" with virtually no fat at all. These new concoctions incorporate a modicum of skim milk (hence the term "dairy") but rely mostly on fat substitutes like gums, emulsifiers, and other stabilizers to approximate the characteristics of ice cream.

Unfortunately, the something-for-nothing combination these products promise is still largely a mirage.

In 1992, *Consumer Reports* tested 50 low-fat and nonfat frozen desserts. Some tasted very good, a few even as good as *Sealtest* ice cream (which was tested for comparison). The best products, alas, also rivaled ice cream in calories and sometimes came uncomfortably close in fat as well. The products that rated highest also tended to have more fat than the lower-rated desserts.

Dairy fat contributes to ice cream's flavor and provides its smooth, creamy texture. Decreasing the fat generally means compromising texture and some taste—a depressing fact that no frozen-dessert manufacturer has overcome.

Rather than fighting this natural law, some manufacturers have chosen to disguise the nature of their products, and liberally use the word "light" on product packaging. But this term is essentially meaningless. *Steve's Gourmet Light* ice milk, for example, has more fat and calories than some regular ice creams.

Knowing whether a product is ice milk or frozen yogurt doesn't tell you much about its nutritional content, either. Frozen yogurt comes in nonfat, low-fat, and full-fat incarnations. The fat content of ice milk, though generally low, also varies from brand to brand, since manufacturers often add cream for its taste and texture.

Frozen dairy desserts do uniformly contain less fat than their competitors, but some approach regular ice cream in calories—sweeteners and fat substitutes add to their calorie count—and none of them tastes good. (The only nonfat product rated good was a frozen yogurt from Sealtest.)

Nutrition Versus Flavor

None of the tested products completely satisfied *Consumer Reports'* standards of excellence, but many were very good—for a low-fat product.

In general, yogurts and ice milks tasted better than the frozen dairy desserts—far better. But the frozen dairy desserts were lower, often much lower, in fat and calories. Once again, it seems there's conflict between the sensual and the sensible.

Or is there?

Many high-rated brands had only 3 or 4 grams of fat per serving. That's roughly half as much as regular *Sealtest* ice cream, and much less than *Häagen-Dazs* ice cream, with 17 grams of fat per half cup.

The Ratings detail the calories and grams of fat in each product, plus the percentage of calories that comes from fat. Conventional nutritional wisdom (including government agencies and *Consumer Reports* medical consultants) holds that you should limit your total fat intake to no more than 30 percent of total calories you consume each day.

By this guideline, a woman who eats 2,200 calories a day should take in no more than about 73 grams of fat a day—roughly 660 calories' worth. (A gram of fat contains nine calories.) For a man who takes in 2,900 calories, the limit is 97 grams of fat. The 3 or 4 grams of fat in a low-fat frozen dessert constitute a small price to pay for a treat.

Dieters, however, would be advised to read the Calories column in the Ratings. Weight loss or gain is determined more by the number of calories you eat than by the amount of fat you take in. Many low-fat desserts have as many calories as regular ice cream does; the sweeteners they use, as well as their fat substitutes, contribute to the high calories.

Another caveat: All the statistics in the Ratings are based on a half-cup serving (4 fluid ounces). That's a serving size many ice-cream lovers would consider miserly.

Finally, watch out for a nutritional trap: Since fat is a large part of what makes food filling, you may feel less full and want to eat more dessert if you choose a low-fat brand.

RATINGS

*As published in the **August 1992** issue of Consumer Reports*

Low-fat frozen desserts

Listed by type. Within each type, listed in order of flavor score. Products with equal scores are listed alphabetically. Products within a few points of each other are very similar in overall quality. *Sealtest* ice cream is listed for comparison purposes only.

1 Flavor. Based on tests by a panel of trained tasters. Desserts were rated by how well they met *Consumer Reports* criteria for excellence of flavor for a reduced-fat dessert.

2 Texture. The higher-scored products were full-bodied: smoother, moderately to very dense, and melted into a liquid similar in consistency to heavy cream. Lower-rated products tended to be weak-bodied—icy, airy, and thin—and/or left a gummy, sticky, or gritty feeling in the mouth.

3 Cost per serving. The estimated national average for a four-fluid-ounce serving, based on prices paid nationally in 1992. Unless noted, cost per serving is based on product purchased in half-gallon carton. An * indicates product was available only in pint-size container.

4 Weight per serving. In grams, as measured by *Consumer Reports*. The higher the weight, the denser the product, indicating less air has been whipped in.

5 Calories per serving. Denser products tend to be higher in calories, as do those that rely heavily on cream, whole milk, and sugar. On average, frozen dairy desserts contained the fewest calories per serving; frozen yogurt, the most.

6 Total fat. Total fat per serving, in grams (one gram of fat contains nine calories). In general, at least half the fat in these products is saturated.

7 % calories from fat. As a rule, no more than 30 percent of daily calories should come from fat.

8 Sensory comments. Unless otherwise noted, all vanilla products had slight to moderate dairy and vanilla-type flavors. The chocolate products had slight dairy and moderate chocolate flavors. All desserts were moderately to very sweet. Products described as "hollow" lacked fullness and complexity in their flavors.

Products described as having weak body tended to be icy, airy, and thin upon melting; those described as having full body were typically smooth, somewhat dense, and thick. Unless noted, all the desserts were slightly airy and icy, somewhat thin upon melting in the mouth, and ranged in gumminess (stickiness) from not at all to slightly gummy.

---

1 *Nutritional content may have changed since our tests, according to manufacturer.*

2 *Data on total fat from Consumer Reports analysis; specific amount not listed on label.*

3 *Name now changed to Edy's/Dreyer's Fat Free.*

4 *Prices for half-gallon cartons of Sealtest Free and Knudsen Free were different.*

● Better ◐ ○ ◐ ● Worse →

	[1] Flavor (P F G VG E, 0–100)	[2] Texture	[3] Cost per serving	[4] Weight per serving	[5] Calories per serving

Brands

CHOCOLATE

Brand	Flavor	Texture	Cost	Weight	Calories
Sealtest Chocolate Ice Cream		◐	$.18	66 g.	140
Frozen yogurts					
Breyers		○	.21	71	150
Honey Hill Farms		◐	.60*	84	147
Elan		◐	.50*	87	130
Crowley Silver Premium		◐	.19	73	120
Edy's/Dreyer's Inspirations [1]		○	.26	72	110
Häagen-Dazs		◉	.63*	100	173
Kemps		○	.20	72	120
Lucerne (Safeway)		○	.18	69	107
Yoplait Soft		○	.51*	75	120
Albertsons		○	.16	68	104
Ice milks					
Kroger D'light		◐	.13	66	100
Breyers Light		○	.22	65	120
Lucerne Light (Safeway)		○	.13	65	120
Albertsons Light		◐	.13	66	123
Frozen dairy desserts					
Weight Watchers Grand Collection (Fat Free)		○	.21	66	80
Simple Pleasures (Fat Free)		○	.57*	94	130
Sealtest Free/Knudsen Free (Nonfat)		◐	.16/.24 [4]	67	100

VANILLA

Brand	Flavor	Texture	Cost	Weight	Calories
Sealtest Vanilla Ice Cream		◐	.18	66	140

Frozen yogurts

Product				
Honey Hill Farms	●	.60*	84	147
Breyers	○	.21	74	140
Edy's/Dreyer's Inspirations [1]	◑	.26	72	110
Hood	◑	.18	73	120
Kemps	◑	.20	72	120
Häagen-Dazs	●	.63*	100	173
Crowley Silver Premium	◑	.19	73	120
Lucerne (Safeway)	◑	.18	72	107
Elan	◑	.51*	91	130
Yoplait Soft	○	.51*	75	120
Sealtest (Nonfat)	◑	.16	74	100
Albertsons	○	.16	68	99
Colombo Gourmet Vanilla Dream	○	.54*	85	120

Ice milks

Product				
Breyers Natural Light	○	.21	68	120
Edy's/Dreyer's Grand Light	●	.27	61	100
Light n' Lively	◑	.17	65	100
Steve's Gourmet Light	○	.56*	108	190
Blue Bell Light	○	.19	66	100
Lucerne (Safeway)	○	.13	64	100
Albertsons Light	○	.13	67	112
Kroger D'light	○	.13	66	100

Frozen dairy desserts

Product				
Weight Watchers Grand Collection (Fat Free)	○	.21	69	80
Edy's/Dreyer's American Dream (Nonfat) [3]	○	.17	71	90
Simple Pleasures (Fat Free)	○	.58*	92	120
Sweet 'n Low (Lowfat)	◑	.40*	67	80
Sealtest Free/Knudsen Free (Nonfat)	◑	.16/.24 [4]	68	100
Ultra Slim Fast (Lowfat)	●	.56*	73	90

Ratings
Continued

Brands	[6] Total fat	[7] % calories from fat	[8] Sensory comments
CHOCOLATE			
Sealtest Chocolate Ice Cream	6 g.	39	Full dairy, well-balanced flavors; airy, light but gummy.
Frozen yogurts			
Breyers	4	24	Yogurty, full dairy, well-balanced chocolate; fairly weak body.
Honey Hill Farms	5	33	Not yogurty, full dark chocolate; full body, fairly gummy.
Elan	3	21	Not yogurty, full dark chocolate, nutty note, a bit bitter.
Crowley Silver Premium	3	20	Not yogurty, smoky, caramel notes; fairly full body but gummy.
Edy's/Dreyer's Inspirations [1]	3	25	Moderately yogurty; somewhat weak body.
Häagen-Dazs	4	21	Not yogurty, dark chocolate with excessive smoky flavor; full body.
Kemps	3	20	Not yogurty, hint of caramel; somewhat weak body.
Lucerne (Safeway)	3	23	Slightly yogurty, low chocolate; somewhat weak body.
Yoplait Soft	3	20	Not yogurty, cherry and alcohol notes; mousselike but gummy.
Albertsons	1	12	Moderately yogurty, low chocolate, variable flavor notes; gummy.
Ice milks			
Kroger D'light	2	18	Some iciness.
Breyers Light	4	30	Somewhat weak body.
Lucerne Light (Safeway)	4	30	Low dairy and chocolate; icy, somewhat gummy.
Albertsons Light	2	15	Hollow and bland, grain flavor; very weak body.
Frozen dairy desserts			
Weight Watchers Grand Collection (Fat Free)	0.5 [2]	5	Hollow, low dairy, slight nondescript off-notes; fairly thick, gummy.
Simple Pleasures (Fat Free)	0.7 [2]	5	Hollow, low dairy, cherry and alcohol notes; fairly full but gummy.
Sealtest Free/Knudsen Free (Nonfat)	0	0	Hollow, little dairy, cherry and alcohol notes; weak body but gummy.
VANILLA			
Sealtest Vanilla Ice Cream	7	45	Fully dairy and vanilla flavors; airy, light but gummy.
Frozen yogurts			
Honey Hill Farms	5	33	Not yogurty, full dairy, some "real" vanilla, alcohol note; full body.
Breyers	4	26	Very yogurty, full dairy, "real" vanilla, alcohol note; somewhat weak

Edy's/Dreyer's Inspirations [1]	3	25	Moderately yogurty, tropical-fruit note.
Hood	3	23	Moderately yogurty, tropical-fruit and alcohol notes.
Kemps	3	20	Moderately yogurty, slight coffee/chocolate and alcohol notes.
Häagen-Dazs	4	21	Slightly yogurty, full dairy, "real" vanilla, strong alcohol; full body.
Crowley Silver Premium	3	20	Slightly yogurty, slight chocolate note.
Lucerne (Safeway)	3	23	Yogurty, tropical-fruit note; somewhat thin texture.
Elan	3	21	Slightly yogurty, low flavor, tropical-fruit note; somewhat thin.
Yoplait Soft	3	20	Not yogurty, slight coffee note, sometimes stale flavor; gummy.
Sealtest (Nonfat)	0	0	Moderately yogurty, hint of "real" vanilla, tropical-fruit and alcohol notes; weak body but gummy too.
Albertsons	1	13	Yogurty, tropical-fruit note, a bit acidic; somewhat weak body.
Colombo Gourmet Vanilla Dream	3	20	Not yogurty, low dairy, vanilla; somewhat weak body but gummy.
Ice milks			
Breyers Natural Light	4	30	Full-dairy, "real" vanilla, alcohol note; somewhat weak body.
Edy's/Dreyer's Grand Light	4	36	Full dairy, low vanilla; somewhat full body.
Light n' Lively	3	27	Alcohol note, eggnoglike character; some iciness.
Steve's Gourmet Light	8	38	Hint of "real" vanilla, alcohol note; full body but gummy.
Blue Bell Light	2	18	Low vanilla; somewhat weak body.
Lucerne (Safeway)	2	18	Low dairy and vanilla, hint of caramel; somewhat weak body.
Albertsons Light	2	16	Low dairy, "artificial" vanilla, off-flavors; somewhat weak.
Kroger D'light	2	18	Strong "artificial" vanilla; somewhat gummy.
Frozen diary desserts			
Weight Watchers Grand Collection (Fat Free)	0.3 [2]	4	Hollow, slightly low dairy, strong "artificial" vanilla; gummy.
Edy's/Dreyer's American Dream (Nonfat) [3]	2	2	Bland, hollow, "artificial" vanilla; somewhat full body but gummy.
Simple Pleasures (Fat Free)	0.9 [2]	7	Bland, hollow, "artificial" vanilla, vitaminlike/chemical off-flavors; somewhat full body but gummy.
Sweet 'n Low (Lowfat)	2	23	Bland, hollow, chemical-like off-flavor, "artificial" vanilla; slightly icy, airy, but also thick, very gummy.
Sealtest Free/Knudsen Free (Nonfat)	0	0	Stale, hollow, low dairy, "artificial" vanilla, somewhat weak; gummy.
Ultra Slim Fast (Lowfat)	0.4 [2]	4	Barely recognizable dairy and vanilla, bitter, mostly off-flavors—vitamin, chemical fishy; very gummy, chalky, gritty.

Recommendations

If you view sweet frozen desserts as an occasional treat, and you have no special reason to limit your fat intake even more sharply than current dietary guidelines suggest, why deny yourself the superior flavor and texture of real ice cream? A small serving of regular or even premium ice cream once in a while won't subvert a diet that usually favors fruits, vegetables, grains, fish, and poultry over red meat, dairy, and sweets.

If fat is a major concern—for example, if you're trying to bring your blood-cholesterol level down—most of these products do offer less fat than regular ice cream, and the ones rated very good are comparable in taste to the real thing. Frozen yogurts from *Breyers* and *Honey Hill Farms* (a West Coast brand) had the best flavor, in both chocolate and vanilla. Unfortunately, they were also among the many low-fat desserts with as many calories as an average ice cream. So if you're counting calories as well as grams of fat, count them out.

Although the frozen dairy desserts have little or no fat, we don't recommend any of them. These products still have a long way to go before they can compete with ice milk or frozen yogurt, let alone ice cream.

FROZEN LIGHT ENTRÉES

In 1993, *Consumer Reports* published an analysis of five best-selling frozen light entrées: chicken enchiladas, glazed chicken, lasagna, Salisbury steak, and turkey. The entrées tested differed from frozen dinners in that they usually include just one side dish, if that; dinners often include two, plus dessert. Regular entrées were also tested from some of the same companies that make light entrées. That way, nutrition as well as taste could be compared.

Nutrition Facts

Most frozen light entrées have a similar nutritional résumé:

- 8 to 10 ounces of food
- 200 to 300 calories, about a tenth of the food energy most people need in a day

- Less than 30 percent of calories from fat, a cap that government guidelines recommend for the diet as a whole
- 50 milligrams or less of cholesterol, against the 300-milligram daily limit many health experts advocate

The Ratings give specific figures for each entrée, including any side dish. They also list the amount of sodium. Sodium in the light entrées ranged from less than 400 milligrams to about 800, but it exceeded 1,000 milligrams in some regular entrées. (The daily limit that government guidelines suggest for the average person is 2,400 milligrams.)

Dish for dish, the regular entrées typically packed twice the fat of the lights. That additional fat can add more than 100 calories and inflate the percentage of calories that comes from fat. Even if you buy a regular entrée, though, you probably needn't be concerned about its cholesterol or saturated fat content. The regular entrées highest in cholesterol supplied less than 80 milligrams. And almost no entrée, regular or light, was burdened by a nutritionally meaningful amount of saturated fat.

There are two concerns about the tested products: One reason they're so low in calories and fat is that they aren't a complete meal; they're not likely to fill up active people or those who are larger than average. And the dishes are very low in fiber. Fiber aids digestion and can make you feel full after a meal.

You'd do well to supplement any frozen entrée with a salad, a baked potato or whole grain bread, and fresh fruit. When you're done, you'll have had a more satisfying and nutritionally sound meal—and one that could still have fewer than 700 calories.

If you're choosing a certain type of meal for its nutrition, buy a light entrée of glazed chicken. Most such entrées get less than 20 percent of their calories from fat.

Far from Homemade

An excellent frozen entrée should have flavors and textures that echo at least vaguely those of freshly prepared food containing minimally processed ingredients. Most of the tested entrées fell far short of food you might cook yourself, buy at a deli counter, or eat in a good coffee shop.

To see if the processing was what degraded flavor and texture, *Consumer Reports* food specialists froze and reheated homecooked and take-out dishes. All were much better than the commercially frozen dinners. Thawing and refreezing in the distribution chain may steal away flavors and textures, but the likelier culprits are low-quality ingredients and sloppy cooking or processing procedures. Some manufacturers choose inexpensive, low-calorie ingredients like cereal fillers, thickeners like starch, gristly meat, or "reconstituted" meat—bits of meat stuck together with the help of binders. Sometimes they simply use too little of the good ingredients.

Only three dishes were rated very good, and two of them were regular entrées. The sensory problems blossom as you read down the Ratings: weird tastes of soap, sulfur, or almond; bouncy or mushy meat; dry or spongy cheese; wet or pasty stuffing; doughy noodles.

The glazed-chicken dishes were generally the best of the lot. Their meat was appropriately chickenlike, and it was intact, not put together with binders. Still, the chicken tasted steamed or boiled, not browned. The turkey dishes weren't bad, but some were rather dry. Worst-tasting of all were the Salisbury steaks. Most had a bland, warmed-over flavor and a texture that was spongy, chewy, or rubbery and reminiscent of hot dogs. Scores for the enchilada and lasagna entrées varied considerably.

Vegetables tended to have a tough or waterlogged texture and a bland taste. Rice was sometimes bland, sometimes well seasoned, but always too crumbly. Turkey stuffings were flavorful enough, courtesy of sage and thyme. Potatoes, commonly paired with Salisbury steak, were often far tastier than the meat.

Recommendations

If you're looking for a convenient way to reduce calories, fat, and sodium, frozen light entrées may suit you just fine—provided your taste buds aren't too demanding. They generally keep the calorie load to under 300, usually with less than 30 percent of those calories coming from fat.

But even the tastiest of the light entrées could claim only a nodding acquaintance with the flavors and textures of freshly
(*continued on page 212*)

RATINGS

As published in the **January 1993** issue of Consumer Reports

Frozen light entrées

Listed by types; within types, listed in order of overall sensory quality. Products within in a few points of each other were similar in overall quality, though not necessarily in flavor characteristics. Products with equal scores are listed alphabetically. Because the entrées within each category were judged by different criteria of excellence, scores of products in different categories are not directly comparable.

1 **Product.** Generally, light entrées, dishes that claim relatively few calories and a favorable nutritional profile, were tested. For comparison, some regular entrés, which make no such claim, were included. They are indicated by a ●

2 **Sensory index.** Based on taste tests by trained sensory panelists. Sensory scores reflect only the entrée, not any side dishes included. All side dishes would have been rated fair to good.

3 **Per serving.** Cost is the estimated average based on prices paid nationally in 1992. **Weight** has been rounded to the nearest quarter-ounce. Most products are sold in a single-serving container you heat in a conventional or microwave oven. Exceptions, in "family"-size packages or boil-in-bags, are footnoted. Nutrition data include side dishes and come from laboratory analyses and from packages and manufacturers' information, which were spot-checked.

4 **Sensory comments.** Unless noted, all entrées lacked fresh character and were slightly to moderately salty. Meats had at least slight warmed-over tastes. Vegetables tended to be bland, with typical frozen-vegetable texture. Some specifics:
   Chicken enchiladas, unless otherwise noted, consisted of somewhat soggy tortillas that tended to crumble and fall apart, slight to moderate amounts of somewhat pasty white and dark meat (shreds or chunks), and sauce with little or no "heat."
   Glazed chicken entrées generally had intact chicken flesh, not re-formed pieces, that was somewhat pasty.
   Lasagnas tended to have mild tomato flavor and fairly thick, soft noodles; their cheese lacked a fresh taste, and their sparse meat wasn't beefy.
   Salisbury steaks, unless otherwise noted, were of ground meat with a moderately chewy texture; when present, mushrooms were rubbery.
   Turkey dishes contained mostly white meat that was somewhat dry.

---

① Packaged in boil-in-bag.

② Packaged in 28-ounce size; suggested serving is one-fourth package.

③ Packaged in 24-ounce size; suggested serving is one-fourth package.

Ratings
Continued

3 Per serving

Better ● ◖ ○ ◑ ● Worse

2 Sensory index — Poor—Excellent

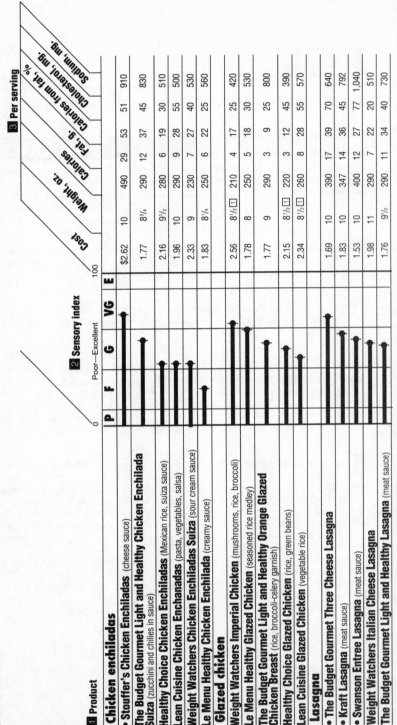

1 Product	Sensory index (P F G VG E)	Cost	Weight, oz.	Calories	Fat, g.	Calories from fat, %	Cholesterol, mg.	Sodium, mg.
Chicken enchiladas								
• Stouffer's Chicken Enchiladas (cheese sauce)	VG	$2.62	10	490	29	53	51	910
• The Budget Gourmet Light and Healthy Chicken Enchilada Suiza (zucchini and chilies in sauce)	G	1.77	8¾	290	12	37	45	830
Healthy Choice Chicken Enchiladas (Mexican rice, suiza sauce)	G	2.16	9½	280	6	19	30	510
Lean Cuisine Chicken Enchanadas (pasta, vegetables, salsa)	G	1.96	10	290	9	28	55	500
Weight Watchers Chicken Enchiladas Suiza (sour cream sauce)	G	2.33	9	230	7	27	40	530
Le Menu Healthy Chicken Enchilada (creamy sauce)	F	1.83	8¼	250	6	22	25	560
Glazed chicken								
Weight Watchers Imperial Chicken (mushrooms, rice, broccoli)	G	2.56	8½ 1	210	4	17	25	420
Le Menu Healthy Glazed Chicken (seasoned rice medley)	G	1.78	8	250	5	18	30	530
The Budget Gourmet Light and Healthy Orange Glazed Chicken Breast (rice, broccoli-celery garnish)	G	1.77	9	290	3	9	25	800
Healthy Choice Glazed Chicken (rice, green beans)	G	2.15	8½ 1	220	3	12	45	390
Lean Cuisine Glazed Chicken (vegetable rice)	G	2.34	8½ 1	260	8	28	55	570
Lasagna								
• The Budget Gourmet Three Cheese Lasagna	VG	1.69	10	390	17	39	70	640
• Kraft Lasagna (meat sauce)	G	1.83	10	347	14	36	45	792
• Swanson Entree Lasagna (meat sauce)	G	1.53	10	400	12	27	77	1,040
Weight Watchers Italian Cheese Lasagna	G	1.98	11	290	7	22	20	510
The Budget Gourmet Light and Healthy Lasagna (meat sauce)	G	1.76	9½	290	11	34	40	730

	Price	oz					
Weight Watchers Lasagna (meat sauce)	2.29	10¼	270	6	20	5	510
Weight Watchers Garden Lasagna	2.00	11	260	7	24	15	430
• **Stouffer's Single Serving Lasagna** (meat and sauce)	2.13	10½	360	13	33	46	784
Healthy Choice Zucchini Lasagna	2.17	11½	240	3	11	15	390
Lean Cuisine Lasagna (meat sauce)	2.00	10¼	260	6	21	25	590
Healthy Choice Lasagna (meat sauce)	2.15	10	260	5	17	20	420
Le Menu Healthy Entree Lasagna (meat sauce)	1.79	10	290	8	25	30	470
Ultra Slim-Fast Lasagna (meat sauce)	2.71	12	330	9	25	55	980
Lean Cuisine Zucchini Lasagna	2.02	11	260	5	17	20	550
• **Banquet Family Entree Lasagna** (meat sauce)	0.88	7[2]	270	10	33	48	564
Le Menu Healthy Garden Vegetable Lasagna	1.86	10½	260	8	28	25	500
Salisbury steak							
• **Kraft Beef Sirloin Salisbury Steak** (gravy, steak fries)	1.85	9	365	19	47	71	1,122
Lean Cuisine Salisbury Steak (gravy, scalloped potatoes)	2.27	9½	240	7	26	45	580
• **Stouffer's Homestyle Favorites Salisbury Steak** (gravy, macaroni, and cheese)	2.60	9¾	350	17	44	45	1,130
The Budget Gourmet Light and Healthy Beef Sirloin Salisbury Steak (red wine sauce, potatoes, carrots, broccoli)	1.76	9	220	6	25	25	680
Le Menu Healthy Salisbury Steak (gravy, mushrooms, potatoes)	1.78	8	210	6	26	25	500
• **Banquet Family Entree Gravy & 6 Salisbury Steaks**	0.54	7[2]	260	19	66	38	596
Turkey							
Healthy Choice Turkey and Mushrooms in Gravy (rice pilaf)	2.16	8½[1]	200	3	14	40	380
Lean Cuisine Sliced Turkey Breast (mushroom sauce, rice pilaf)	2.26	8[1]	220	6	25	40	550
Le Menu Healthy Traditional Turkey (gravy, stuffing, vegetables)	1.82	8¼	200	5	23	25	610
• **Stouffer's Homestyle Favorites Turkey Breast** (gravy, stuffing)	2.60	8	300	13	39	37	850
Weight Watchers Stuffed Turkey Breast (gravy, vegetables)	2.57	8½	270	8	27	60	520
Lean Cuisine Sliced Turkey Breast (gravy, dressing, vegetables)	2.29	8	200	5	23	25	590
• **Banquet Family Entree Gravy & Sliced Turkey**	0.52	6[3]	120	6	45	19	529

Ratings
Continued

1 Product	4 Sensory comments
Chicken enchiladas	
• **Stouffer's Chicken Enchiladas** (cheese sauce)	Tortilla with distinct corn flavor; plentiful shredded chicken; lots of sauce; mild cheddar, sour cream, green chili.
The Budget Gourmet Light and Healthy Chicken Enchilada Suiza (zucchini and chilies in sauce)	Flaky corn tortilla; little chicken; lots of sauce; sour creamlike, green chili.
Healthy Choice Chicken Enchiladas (Mexican rice, suiza sauce)	Filling mostly rice, very little chicken; scant, flat-tasting sauce; sour cream, cumin, a bit hot.
Lean Cuisine Chicken Enchanadas (pasta, vegetables, salsa)	Doughy pasta; vegetable filling, little meat; lots of chunky tomato sauce; chili powder, oregano.
Weight Watchers Chicken Enchiladas Suiza (sour cream sauce)	Pasty, mostly white chicken; green chili, scant sour cream and cheddar sauce, thickeners.
Le Menu Healthy Chicken Enchilada (creamy sauce)	Little chicken; "hollow-tasting" green chili sauce; soapy off-taste, lots of thickeners.
Glazed chicken	
Weight Watchers Imperial Chicken (mushrooms, rice, broccoli)	Soft chunks of flavorful teriyaki-mushroom sauce; relatively crisp, tasty broccoli.
Le Menu Healthy Glazed Chicken (seasoned rice medley)	Chicken chunks (sometimes fatty) in sweet fruity oriental sauce; rice with dried-onion flavor.
The Budget Gourmet Light and Healthy Orange Glazed Chicken Breast (rice, broccoli-celery garnish)	Soft fillets in flavorful but very sweet orange-mustard sauce, thickeners; seasoned yellow rice.
Healthy Choice Glazed Chicken (rice, green beans)	Soft, pasty, "steamed" fillets in bland mushroom sauce, lightly spiced; bland rice and vegetables.
Lean Cuisine Glazed Chicken (vegetable rice)	Soft, pasty fillets, some grilled taste, bland mushroom sauce; almond-oil-like note; bland rice and vegetables.
Lasagna	
• **The Budget Gourmet Three Cheese Lasagna**	Light, chunky sauce with wine; moist cheese with hint of fresh flavor.
• **Kraft Lasagna** (meat sauce)	Skimpy, bland cheese; meat less processed-tasting than most.
• **Swanson Entree Lasagna** (meat sauce)	Thick doughy noodles; distinct basil; bland cheese; meat less processed-tasting than most.
Weight Watchers Italian Cheese Lasagna	Thick tomato sauce; oregano, basil; very bland, dry, spongy cheese.
The Budget Gourmet Light and Healthy Lasagna (meat sauce)	Light chunky sauce; little spice; skimpy, bland, moist cheese; soft veal; less processed-tasting than most.
Weight Watchers Lasagna (meat sauce)	Thick tomato sauce, oregano, basil; very bland, dry, spongy cheese; meat less processed-tasting than most.

Product	Description
Weight Watchers Garden Lasagna	Thick tomato sauce; bland, dry, spongy cheese; flavorful zucchini and spinach mixed with cheese.
• **Stouffer's Single Serving Lasagna** (meat and sauce)	Thick, soft, doughy noodles; bland with little tomato and spice taste; few cheese curds; greasy.
Healthy Choice Zucchini Lasagna	Soft, doughy noodles; bland, with thin light sauce; few and tasteless cheese curds; tough zucchini.
<u>**Lean Cuisine Lasagna**</u> (meat sauce)	Bland sauce with thickeners; little tomato; few and tasteless spongy cheese curds; chewy meat.
Healthy Choice Lasagna (meat sauce)	Doughy noodles; bland, dried-up sauce; few and tasteless cheese curds; chewy, dry meat.
Le Menu Healthy Entree Lasagna (meat sauce)	Thick, doughy noodles; little tomato, harsh spice, lots of thickeners; moist cheese, "artificial" dairy flavor.
Ultra Slim-Fast Lasagna (meat sauce)	Doughy noodles; gravylike sauce with processed-meat taste; no cheese.
Lean Cuisine Zucchini Lasagna	Soft noodles; bland sauce with thickeners, harsh oregano, little tomato; few and tasteless, spongy cheese curds.
• **Banquet Family Entree Lasagna** (meat sauce)	Very salty gravylike sauce, lots of thickeners; bland spongy cheese; soft, chewy, processed-tasting meat.
Le Menu Healthy Garden Vegetable Lasagna	Thick, doughy noodles; harsh spice, lots of thickeners, little tomato; "artificial" dairy flavor; sulfury vegetables.

Salisbury steak

Product	Description
• **Kraft Beef Sirloin Salisbury Steak** (gravy, steak fries)	Warmed-over flavor, little beef taste (some samples with filler); salty; flavorful potatoes with skin.
Lean Cuisine Salisbury Steak (gravy, scalloped potatoes)	Bland beef with warmed-over flavor; cubed potatoes in creamlike sauce.
• **Stouffer's Homestyle Favorites Salisbury Steak** (gravy, macaroni, and cheese)	Bland beef with warmed-over flavor, some gristle; soft pasta with packaged taste.
The Budget Gourmet Light and Healthy Beef Sirloin Salisbury Steak (red wine sauce, potatoes, carrots, broccoli)	Pressed meat, nondescript flavor, filler, breakfast-sausage spices; little gravy; soft potato chunks; flavorful but tough, fibrous carrot slices.
Le Menu Healthy Salisbury Steak (gravy, mushrooms, potatoes)	Chewy meat, some gristle, filler, and bolognalike taste; soft, slightly raw-tasting potatoes with skins.
• **Banquet Family Entree Gravy & 6 Salisbury Steaks**	Nondescript meat with filler; soft, pasty, spongy texture; bouillon-flavored gravy; greasy; salty.

Turkey

Product	Description
Healthy Choice Turkey and Mushrooms in Gravy (rice pilaf)	Small, bland meat medallions with soft, pasty texture, mushroom sauce; bland rice; tasteless carrots.
Lean Cuisine Sliced Turkey Breast (mushroom sauce, rice pilaf)	Dry, stringy turkey; mushroom gravy with orange zest; flavorful rice with bland vegetables.
Le Menu Healthy Traditional Turkey (gravy, stuffing, vegetables)	Sometimes intact, sometimes pressed turkey; mild poultry spice; heavy, pasty stuffing; soft vegetables.
• **Stouffer's Homestyle Favorites Turkey Breast** (gravy, stuffing)	Pressed turkey with spice but little turkey flavor; light, tasty stuffing.
Weight Watchers Stuffed Turkey Breast (gravy, vegetables)	Pressed meat around dense, pasty, but flavorful stuffing; chalky gravy; soft vegetables.
Lean Cuisine Sliced Turkey Breast (gravy, dressing, vegetables)	Pressed meat with little turkey flavor, little gravy; light corn stuffing; seasoned carrots.
• **Banquet Family Entree Gravy & Sliced Turkey**	Pressed dark and white meat, pasty with warmed-over off-notes; greasy gravy.

prepared food. And their shortcomings cannot be blamed entirely on their low fat and salt content. Many regular dishes, with more fat and salt, suffered the same sensory defects. Blame the entrées' sorry showing instead on inferior ingredients, second-rate recipes, and excessive processing.

Again, for occasional quick meals, try glazed-chicken entrées. They offered the best combination of taste and nutrition. A turkey entrée would be second choice. The best idea for a meal that's quickly prepared, nutritious, and flavorful is cooking extra food occasionally, so you have leftovers to freeze and reheat.

HOT DOGS

Hot-dog makers have tried in recent years to lighten up the image of the fatty, salty frankfurter. Today you can buy hot dogs that advertise themselves as being 80 to 97 percent "fat free" or having 25 to 33 percent "less fat." You can find a dog made from poultry or even from tofu. Is mustard's best friend headed for the health-food aisle?

Not quite.

Regular franks have so much fat to begin with that even most reduced-fat versions can have more fat than many other meats. An "80 percent fat-free" frank gets 20 percent of its weight from fat.

Poultry franks aren't much better. Skinless chicken breast does contain much less fat than beef or pork, but chicken or turkey that's been processed and seasoned to become a hot dog loses much of the nutritional advantage it had on the wing.

Nutritionally, there's not much difference between beef franks, "meat" franks (made from beef, pork, poultry, or a combination of those meats), and poultry franks. Nor is there much difference between regular and reduced-fat varieties. The newest type of hot dog in the supermarkets—listed as "minimal fat" products in the Ratings—is the only dog that differs substantially from the nutritional norm. (They're beef and meat franks processed to keep the fat to a minimum.)

Reduced-fat and poultry franks do differ from regular hot dogs in taste, however. When the manufacturers squeeze fat from their franks, they also squeeze out flavor and juiciness, leaving a hot dog with a more rubbery feel in the mouth. At the same time, they may add salt to enhance the flavor.

What's in a Frank?

According to U.S. Department of Agriculture standards, a frankfurter is a blended semisolid sausage prepared from beef, pork, poultry, or a combination of those meats, with the predominant ingredient listed first on the label. A hot dog also includes binders such as dried skim milk or soy flour, as well as salt, sweeteners, and seasonings such as garlic. A small amount of the curing agent sodium nitrite gives franks their characteristic color and distinctive cured-meat flavor, and also helps prevent botulism. Every hot dog also contains some added water, used to cool the meat as it's ground.

Hot dogs are formed in a casing, then fully cooked. The casing is usually stripped away before the franks are packaged. That distinctive "snap" you feel when you bite into a hot dog actually comes from a skin of protein that forms in the cooking.

Fat, Calories, and Sodium

It helps to know a hot dog's nutritional profile, if only to decide whether you can get away with an extra frank or a second helping of potato salad.

Fat. The USDA says a frank may be up to 30 percent fat by weight. Reduced-fat and poultry franks are about 20 percent fat by weight. The percentage of *calories* derived from fat, however, is more meaningful. The government's dietary guidelines recommend a limit of 30 percent of calories from fat for all the food you eat in a day; some nutrition experts say a lower limit would be optimal. In most hot dogs, at least 70 percent of the calories comes from fat.

As the Ratings indicate, there's little nutritional difference between franks that were close to the USDA limit of 30 percent fat by weight and those that were around 20 percent fat by weight. Most of the reduced-fat franks replace some or all of the missing fat with water, which has no calories, so the percentage of calories from fat stays fairly constant.

Here, the "minimal fat" franks stand out, with less than 50 percent of their calories from fat.

Most regular hot dogs have at least 5 grams of saturated fat, 25 percent of the government's recommended daily allowance. Reduced-fat hot dogs have somewhat less, and "minimal fat" franks have no more than 2 grams of saturated fat.

Cholesterol. None of these hot dogs contributes much cholesterol to the diet: On average, they supply less than 20 percent of the recommended daily limit.

Calories. Regular franks averaged more than 150 calories each, whereas the reduced-fat varieties ranged between 70 and 150. The minimal-fat franks had 45 to 80 calories each.

Sodium. It ranged from 261 milligrams per frank to 783 milligrams. *Consumer Reports* medical consultants believe that most readers don't have to bother about their sodium intake, but the Ratings list sodium values for those who must. (According to current government guidelines, the recommended daily allowance for the average adult is 2,400 mg of sodium.) As a rule, the reduced-fat and poultry franks had the most sodium.

A Matter of Taste

Americans eat 50 million hot dogs a day, or about 80 per person per year. Most of the country prefers a meat frank, though New Yorkers more often choose beef. Judging from tests of 45 franks by *Consumer Reports* in 1993, New Yorkers may be on to something.

A panel of trained tasters sampled each frank—plain, with no mustard, relish, or bun, so the flavor and texture would come through clearly—and described its characteristics. The Ratings order was derived by comparing those descriptions to the characteristics for an ideal hot dog.

A range of distinct flavors was allowed—garlic, onion, smoke, or a slight sweetness—and credit was given to hot dogs with a full flavor unsullied by off-notes. Points were subtracted for any hint of sourness or "old meat" and "old fat" flavors. The ideal

(*continued on page 220*)

RATINGS

As published in the **July 1993** issue of **Consumer Reports**

Hot dogs

Listed by types; within types, listed in order of overall sensory quality. Products that scored within a few points of each other are similar in quality. Products with identical scores are listed alphabetically.

1 Sensory score. Based on taste tests by trained sensory panelists who measured the intensity of numerous flavor and texture characteristics. An excellent hot dog should be full-flavored and fairly salty. The hot dog can be a bit sweet and may have onion and garlic flavors. It should also taste fresh, with no old-meat or old-fat flavors, no sour or fermented tastes. It can have a smoky flavor, provided that doesn't overwhelm other flavors or taste ashy. The hot dog should snap with the first bite and be juicy inside. The texture should be slightly springy but not rubbery, and there should be no gritty particles.

2 Price/nutrition per hot dog. The **cost** is the estimated average, based on prices paid nationally in 1993. The figures for **calories, fat, saturated fat,** and **sodium** come from package labels, except as noted in footnotes. The **percentage of calories from fat** is a calculation made by *Consumer Reports* technical staff. It's a more meaningful guide to this aspect of nutritional quality than the percentage of fat listed on many product labels, which is based on weight.

3 Taste and texture comments. Noteworthy attributes, from the sensory panel's data. Except as noted, all hot dogs were salty and moderately to highly seasoned. They had a little snap on the first bite, and were somewhat juicy. The beef hot dogs tended to have more garlic and onion flavors, less smoke flavor and sweetness. All the poultry hot dogs had a slight old-meat flavor. According to government standards, meat hot dogs can be made from beef, pork, poultry, or combinations of those meats. In general, the meat that accounts for the greatest percentage of weight is listed first on the label. Because the mix of meats may change and because some manufacturers sell more than one type of "meat" hot dog, the meat listing from the package label after the brand names is included.

---

1 *Based on analysis by* Consumer Reports.

2 *From manufacturer's data.*

3 *Less than 1 gram.*

Ratings
Continued

Sensory Score scale: Poor — Excellent (F | P | G | VG | E) [1]

[2] Per hot dog

Product	Sensory Score	Franks per pkg.	Cost	Weight, oz.	Calories
Beef hot dogs					
Brunckhorst's Boar's Head Natural Casing	E	7	51¢	2.3	170 [1]
Eckrich Jumbo	VG	8	26	2.0	180
Hebrew National Kosher	VG	7	41	1.7	149 [2]
Kahn's	VG	10	25	1.6	130
Armour Premium	VG	10	21	1.6	149 [1]
Oscar Mayer	VG	10	26	1.6	140
Ball Park	VG	8	30	2.0	167 [2]
Hebrew National Kosher Lite	VG	7	41	1.7	110
Best's Kosher (Lower salt & fat)	VG	8	47	1.5	100
Lady Lee	VG	10	18	1.6	126 [2]
Nathan's Famous 8 Skinless	VG	8	34	2.0	176 [2]
Pathmark Deli Style Skinless	G	8	35	2.0	176 [1]
Meat hot dogs					
Safeway Our Premium	VG	8	29	2.0	180 [2]
Lykes Meaty Jumbo	VG	8	19	2.0	180 [2]
Oscar Mayer (Pork & turkey)	VG	10	19	1.6	150
Armour Premium (Pork, turkey, & beef)	VG	10	15	1.6	147 [1]
Kahn's Jumbo	VG	8	25	2.0	180
Eckrich Bunsize (Pork, turkey, & beef)	VG	8	20	2.0	180
Oscar Mayer Light	VG	8	25	2.0	130

Hormel Wranglers		8	36	2.0	180
Bryan Juicy Jumbos		8	27	2.0	180 [2]
Ball Park (Beef & pork, turkey)		8	25	2.0	177 [2]
Ball Park Lite (Beef & pork, chicken)		8	28	2.0	140
Bar S Jumbo (Chicken, pork, & beef)		8	12	2.0	216 [2]
Farmer John		10	16	1.6	130 [2]
Rath Blackhawk Biger-Than-The-Bun (Chicken, pork, & beef)		8	14	2.0	170
Kahn's Light & Mild (Beef & turkey)		8	29	2.0	110
Dubuque (Chicken & pork)		10	7	1.2	108 [1]
Wilson Jumbos (Chicken & pork)		8	13	2.0	180
John Morrell (Chicken, pork, & beef)		10	17	1.2	109 [1]
Hygrade's (Chicken & pork)		8	13	2.0	181 [1]
Janet Lee (Chicken, beef, & pork)		10	9	1.2	101 [2]
Shoprite (Chicken & pork)		10	11	1.6	120 [1]
Poultry hot dogs					
Louis Rich Bun-Length Turkey		8	21	2.0	130
Lady Lee Chicken		10	12	1.2	79 [1]
Butterball Bun Size Turkey		8	18	2.0	130
Gwaltney Great Dogs Turkey		8	12	2.0	150
Grillmaster Chicken		8	14	2.0	130
Jennie-O Turkey		10	8	1.2	70
Mr. Turkey Bun Size		8	16	2.0	130
Wampler-Longacre Turkey		10	12	1.6	110
Minimal-fat hot dogs (Beef and meat)					
Armour Premium Lean Beef Jumbo		8	31	2.0	80
Healthy Choice		10	27	1.6	50
Hormel Light & Lean 97		10	27	1.6	45
Oscar Mayer Healthy Favorites		8	30	2.0	60

Ratings
Continued

Product	Fat, g.	% calories from fat	Saturated fat, g.	Sodium, mg.	Taste and texture comments
Beef hot dogs					
Brunckhorst's Boar's Head Natural Casing	15.0 [2]	79	6.1 [1]	576 [1]	Full flavor; lots of garlic, onion; juicy; big snap.
Eckrich Jumbo	17.0	85	7.8 [1]	490	Full flavor; smoky; juicy.
Hebrew National Kosher	14.0 [2]	85	6.2 [2]	410 [2]	Full flavor with lots of garlic; juicy.
Kahn's	12.0	83	5.5 [2]	450	Smoky; juicy.
Armour Premium	14.0 [1]	85	6.1 [1]	502 [1]	Full flavor; smoky; juicy; slightly soft.
Oscar Mayer	13.0	84	5.6 [2]	470	Smoky; slightly sweet; juicy.
Ball Park	15.6 [2]	84	7.4 [1]	545 [2]	Juicy.
Hebrew National Kosher Lite	10.0	82	4.2 [2]	360	Full flavor with lots of garlic; juicy.
Best's Kosher (Lower salt & fat)	8.0	72	3.6 [1]	270	Lots of garlic and onion; juicy.
Lady Lee	11.0 [2]	79	4.7 [2]	436 [2]	Full flavor with lots of garlic and onion; slight old-fat flavor; juicy.
Nathan's Famous 8 Skinless	16.0 [2]	82	3.0 [2]	463 [2]	Full flavor with lots of garlic and onion; slight old-fat flavor; juicy.
Pathmark Deli Style Skinless	16.0 [1]	82	7.1 [2]	394 [1]	Lots of garlic and onion; old-meat and old-fat flavors; juicy.
Meat hot dogs					
Safeway Our Premium	16.5 [2]	83	6.1 [2]	635 [2]	Full flavor; salty; juicy.
Lykes Meaty Jumbo	16.7 [2]	84	6.7 [1]	600 [2]	Smoky.
Oscar Mayer (Pork & turkey)	14.0	84	5.0 [2]	430	Smoky; slightly sweet.
Armour Premium (Pork, turkey, & beef)	13.0 [1]	80	4.9 [1]	466 [1]	Smoky; salty; very little snap.
Kahn's Jumbo	16.0	80	6.5 [1]	560	Ashy smoke flavor; salty.
Eckrich Bunsize (Pork, turkey, & beef)	17.0	85	6.5 [1]	510	Smoky.
Oscar Mayer Light	11.0	76	3.9 [2]	630	Smoky; slightly rubbery.
Hormel Wranglers	16.0	80	6.0	500	Full flavor; smoky; very juicy and greasy; coarse.

[2] Per hot dog

[3] Taste and texture comments

Product					Description
Bryan Juicy Jumbos	17.0 [2]	85	6.9 [1]	600 [2]	Ashy smoke flavor; salty.
Ball Park (Beef & pork, turkey)	16.5 [2]	84	6.1 [1]	707 [1]	Mild; airy; slightly gritty.
Ball Park Lite (Beef & pork, chicken)	12.0	77	4.3 [1]	698 [1]	Mild; slightly rubbery and gritty.
Bar S Jumbo (Chicken, pork, & beef)	17.7 [2]	74	6.9 [1]	625 [2]	Slightly soft and airy; gritty.
Farmer John	11.0 [2]	76	4.5 [1]	459 [2]	Ashy smoke flavor; slightly soft and airy; very little snap.
Rath Blackhawk Biger-Than-The-Bun (Chicken, pork, & beef)	15.0	79	6.0 [1]	670	Gritty; very little snap.
Kahn's Light & Mild (Beef & turkey)	8.0	65	3.5 [1]	630	Slight old-meat flavor; slightly rubbery.
Dubuque (Chicken & pork)	10.0 [1]	83	3.6 [1]	414 [1]	Ashy smoke flavor; slight old-meat flavor; gritty; very little snap.
Wilson Jumbos (Chicken & pork)	17.0	85	7.8 [1]	616 [1]	Smoky; slightly soft; gritty; very little snap.
John Morrell (Chicken, pork, & beef)	10.0 [1]	83	3.8 [1]	391 [1]	Bland; gritty; very little snap.
Hygrade's (Chicken & pork)	17.0 [1]	85	6.2 [1]	561 [1]	Bland; slight old-meat flavor; airy; gritty; very little snap.
Janet Lee (Chicken, beef, & pork)	10.0 [2]	89	3.8 [1]	350 [2]	Old-meat and sour flavors; slightly soft and spongy; gritty.
Shoprite (Chicken & pork)	10.0 [1]	75	3.9 [1]	261 [1]	Spoiled flavor; spongy; gritty.
Poultry hot dogs					
Louis Rich Bun-Length Turkey	11.0	76	3.3 [2]	660	Slightly rubbery and gritty.
Lady Lee Chicken	6.0 [1]	68	2.1 [1]	386 [1]	Slightly rubbery; gritty.
Butterball Bun Size Turkey	10.0	69	3.1 [1]	630 [2]	Slight medicinal flavor; gritty.
Gwaltney Great Dogs Turkey	13.0	78	4.2 [1]	783 [2]	Slightly dry; rubbery; gritty.
Grillmaster Chicken	11.0	76	3.5 [1]	641 [2]	Ashy smoke flavor; slightly dry, rubbery; gritty.
Jennie-O Turkey	6.0	77	1.4 [2]	330	Bland; slightly dry and rubbery; gritty.
Mr. Turkey Bun Size	11.0	76	3.6 [2]	640	Bland; slight medicinal flavor; slightly dry; rubbery; gritty.
Wampler-Longacre Turkey	9.0	74	2.6 [1]	419 [2]	Strong medicinal flavor; slightly dry; rubbery; gritty; very little snap.
Minimal-fat hot dogs (Beef and meat)					
Armour Premium Lean Beef Jumbo	4.0	45	2.0 [1]	640	Slight old-meat and old-fat flavors; slightly rubbery.
Healthy Choice	1.0	18	[3]	460	Ashy smoke flavor; slightly dry and rubbery.
Hormel Light & Lean 97	1.0	20	0.0 [2]	390	Burnt aroma; distinct black-pepper flavor; slightly dry; rubbery.
Oscar Mayer Healthy Favorites	2.0	30	0.6 [2]	520	Extremely bland; ashy smoke and slight old-meat flavors; slightly dry; rubbery.

frank should have some snap when you first bite into it. It should be juicy and slightly springy, not dry or rubbery. And it shouldn't contain fine bits of bone, gristle, or grit.

Beef hot dogs earned the highest scores overall because they were full-flavored and juicy. Many tended to be less sweet and smoky than the other types, and more often had a distinct garlic and onion flavor. All but one of the remaining beef franks were rated very good.

The meat hot dogs ran the gamut. The best earned a score that would rank it with the best beef franks. The worst had so many off-flavors that it barely earned a score at all. The lowest-scoring meat hot dogs tasted of old meat and contained gritty particles reminiscent of finely ground bone meal.

The best of the poultry franks mustered only a good sensory score. Most were rated fair. Many lost points for tasting somewhat like leftover turkey that had been kept a little too long. None of the chicken and turkey franks were very juicy, all were somewhat gritty, and most were rubbery.

Overall, the minimal-fat franks were comparable to the poultry franks: rubbery and slightly dry.

Recommendations

You could dine on sirloin steak and take in less fat, calories, and sodium than you would with a couple of hot dogs. The "minimal-fat" franks are an option: They are nutritionally better, but they exact a big compromise in taste. Most people would probably be happier having hot dogs that really taste good and eating them less often.

OLIVE OIL

Olive oil became *the* fashionable condiment in the mid-1980s. That was when medical research began to suggest that olive oil could be good for the heart because it lowers LDL, the "bad" form of cholesterol. Moreover, the monounsaturated fats it contains seemed even better than the polyunsaturates in other vegetable oils. Sales more than doubled between 1985 and 1990.

A shopper choosing from the confusing array of bottles available will find that labels are only an imprecise guide to the contents. Label grades like "Pure" and "Light" are words developed for the American market, descriptive but not carefully defined designations. "Extra Virgin," however, means the same thing here that it does in Europe. Here's what each grade means:

Extra Virgin

Under the government rules that prevail in Europe, Extra Virgin is the highest grade and must come from top-quality olives. The fruit is hand-harvested, washed, blended, and mashed. The mash is squeezed at room temperature in a hydraulic press—"cold pressed." Today, the juice is spun in a centrifuge to separate the oil from the watery part.

After separation, the oil is graded by acidity and by taste. It can be called Extra Virgin only if it meets certain standards for color, aroma, and flavor, and passes a chemical test: It must contain less than 1 percent free oleic acid, a fatty acid that can damage olive oil's flavor. If the acidity is a little higher, or if the color and taste are not absolutely "perfect" (the term used in Europe), the oil can be designated Virgin or Superfine Virgin. (Little of either shows up in the United States, though.)

Pure

Oil that can't pass for virgin, and oil from less carefully culled fruit, is refined to create the everyday olive oil known in this country as "Pure" and in Europe simply as "olive oil." After the olives are pressed and centrifuged, the manufacturer may add a solvent to extract the free acids and other impurities. Then the oil is heated, which drives off the solvent and leaves a nearly colorless—and flavorless—oil.

The maker adds back a portion of Extra Virgin oil, between 5 and 25 percent, to give the product the desired olive flavor.

Light

So-called Light or Extra Light olive oil is simply refined oil that hasn't had much Extra Virgin added back for flavor.

A Tasting of Oils

In 1991 a trained *Consumer Reports* taste panel evaluated at least six samples each of 27 olive oils bought at grocery stores, specialty shops, and by mail. The oils came in Extra Virgin, Pure, and Light varieties.

The panelists took their oil straight, sipping samples from coded cups. They recorded the intensity of the flavors they found and any defects they noted.

An excellent olive oil should have a "clean" oil flavor, one that clears out of the mouth fairly quickly. It should be free of any taste defects such as a paintlike or linseed-oil taste, off-flavors arising from oxidation. However, a wide range of olive flavors (depending on the type) and other taste characteristics were judged as acceptable, from very pronounced for Extra Virgins to barely perceptible for Extra Lights.

All the oils were judged to be high-quality products, and for this reason they are listed alphabetically. There were instances of off-flavors in some samples, probably attributable to improper handling somewhere along the line, but the defects were not consistent enough from sample to sample to lower the estimation of any brand.

As one might expect, the Extra Virgins had both the greatest intensity of olive flavor and the largest range of different flavors. Whereas all the oils except some Lights had a distinct olive flavor, some were enhanced with various other flavor notes.

For instance, two of the Spanish oils had a light but sharp evergreen-and-herbal note. Some people could find that too aggressive or even experience a slight burning sensation in the throat, whereas others no doubt will savor the experience. The tasters also found oils with slight fruity notes and nut-like flavors. The fruitiness ranged from "green," like an unripe melon, to something reminiscent of a ripe peach or banana.

The Pure olive oils all had markedly less olive flavor intensity than did the Extra Virgins, although olive character was still there. The Light varieties tasted much less of olives, with few if any nuances of taste.

Recommendations

Olive oil is a versatile cooking ingredient, one that can substitute for just about any oil in any recipe. Good for panfrying and sautéing, olive oil is also a good emulsifier, making the Lights, at least, suitable for baking cakes or brownies.

Save the Extra Virgins for cold uses—their flavor will probably be lost if you fry with them. Used sparingly, they can add interesting flavors when drizzled on fresh pasta or green salad, added to a sauce at the very end, or used instead of butter as a dip for bread. The sensory comments in the Ratings can point you toward flavor nuances you might want to try.

If you don't care for the taste of olives but want to use olive oil as a substitute for other fats in your diet, consider *Bertolli Lucca Extra Light* or *Filippo Berio Mild & Light*. They had the least olive flavor.

Prices vary widely. Although some Extra Virgins, especially mail-order and specialty-shop products, are absurdly expensive, others are surprisingly moderate. For instance, *Giralda, Italica,* and *Pope* Extra Virgins cost only about 10 cents a serving (one tablespoon), approximately the same as a typical Pure variety.

In general, olive oil costs quite a bit more than such cooking oils as corn or soybean oil—roughly 2 to 10 times as much. However, the significance of the extra expense depends on how much you plan to consume. Used as a flavoring, a little Extra Virgin oil can go a long way. Keep the bottle tightly capped in a cool, dark place, and it should last up to two years after it's opened.

PANCAKES

For a 1992 report, *Consumer Reports* food specialists took 28 mixes and frozen pancakes, then cooked (or warmed up) some 1,100 pancakes and tasted them unadorned. Nine of the test products were from Aunt Jemima, a Quaker Oats brand that accounts for nearly half the total market. Included were some mixes made with buttermilk, among them that old standby *Bisquick*, as well as "lite" mixes. Flavored pancakes were also tested.

To make sure no mix had an advantage, *Consumer Reports* food

(continued on page 226)

RATINGS

As published in the October 1991 issue of Consumer Reports

Olive oils

Listed by types. Within types, listed in alphabetical order. All were judged very good in overall quality for their type. All are nutritionally similar and contain about 125 calories per tablespoon.

1 Olive flavor intensity. Bars show the tasters' judgments of the intensity of olive flavor, which ranged from decidedly pronounced to barely perceptible. Although Extra Virgin products generally exhibited more intense olive flavor, that is not in itself an indicator of quality.

2 Price per bottle. Prices are the average found in a nationwide survey of supermarkets in 1991. For specialty-shop or mail-order brands—marked with an asterisk—prices are what was paid.

3 Size. The oil was bought in the size closest to a pint that we could find available. Imported oil tends to come in metric sizes (17 fluid ounces is half a liter, just over a pint). All came in glass or plastic bottles.

4 Cost per serving. Calculated for a serving size of one tablespoon, about half a fluid ounce.

5 Sensory comments. Colors varied from a fairly deep green with a tinge of yellow to a very pale yellow. All the Extra Virgin and Pure varieties had

an easily detectable olive flavor; the Pure products showed a considerable range of olive flavor intensity, however. Beyond that there were certain flavor nuances specific to growing region, degree of ripeness, and so forth. "Green" refers to the flavor of green, slightly unripe fruit. "Fruity" is a complex of ripened fruit flavors, sometimes undifferentiated and sometimes reminiscent of melon, peach, or green-to-ripe banana. "Evergreen/herbal" is a flavor like fresh herbs with a pinelike character. Some Extra Virgins and Pures also exhibited a slight bitterness or astringency, and some produced a sensation called throat burn—a slight tingling or burning impression in the back of the throat. Those are allowable attributes in a good-quality oil.

Product	1 Olive flavor intensity	2 Price per bottle	3 Size, fl. oz.	4 Cost per serving	5 Sensory comments
Extra Virgin					
Bertolli Lucca		$ 5.07	17	15¢	Slight green fruity note.
Carapelli		5.14	17	15	Slight green fruity note.
Extra Virgin Olive Oil Product of France 1 2		23.00*	33.8	34	Slight green fruity note, bitter, astringent.
Filippo Berio		5.04	17	15	Unripe, fruity note.
Giralda		3.75	17	11	Distinct, sharp evergreen/herbal note; slight peachlike note.

Product	Rating			Comments
Italica Spanish		3.14	17	9	Hint of evergreen/herbal.
Pompeian		4.18	16	13	Hint of evergreen/herbal.
Pope		2.95	17	9	Slight green fruity note.
Robert Rothschild Gourmet [3]		8.27*	12.7	33	Distinct green Spanish-olive flavor, slight sharp vinegar flavor; less bitter than most.
Star		3.88	8.3	23	Slight green fruity note.
Tenuta Di Cerreto Marchese Emilio Pucci [2]		39.00*	33.8	57	Slight ripe fruity note.

Pure

Bertolli Lucca Classico	4.52	17	13	—
Carapelli	5.04	17	15	—
Filippo Berio	4.29	17	13	—
Giralda	3.37	17	10	Hint of evergreen/herbal; a bit more astringent than most.
Italica Spanish	3.32	17	10	—
Pompeian	3.79	16	12	Hint of evergreen/herbal.
Pope	2.87	17	8	Slight nutlike note.
Progresso Pure Imported	4.47	25	9	—
Star	3.66	17	11	Fruity, green-melon note.
Vigo	2.82	17	8	—

Light

Bertolli Lucca Extra Light	4.38	17	13	Virtually tasteless.
Carapelli Extra Light	3.49	17	10	—
Filippo Berio Mild & Light	4.40	17	13	Virtually tasteless.
Pompeian Extra Light	3.97	16	13	—
Progresso Select Imported Extra Light	2.65	12	11	—
Star Extra Light	3.77	17	11	—

1 *This product is further identified on a small label by the words "Moulin de Haute Provence."*

2 *Purchased from Williams-Sonoma (800-541-2233).*

3 *Purchased at Bloomingdale's, New York City.*

technicians conducted pilot tests, measuring and weighing the ingredients and determining optimum cooking procedures for each product. Cooking instructions were precise. For example, each mix had to be whisked for 80 strokes and any lumps stuck inside the whisk had to be tapped off after 20 strokes.

A panel of trained tasters evaluated each pancake's appearance, texture, and flavor. *Consumer Reports* statisticians then compared the panel's data with the criteria for pancake excellence. The Ratings were based on the results.

Griddle Grades

A pancake should be more than a sponge for soaking up butter and syrup. It should contribute a flavor of grain, subtle yet full. A hint of egg and dairy flavors may be present, along with a slight sweetness, saltiness, or sourness. A pancake should also be tender, slightly moist, and moderately dense. What's a bad pancake? One that tastes like raw dough, chemical leavening, or cardboard, or one whose texture is gummy, tough and chewy, leaden, crumbly, or full of particles that resemble sawdust.

Although a truly perfect pancake never appeared, a number of mixes turn out very good pancakes. These pancake products fall into a neat pattern: The more you do yourself, the better the pancake. The standard, add-everything mixes made up the top third of the Ratings, followed by most of the complete mixes. With one exception, the frozen variety just didn't stack up.

Recommendations

Standard mixes produced pancakes that came closest to *Consumer Reports* definition of excellence, and they're relatively inexpensive—between 14 and 26 cents per three-pancake serving (including the ingredients you add). *Hungry Jack Buttermilk* and *Hungry Jack Extra Lights* topped the Ratings. Use these for flavored pancakes, too, adding your own blueberries, bananas, nuts, and the like.

If adding oil, egg, and milk is too much hassle, try a high-rated complete mix; all you add is water. The complete mixes cost between 5 and 43 cents a serving—and the ones you just shake and pour were most expensive. *Betty Crocker Buttermilk*, at only 9 cents a serving, was the best.

The frozen pancakes, convenient through they are, were generally tough and chewy, and they cost as much as 53 cents a serving.

When it's wearing its typical coating of butter and syrup, the pancake inspires the kind of guilt you never get from a bowl of bran-something and skim milk. The guilt is really unwarranted, as the Ratings charts below show. A serving of three 4-inch pancakes topped by a teaspoon of butter and four tablespoons of syrup has about 450 calories. That's less than a quarter of the calories an average woman should eat in a day.

The fat in a serving from the tested products ranges from 5 to 16 grams, counting added oil, egg, milk, and butter. With most products, fat content is about 9 grams, which comes to only 18 percent of the meal's total calories.

If you're pouring a typical unmaple syrup (see "Pancake Syrups"), your pancake breakfast will contain about 800 milligrams of sodium. You can decrease the sodium level somewhat by using a real maple syrup.

To lower fat, calories, cholesterol, and sodium even further, make your own batter and leave out the egg yolk, the salt, the sugar, and perhaps some of the oil. You can also use skim milk.

The top-rated mix, plus skim milk, egg white, and half the oil called for in the instructions, resulted in pancakes that were still quite good, although they were thinner and a little tougher than they would have been with the usual mix-ins.

For perfect (almost) pancakes, don't overmix the batter; you'll get tough pancakes. And let the batter stabilize for a few minutes before cooking. Use the batter you make; batter refrigerated for a day or so will yield thin, tough pancakes.

You can make waffles from most pancake mixes by adding a bit more oil. This helps keep batter from sticking to the iron.

PANCAKE SYRUPS

The so-called pancake syrups are a mixture of corn syrup, water, thickeners, flavorings, preservatives, and perhaps a smidgen of

(*continued on page 232*)

RATINGS

As published in the January 1992 issue of Consumer Reports

Pancakes

Listed in order of overall sensory quality, based on taste tests by a trained panel.

1 Type. Standard mixes (**S**) were tested that generally require the addition of eggs, oil, and milk; complete mixes (**C**) that need only water; complete shake-and-pour mixes (**C/SP**) that come in a container to which you add water; and frozen, precooked pancakes (**F**) you heat in a microwave oven.

2 Sensory index. The measurement of overall sensory quality. Products lost points for flaws in taste, appearance, and texture. Products within a few points of each other differed little in overall quality. Those with identical scores are listed alphabetically.

3 Price. The estimated national average, based on prices paid nationally. Price for each standard mix includes added ingredients.

Product	Type 1	Sensory index 2	Size, oz.	Price 3
Hungry Jack Buttermilk	S		32	$1.51
Hungry Jack Extra Lights	S		32	1.41
Lady Lee Old Fashioned	S		32	1.27
Aunt Jemima The Original	S		32	1.50
Mrs. Butterworth's Old Fashioned	S		32	1.48
Pepperidge Farm Buttermilk	S		16	2.00
Aunt Jemima Buttermilk	S		32	1.75
Bisquick (with buttermilk)	S		40	1.98

Sensory index scale: Poor—Excellent, 0 to 100 (P, F, G, VG, E)

Product	Type		Size	Price
Betty Crocker Buttermilk	C		32	1.51
Pepperidge Farm Home Style	S		16	2.16
Hungry Jack Buttermilk	C		32	1.52
Aunt Jemima Buttermilk	C		32	1.71
Hungry Jack Extra Lights	C		32	1.57
Aunt Jemima Buttermilk	F		13¾	1.98
Aunt Jemima Pancake Express Original	C/SP		4½	.85
Martha White FlapStax Buttermilk	C		5½	.42
Mrs. Butterworth's Buttermilk	C		32	1.69
Aunt Jemima	C		32	1.73
Aunt Jemima Original	F		13¾	1.98
Aunt Jemima Lite Buttermilk	F		13¾	2.13
Hungry Jack Original [1]	F		15⅓	1.88
Krusteaz Buttermilk	C		32	1.72
Mrs. Butterworth's	C		32	1.66
Kroger Buttermilk	C		32	1.25
Hungry Jack Buttermilk [1]	F		15⅓	1.86
Krusteaz Buttermilk	F		19	1.88
Bisquick Shake 'n Pour Original	C/SP		7	1.09
Aunt Jemima Lite Buttermilk	C		21	1.82

[1] New, "fluffier" versions came out after our tests. In an informal taste test, the new pancakes were indeed fluffier—and less tough and chewy—than the old, although their flavors were similar.

Ratings
Continued

4 Cost per serving. Based on a serving of three four-inch pancakes.

5 Calories. Per serving, without butter and syrup. A teaspoon of butter adds 36 calories;

four tablespoons of syrup add 200. With standard mixes, the milk was 2 percent fat. You can reduce calories, fat, and cholesterol by using skim milk and egg whites.

6 Sodium. Per serving. Recommended daily sodium intake for an average adult is 2,400 mg.

7 Sensory comments. Except as noted,

all the pancakes had only slight grain flavor and were only very slightly sweet and very slightly salty.

The standard-mix pancakes had a hint of egg and wheat flavor. The complete-mix pancakes had little egg flavor and a slight raw-dough flavor. The frozen pancakes had little egg flavor.

Product	4 Cost per serving	5 Calories	6 Sodium, mg.	7 Sensory comments
Hungry Jack Buttermilk	16¢	210	560	Balanced flavors, subtle grain flavor, slightly eggy, a bit sweet; tender.
Hungry Jack Extra Lights	14	190	490	Balanced flavors, subtle grain flavor, very slightly eggy, a bit sweet; tender.
Lady Lee Old Fashioned	17	258	614	Balanced flavors, subtle grain flavor, very slightly eggy, a bit sweet; tender.
Aunt Jemima The Original	14	200	590	Subtle grain flavor; tender.
Mrs. Butterworth's Old Fashioned	14	190	570	Subtle grain flavor, very slightly eggy; tender.
Pepperidge Farm Buttermilk	24	239	579	Subtle grain flavor, slight dried-buttermilk flavor; tender.
Aunt Jemima Buttermilk	16	220	760	Subtle grain flavor; tender.
Bisquick (with buttermilk)	18	300	780	Subtle grain flavor, slight raw-dough flavor.
Betty Crocker Buttermilk	9	210	500	Sweet taste, very slight cardboard off-flavor; a bit gummy.
Pepperidge Farm Home Style	26	191	503	Subtle grain flavor, slight raw-dough flavor, a bit soggy inside, gummy.
Hungry Jack Buttermilk	9	180	720	Subtle grain flavor, slight corn flavor, slight cardboard off-flavor; a bit gummy.

Product			Comments
Aunt Jemima Buttermilk	12	230	610	Slight cardboard off-flavor, a bit sweet; a bit gummy.
Hungry Jack Extra Lights	9	190	710	Slight corn flavor, slight cardboard off-flavor; a bit gummy.
Aunt Jemima Buttermilk	50	210	860	Slight "fried-doughnut" flavor, sweet; tough and chewy.
Aunt Jemima Pancake Express Original	43	250	910	Slight corn flavor, hint of cardboard off-flavor, a bit salty; a bit gummy.
Marth White FlapStax Buttermilk	5	240	960	Slight corn flavor, hint of cardboard off-flavor, a bit bitter; a bit gummy.
Mrs. Butterworth's Buttermilk	10	190	660	Slight corn flavor, hint of cardboard off-flavor, a bit salty; a bit gummy.
Aunt Jemima	13	250	910	Slight corn flavor, slight cardboard off-flavor; a bit gummy.
Aunt Jemima Original	50	210	800	Slight "fried-doughnut" flavor, sweet; tough and chewy.
Aunt Jemima Lite Buttermilk	53	140	860	More grain flavor than other frozen products; a bit tough and chewy, some sawdustlike particles.
Hungry Jack Original [1]	47	240	570	"Fried-doughnut" flavor, a hint of freezer flavor, sweet; tough and chewy.
Krusteaz Buttermilk	10	200	770	Distinct cardboard off-flavor; a bit gummy.
Mrs. Butterworth's	10	190	700	Slight corn flavor, hint of cardboard off-flavor, salty; a bit gummy.
Kroger Buttermilk	7	180	630	Distinct cardboard off-flavor, slight raw-dough flavor; gummy.
Hungry Jack Buttermilk [1]	47	260	590	"Fried-doughnut" flavor, slight freezer flavor, sweet; tough and chewy.
Krusteaz Buttermilk	47	290	900	Little grain flavor, slight raw-dough flavor, "fried-doughnut" flavor, strong freezer flavor, sweet; a bit tough and chewy.
Bisquick Shake 'n Pour Original	36	250	880	Little grain flavor, distinct burned-plastic off-flavor, bitter, slightly sweet.
Aunt Jemima Lite Buttermilk	13	130	570	Distinct cardboard off-flavor, slight raw-dough flavor; gummy, a bit soggy inside, many sawdustlike particles.

butter. Some derive their "maple" taste from a variety of flavors: coffee, chocolate, vanilla, and fenugreek, the seeds of an Asian plant also used as an ingredient in curry powder. Others are blends that contain 15 percent real maple plus other sugar syrups.

Falling farthest from the tree are diet syrups, which replace much of the sugar with gums and water. Most diet syrups have 100 calories per 4-tablespoon serving, rather than the 200 calories of the regular products.

There's no mystery about the appeal of pancake syrup versus the real thing: price. The high price of maple syrup reflects the realities of a small-scale manufacturing process and the North's capricious weather as much as it does the demands of the marketplace.

All the Options

For a 1992 report, *Consumer Reports* tested 10 real maple syrups, including six products sold through the mail; two blends; 12 pancake syrups; and eight diet syrups. *Vermont Powdered Maple* is unique. It's sold as maple sugar. To turn it into syrup, you add it to boiling water.

Trained sensory panelists tasted the syrups straight, not atop pancakes or anything else that might prove distracting. The ideal syrup should have a distinct maple flavor that is at least reminiscent of real maple. Nuances of woody, chocolate, coffee, and vanilla flavors can be present. Points were taken off if a syrup tasted tinny or burned; if it tasted of cherry, mint, or artificial sweeteners; or if it tasted like pencil shavings, a flaw that cropped up in a couple of syrups. The butter flavor of a butter-flavored syrup should taste fresh and real—not like the imitation stuff on some movie-house popcorn.

Allowances were made for the small differences commonly found between a maple syrup and an imitator. A very slight bitterness is characteristic of real maple syrup, for instance; a slight taste of salt is acceptable in the others.

The color can range from straw to dark brown. The texture can vary from thin to thick, but a syrup should not be slippery or gelatinous. Residual stickiness should clear quickly from the mouth.

Recommendations

The tests showed that the forest is still a better source of syrup than the factory. On the whole, the more real maple a syrup had, the better it tasted.

Vermont Maple Orchards, L.L. Bean, Williams-Sonoma, and *The Dakin Farm,* all pure maples, were excellent syrups.

Vermont Maple has an edge: at 77 cents a 4-tablespoon serving, it's less expensive than the others. (*Williams-Sonoma,* for instance, costs $1.38 a serving—you would shell out $22 for a 32-fluid-ounce can.) *Vermont Maple* is sold in stores in New York and New England; the other three brands are sold only by mail order.

The rest of the real maple syrups were very good. They sometimes had less maple flavor than the top-rated products, a caramel flavor that overpowered the maple, or a fermented or tinny taste.

Both maple blends were very good, and they were also good buys. *Giant Cane and Maple Sugar* cost only 25 cents a serving, the same as many unmaple syrups; a serving of *Steeves Maples* costs 32 cents.

Recommendations

Using a pancake syrup is cheaper. Per serving, some cost less than one-tenth as much as maple. But flavor is a lot lower, too. Nonetheless, people who have grown up with pancake syrup may think the taste is good enough. And once you've poured the syrup on pancakes, French toast, ice cream, or whatever, the sacrifice may not be as noticeable as it was to the tasters, who sipped the syrups neat. Still, the best of the imitators was rated no better than good. Often, their mock maple flavors—and off-flavors of plastic, perfume, or pencil shavings—were evident.

The top pancake syrup, *Vermont Maid,* 20 cents a serving, had 2 percent maple syrup, and its presence showed—just barely—in the taste. Five other syrups with just a dollop of maple didn't fare as well.

The water used to make the diet products "lite" and the vegetable gums that keep them thick can result in a less-sweet syrup with a gelatinous texture rather like that of raw egg whites. As a group, the diet products were lowest-rated. The best of the bunch was *Log Cabin Country Kitchen Lite*, at 16 cents a serving. The worst diet syrup—and the worst overall—was *Cary's Sugar Free*, which scored a paltry 8 points on our 100-point sensory index. If you're that concerned with keeping weight off, it might be best to skip syrup completely.

Syrup is basically sugar and water, and provides virtually nothing but calories. The pancake syrups often use salt to beef up their flavor. *Hungry Jack Lite* had the highest sodium content, 230 milligrams per 4-tablespoon serving.

SPAGHETTI

There may seem to be a large number of pasta brands on supermarket shelves these days. But, in truth, three companies make most of them: Borden (*Creamette, Prince, Luxury*, and others); Hershey (*Ronzoni, American Beauty, San Giorgio*, and others); and CPC International (*Mueller's*). Most are marketed regionally: *Prince* in Boston, *Golden Grain* in San Francisco, *Skinner* in Houston, *Luxury* in New Orleans. *Creamette* and *Mueller's* are more widely sold. In a 1992 test, *Consumer Reports* food specialists cooked a variety of packaged spaghettis. They were served, *al dente*, to an expert panel of taste testers.

They found only subtle differences. Top-rated brands like *Master Choice* and *Pathmark* had slightly more grain flavor and hardly any starchiness. Brands with more starchy flavor placed lower in the Ratings. Three had noticeable flavor flaws: *American Beauty* and *Janet Lee* had slightly fruity off-notes; *Ferrara Lite* tasted of wet cardboard. However, with the possible exception of the last brand, flavor differences between higher- and lower-rated brands weren't so great that you would notice them in the presence of a robust marinara or *fra diavolo* sauce.

One spaghetti that did taste somewhat different was *Buitoni High Protein*, the only brand with wheat germ. It had a slightly sweet and nutty bran flavor reminiscent of whole wheat.

Textural differences were subtle too. Most brands came fairly

(continued on page 240)

RATINGS

*As published in the **January 1992** issue of* **Consumer Reports**

Pancake syrups

Listed in order of overall sensory quality, based on taste tests by a trained panel.

1 Type. Pure maple syrups (**M**); blends (**B**) with 15 percent maple syrup; "unmaple" syrups (**U**) that contain little or no real maple syrup; and reduced-calorie diet syrups (**D**) were tested. Except where noted, diet syrups have about 100 calories per four-tablespoon serving, as opposed to 200 calories for the other types.

2 Sensory index. Measurement of overall sensory quality. Syrups within a few points of each other differed little in overall quality. Those with identical scores are listed alphabetically.

3 Price. The estimated average, based on prices paid nationally in 1991. For mail-order brands, the catalog price.

4 Cost per serving. Based on a four-tablespoon (two-fluid-ounce) serving.

5 Sodium. Per serving. Maple syrup naturally contains very little sodium. The unmaple syrups use salt to enhance flavor, but only a few have significant amounts of sodium. A dash indicates less than 20 mg.

6 Packaging. Glass (**G**) and metal (**M**) are easiest to recycle. High-density poly-ethylene (**PE**) is accepted at a growing number of recycling centers, but few currently recycle polypropylene (**PP**). The powdered product comes in an unrecycled-paper bag (**P**).

7 Sensory comments. Except as noted, all maple syrups had a medium-brown color and were slightly to moderately thick. Flavor was complex and delicate, with a bit more real maple flavor than caramel flavor. The maple flavor sometimes had chocolate/coffee and woody-bark notes. All maple syrups were very sweet, a bit bitter, and slightly astringent.
   Except as noted, all other syrups were medium-brown, moderately thick, and a bit slippery or gelatinous. They had no obvious real maple flavor but had a distinct imitation maple flavor with vanilla and chocolate/coffee notes. There was slightly less caramel flavor and sweetness than in a typical maple syrup, and usually a bit of saltiness.

Ratings
Continued

Product	Type [1]	Sensory index [2] Poor—Excellent (0–100)	Size, fl. oz.	Price [3]
Vermont Maple Orchards (U.S. Grade A Dark Amber)	M	● E	8½	$ 3.29
Williams-Sonoma (Vermont Fancy Grade) [1]	M	● E	32	22.00
L. L. Bean (U.S. Grade A Medium Amber) [1]	M	● E	16	7.25
The Dakin Farm (Vermont Fancy Grade) [1]	M	● E	16	8.08
Reese (U.S. Grade A Dark Amber)	M	● E	8	4.50
The Vermont Country Store (Grade A Medium Amber) [1]	M	● E	16	8.50
Camp (U.S. Grade A Dark Amber)	M	● VG–E	8½	3.07
Cary's (U.S. Grade A Dark Amber)	M	● VG–E	8	3.64
Giant Cane and Maple Sugar	B	● VG	24	2.99
The Vermont Country Store Vermont Powdered Maple [1]	M	● VG	32 [4]	15.90
American Spoon Foods—Michigan [1]	M	● VG	8	5.95
Steeves Maples	B	● VG	8⅗	1.36
Vermont Maid (2% maple)	U	● G	24	2.43
A&P Pancake & Waffle	U	● G	24	1.14
Log Cabin Country Kitchen	U	● G	24	1.90

Brand		U/D		Price
Hungry Jack (unspecified amt. of maple)		U	24	2.56
Mrs. Butterworth's (.4% butter)		U	24	2.71
Empress (Safeway) (2% maple)		U	24	1.82
Kroger (2% maple)		U	24	2.09
Cost Cutter (in Kroger stores)		U	24	1.14
Golden Griddle		U	24	2.76
Log Cabin (2% maple)		U	24	2.82
Aunt Jemima Original		U	24	2.90
Log Cabin Country Kitchen Lite		D	24	1.92
Weight Watchers		D	24	2.52
Hungry Jack Lite (unspecified amt. of maple)		D	24	2.60
Aunt Jemima Lite		D	24	2.89
Log Cabin Lite		D	24	2.82
Aunt Jemima Butter Lite		D	24	2.93
Mrs. Butterworth's Lite [2]		D	24	2.73
Karo		U	16	1.41
Cary's Sugar Free [3]		D	12	1.75

[1] Mail-order brand.

[2] 124 calories per serving.

[3] 40 calories per serving.

[4] Ounces by weight, not volume.

Phone numbers for mail-order brands:

American Spoon Foods................800-222-5886
The Dakin Farm..........................802-425-3971

L. L. Bean.................................800-221-4221
(Tel. Device for the Deaf.......800-545-0090)
The Vermont Country Store 802-362-2400
Williams-Sonoma 800-541-2233

Ratings
Continued

Product	Cost per serving [4]	Sodium, mg. [5]	Packaging [6]	Sensory comments [7]
Vermont Maple Orchards (U.S. Grade A Dark Amber)	$ .77	—	G	Clean taste, no off-flavors.
Williams-Sonoma (Vermont Fancy Grade) ⊞	1.38	—	M	Light color; clean taste, no off-flavors, mostly maple flavor, less caramel.
L. L. Bean (U.S. Grade A Medium Amber) ⊞	.91	—	PE	Hint of burned flavor.
The Dakin Farm (Vermont Fancy Grade) ⊞	1.02	—	M	Light color, mild flavor, mostly maple, less caramel.
Reese (U.S. Grade A Dark Amber)	1.13	—	G	Very slight tinny taste in some samples.
The Vermont Country Store (Grade A Medium Amber) ⊞	1.06	—	M	Mild flavor, more caramel, less maple; very slight tinny taste in some samples.
Camp (U.S. Grade A Dark Amber)	.72	—	G	Very slight fermented taste in some samples.
Cary's (U.S. Grade A Dark Amber)	.91	—	G	Very slight tinny taste in some samples.
Giant Cane and Maple Sugar	.25	—	PP	Dark brown; slight real maple flavor, mostly brown sugar/caramel, very slight burned flavor, hint of prune flavor.
The Vermont Country Store Vermont Powdered Maple ⊞	.94	—	P	Dark brown; strong overall flavor but less maple, mostly brown sugar/caramel, slight burned flavor.
American Spoon Foods—Michigan ⊞	1.49	—	PE	Dark brown; strong overall flavor but less maple, mostly molasses/caramel, slight burned flavor; bitter.
Steeves Maples	.32	—	G	Very slight real maple flavor, some imitation maple; slightly perfumy.
Vermont Maid (2% maple)	.20	20	PP	Fairly light color; close to texture of real maple syrup; very slight real maple flavor with a slight pencil-shavings taste.

Product				
A&P Pancake & Waffle	.10	40	PP	—
Log Cabin Country Kitchen	.16	40	PP	Close to texture of real maple syrup; hint of cherry.
Hungry Jack (unspecified amt. of maple)	.21	50	PP	Hints of cherry and mint.
Mrs. Butterworth's (.4% butter)	.23	64	G	Slight old-butter flavor.
Empress (Safeway) (2% maple)	.15	38	PP	Fairly light color; hints of cherry and mint.
Kroger (2% maple)	.17	46	PP	—
Cost Cutter (in Kroger stores)	.10	46	PP	Hint of mint.
Golden Griddle	.23	60	PP	Thick and sticky; a bit low in overall flavor, hint of plastic.
Log Cabin (2% maple)	.24	70	PP	Hint of mint.
Aunt Jemima Original	.24	120	PP	Hint of buttery flavor, slight pencil-shavings taste, hint of plastic.
Log Cabin Country Kitchen Lite	.16	170	PP	Slightly perfumy.
Weight Watchers	.21	160	PP	Fairly light color; slightly slippery/gelatinous; hint of cherry.
Hungry Jack Lite (unspecified amt. of maple)	.22	230	PP	Slightly slippery/gelatinous; hints of cherry and plastic.
Aunt Jemima Lite	.24	180	PP	Slightly slippery/gelatinous; hints of buttery flavor and plastic; perfumy.
Log Cabin Lite	.24	180	PP	Quite slippery/gelatinous; hint of cherry.
Aunt Jemima Butter Lite	.24	180	PP	Slightly slippery/gelatinous; slight imitation-butter flavor with hints of perfume and plastic.
Mrs. Butterworth's Lite ②	.23	126	G	Quite slippery/gelatinous; slight imitation-butter flavor.
Karo	.18	140	G	Very pale; very thick and sticky; little overall flavor.
Cary's Sugar Free ③	.29	80	PP	Light color; quite slippery/gelatinous; little overall flavor, artificial-sweetener taste; less sweet than others; slightly bitter, very slightly astringent; hint of plastic.

239

close to the ideal. Those near the bottom of the Ratings weren't "bouncy" or springy enough to the bite, or were too pasty, rather like uncooked dough, or too crumbly, falling apart into small pieces. Despite repeated attempts, the bottom three brands— *American Beauty*, *Mueller's*, and *Ferrara Lite*—couldn't be cooked al dente.

Status Starches

As pasta has become more popular, manufacturers have tried to tempt pasta lovers with refrigerated "fresh" pasta, or pasta that's more "natural" and less refined, or pasta with exotic flavors like wild mushroom. Three fresh linguines and four whole wheat pastas were included in the taste test.

Fresh linguine. Two of the bigger names in refrigerated pasta— *Contadina* and *Di Giorno*—plus an offering from an upscale New York City supermarket chain—D'Agostino—were bought and tested. *Creamette* dry linguine served as a comparison pasta. Prices for the refrigerated brands ranged from 40 to 44 cents per 5-ounce cooked serving, compared with 11 cents for the *Creamette*.

None of the fresh linguines was very good. All had a sulfurlike taste reminiscent of old eggs. *Contadina* and *Di Giornio* also tasted starchy. The grain flavor of all three was faint, which is typical of fresh pasta. *Creamette* had more grain flavor.

Texture wasn't any better than taste—the sensory panelists said that eating the stiff *Contadina* and *Di Giorno* was like chewing on rubber bands. To improve the texture, they were given longer cooking times, but they proved beyond redemption. The D'Agostino brand had its own problems—it was a little too soft and pasty, even for a fresh pasta. *Creamette* linguine could be cooked to a nice al dente.

Nutrition

Nutritionally, pasta is good food. It's low in fat and calories. The 5-ounce cooked serving that many labels recommend provides just 210 calories. Pasta also contains zero sodium, unless you add it to the cooking water. Of course, most people pour on sauce, which adds some fat, calories, sugar, and sodium. And many eat closer to 8¼ ounces of pasta when it's the main dish. Even then, pasta (and sauce) is a healthful meal.

Most packaged pastas are nutritionally similar. *Buitoni High Protein* contains 50 percent more protein than the other brands, as its package claims, but that hardly makes *Buitoni* worth a premium price. Most Americans already have an abundance of protein in their daily diet. Besides, the protein in *Buitoni* or any pasta is nutritionally incomplete. You would get more useful protein from any brand of spaghetti simply by adding cheese.

Since all pastas are nutritionally similar, manufacturers have very little to shout about. That doesn't stop some from emblazoning boxes with "sodium-free" claims or "no cholesterol" starbursts.

SPAGHETTI SAUCES

The spaghetti-sauce business is subject to the same fashion trends that have brought us Dijon mustard, home-brewed espresso, and fresh pasta. So when *Consumer Reports* tested sauces in 1992, a spaghetti sauce from a winery, *Sutter Home Italian Style with Zinfandel Wine*, as well as costly refrigerated versions made by *Contadina*, were included.

To find the best of the store-bought species, *Consumer Reports* trained panel of sensory testers tasted 48 spaghetti sauces. The products came with and without meat or "meat flavor"; spiced with onion, garlic, oregano, or basil; in textures that varied from chunky to velvet smooth; and in viscosities ranging from rather watery to something approaching ketchup. The sensory panelists also sampled three dry packaged mixes.

A Question of Style

A gourmet cook could say that sauce is an artistic creation, with many interpretations but no definition. Take the word "marinara," roughly translated from the Italian as "sailor style." Several manufacturers were asked how their marinara sauce differed

(*continued on page 244*)

RATINGS

As published in the May 1992 issue of Consumer Reports

Spaghetti

Listed in order of overall sensory quality. Products within a few points of each other were similar in quality. Those with equal scores are listed alphabetically.

1 Product. The only national brand, *Creamette*, and 23 regional brands were tested. Four of the tested brands are imports: *Spigadoro*, *Da Vinci*, *De Cecco* and *Ferrara Lite*. Several more are supermarket brands. Some supermarket brands come from more than one supplier. The tested *Town House* was bought in California, the *Janet Lee* in Louisiana

and Texas. The same brands from other parts of the country may differ in quality.

2 Sensory index. How close each tested product came to the criteria for excellence, based on measurements by the trained sensory panel. To score well, a product had to both exhibit good qualities (such as bounciness and a mild grain flavor) and be free of flaws (such as a very pale color, off-notes, pastiness).

3 Price. The estimated average, based on prices paid nationally in 1991. Four brands—*Pathmark*, *Prince*, *Shop Rite*, and *A & P*—earned Best Buy status for their combination of high quality and low price.

Note that pasta is often a sale item; you may find other high-rated brands at even better prices.

4 Cost per serving. For a five-ounce serving of cooked spaghetti.

5 Sensory comments. Except as noted, spaghettis were cream or pale yellow in color, with a mild grain and very slight starchy flavor. Cooked al dente, they had a very slight starchy mouthfeel, were slightly bouncy and moderately firm, sheared cleanly between the teeth, and became only a little bit pasty when chewed. Sensory differences were small but, in general, the lower the score, the less bouncy, firm, clean-shearing, and grainy flavored the spaghetti.

1 Product	2 Sensory index Poor—Excellent P F G VG E	Size, oz.	3 Price	4 Cost per serving	5 Sensory comments
Master Choice No. 8		16	$ .84	11¢	Bouncy; full grain flavor.
Pathmark No. 8, A Best Buy		16	$ .55	7	Bouncy; full grain flavor.
Kroger		16	.74	9	—
Prince, A Best Buy		16	.50	6	Bouncy.

242

Product		oz	$	cents/oz	Comments
Buitoni High Protein		8	.92	23	Beige color; thick strands; quite bouncy; distinct grain flavor; whole wheat and nutty/bran character; very slightly astringent.
Golden Grain		16	.99	12	—
Shop Rite No. 8, A Best Buy		16	.58	7	—
A & P No. 6, A Best Buy		16	.58	7	—
San Giorgio No. 8		16	.67	8	Bouncy.
Ronzoni No. 8		16	.71	9	—
Spigadoro No. 3		16	.70	9	Paler color.
Creamette Italian Style		16	.90	11	—
Da Vinci		16	.86	11	—
Anthonys La Paloma		16	.86	11	Thin strands.
Luxury No. 4		16	.81	10	A bit less bouncy.
Lady Lee		16	.89	11	A bit less bouncy.
Skinner		12	.78	13	—
De Cecco No. 12		16	1.41	18	Thick strands.
Town House Long		16	.90	11	Slight fruity off-note.
Ravarino & Freschi (R*F)		12	.68	11	Thick strands; doesn't shear cleanly.
Janet Lee Long		12	.68	11	Somewhat thick strands; a bit pasty; slight fruity off-note.
American Beauty		24	1.29	11	Somewhat thick strands; a bit less bouncy; a bit pasty; starchy flavor; with slight fruity off-note.
Mueller's		16	.66	8	Paler color; a bit less bouncy, doesn't shear cleanly, a bit pasty; starchy and low grain flavor.
Ferrara Lite 2 Minute Pasta		16	1.23	15	Paler color; thin strands, becomes sticky quickly; soft, not very bouncy, a bit crumbly, not pasty; low grain flavor, slight wet-cardboard note.

from a plain meatless spaghetti sauce. Each gave a different answer. Ragù said its marinara has a more distinctive olive-oil flavor. Prego's marinara contains no corn-syrup sweetener. Contadina said its marinara is "traditional" and contains anchovies. And *Newman's Own Venetian Marinara* is identical to its regular spaghetti sauce. As a result, the Ratings include all the meatless and marinara sauces in one group.

The Ratings divide the sauces into meatless and meat types because they are fundamentally different products. The sauces are further divided into three styles, depending primarily on how long the tomato base was judged to have been cooked:

- *Long-cooked* sauces were generally thick, hearty, and sweet, with a notable flavor of basil or oregano, or both. They were a bit reminiscent of tomato paste.
- *Moderately cooked* sauces were less sweet, generally a little thinner, and exhibited a blended spice flavor. They were reminiscent of tomato puree.
- *Slightly cooked* sauces were more like a crushed-tomato product or even like a ratatouille, with small chunks of tomato swimming in a thin base. The fundamental flavor was a bit more like uncooked tomato than were the other sauces.

The words on the label are not an infallible guide to what you find in the jar. Terms like "homestyle" and "thick and hearty" are common. Those essentially nondescriptive adjectives often denote a thick, long-cooked sauce. "Original" and "traditional" usually turns out to mean a slightly thinner, moderately cooked sauce. With the canned *Hunt's* brands, though, it was the other way around: *Hunt's Traditional* was the hearty one while *Hunt's Homestyle Traditional* was thinner.

Consider the Sauce

To test the spaghetti sauces, trained tasters sampled the freshly heated sauces neat, without pasta. Their sensory descriptions of each product were then compared statistically with the profile of an "ideal" sauce.

The testers expected a sauce to have a moderately intense to-mato flavor. They also looked for a well-blended balance of what-ever spices, vegetables, cheese, or other ingredients were used. Points were taken off if some flavor overwhelmed the others, or for a flavor flaw, such as the taste of stale, dried onion or garlic.

Other features that could earn a sauce negative points: a self-proclaimed "chunky" sauce that lacked chunks, a sauce calling itself garlic- and basil-flavored but tasting of neither garlic nor basil, or a sauce that looked greasy or gelatinous.

The standards for meat sauce were similar to those for meatless products, including flavors associated with freshly cooked meat and meat juices. (Under federal regulations, a sauce has to con-tain at least 6 percent meat to call itself a meat sauce. Anything less is "meat flavored.") *Consumer Reports* thinks these sauces should contain identifiable meat or at least have a meat flavor. That was not normally the case. Most contained very small quan-tities of finely ground meat that tasted overprocessed, like canned meat, if it tasted of anything at all. It was usually impossible even to tell the origin of the meat—beef or pork—without looking at the label.

The dry mixes—aimed at people who want a packet of pre-mixed spices to add to a basic tomato sauce—were the most dis-appointing.

How Nutritious?

Spaghetti sauce is a reasonably good source of vitamins A and C. In most sauces, the calories come mainly from carbohydrates. The meatless sauces contain no cholesterol, and even the meat sauces contain cholesterol in negligible quantities—testimony to the paucity of meat. In fact, the nutritional profiles of meatless and "meat" sauces were virtually identical.

Spaghetti sauce tends to contain a good deal of salt, averaging about 540 milligrams of sodium in the 4-ounce serving most la-bels recommend. (Note that most people eat larger servings of sauce—about 6 ounces—when serving pasta as a main dish.) For people on a sodium-restricted diet, a regular spaghetti sauce is something to avoid. Two low-sodium sauces, *Prego No Salt Added* and *Pritikin Original,* were also tested. Since salt is a flavor enhancer, it's tough to forgo it and have a full-flavored sauce. Instead, the two sauces tasted a bit "hollow." Nonetheless, for low-salt sauces, both were fairly good.

Tomato products naturally contain large amounts of sugars. For instance, half a cup of tomato paste contains the equivalent of 4 teaspoons of table sugar. During cooking, many manufacturers (and some home cooks) add additional sweeteners. A glance at the labels tells us that commercial sauces often contain added corn syrup, dextrose, or sugar. In fact, a 4-ounce serving of the tested sauces contains the equivalent of 1½ teaspoons of sugar. People on a sugar-restricted diet should probably avoid spaghetti sauces. That includes the diet-brand *Pritikin Originals,* which list fruit juice concentrate as an ingredient. As far as the body is concerned, that's the same as sugar. (The Ratings note sauces that contain no added sugars.)

Although spaghetti sauce is a fairly low calorie food to start with, Weight Watchers tries to lower it even more. *Weight Watchers* meat-flavored sauce is indeed low in fat, and the nutrition label lists calories at only 50 per serving. However, it accomplishes that by using a nonstandard serving size of only one-third cup. In a standard 4-ounce serving (about a half cup) *Weight Watchers* delivers 73 calories—about the same as many brands that do not tout themselves as diet sauces. *Weight Watchers* is also quite high in sodium—646 milligrams per 4-ounce serving.

If fat is a concern, several products could take the place of the two diet sauces. *Aunt Millie's Family Style Chunky Tomato & Italian Spices* and *Master Choice Pomodoro* did better than the diet brands in the sensory tests, and they have little fat. If both fat and sodium are considerations, you might consider *Enrico's,* a Best Buy.

Recommendations

None of the sauces earned excellent scores. Excellence would have required—at least—fresh ingredients, unlikely to be found in a commercial preparation. But many of the meatless sauces were very good, if a little too sweet.

Three Ragù products topped the Ratings: *Chunky Gardenstyle Extra Tomatoes, Garlic & Onion, Slow-Cooked Homestyle Tomato &*

(continued on page 252)

RATINGS

As published in the **May 1992** issue of **Consumer Reports**

Spaghetti sauce

Listed by types; within types, listed in order of overall sensory quality. Sauces within a few points of each other were similar in quality. Those with equal scores are listed alphabetically.

1 Product. The first group comprises meatless sauces, variously known as plain, meatless, or marinara. Sauces with meat or meat flavoring as a group fared less well than meatless varieties. All sauces come in a glass jar unless otherwise noted.

2 Style. The sauces were categorized according to how long-cooked the tomato base seemed to the tasters. For the most part that assessment also indicated the texture and consistency of the sauce. Long-cooked (**L**) sauces tended to be thick and sweet, with a notable herb flavor. Moderately cooked (**M**) styles were thinner and less sweet, with a blend of spices. Slightly cooked (**S**) sauces were notably thin and less sweet, and contained chunks of tomato and, often, of onion.

3 Sensory index. The score here shows how close each product came to the criteria for excellence, based on measurements by our trained sensory panel. To score well, a sauce had to exhibit good flavor and texture and be free of such defects as off-tastes or a greasy or congealed appearance.

4 Price. Except as noted, these are estimated national averages, based on prices paid in 1991. An * denotes the price paid. *Hunt's Traditional* earned Best Buy status for its combination of high quality and low price.

5 Per serving. Testers used a four-ounce serving, suggested on many labels (but note that surveyed readers said they often use more—perhaps six ounces). **Cost** was usually less than 27 cents for four ounces. **Calories** averaged about 80. **Sodium** is based on manufacturers' information and was spot-checked by *Consumer Reports.*

6 Sensory comments. Except as noted, descriptions in **"Style"** (above) apply. Beyond that, meatless sauces usually had a moderate tomato, herb/spice, and onion/garlic flavor, with only small quantities of finely ground tomato. Chunky sauces had small chunks of tomato and onion. As the comments show, most meat and meat-flavored sauces contained little meat and had little meat flavor. A few had a processed-meat flavor, almost like canned meat.

---

1 *Now available as* **Ragù Fino Italian.**
2 *Packaged in a can.*
3 *Contains no added sugars.*
4 *Now available as* **Contadina Plum Tomato.**
5 *Packaged in a plastic tub.*
6 *Now available as* **Contadina Marinara.**

Ratings
Continued

[1] Product	[2] Style	[3] Sensory index (Poor—Excellent: P F G VG E)	Size, oz.	[4] Price
Meatless sauces				
Ragù Chunky Gardenstyle Extra Tomatoes	M	VG	30	$1.75
Ragù Slow-Cooked Homestyle Tomato/Herbs [1]	L	VG	28	1.91
Ragù Fresh Italian Tomato & Herbs [1]	S	VG	28	1.73
Hunt's Traditional, A Best Buy [2]	L	VG	27½	1.04
Enrico's	L	VG	32	2.85
Prego Extra Chunky Tomato, Onion & Garlic	L	VG	30	1.84
Progresso Marinara [3]	S	VG	15½	1.47
Aunt Millie's Family Style Italian Spices	L	VG	26	1.63
Aunt Millie's Traditional [3]	M	VG	26	1.60
Master Choice Pomodoro	L	VG	32	1.74
Ragù Thick & Hearty	L	VG	30¾	1.71
Aunt Millie's Marinara [3]	M	VG	26	1.56
Prego	L	VG	30	1.82
Contadina Fresh Plum Tomato with Basil [3][4][5]	S	VG	15	3.67
Progresso	S	G	32	1.50
Francesco Rinaldi Marinara	M	G	30	1.76
Newman's Own Venetian/Marinara	M	G	26	2.34
Classico di Napoli Tomato & Basil [3]	S	G	26	2.45
Prego Marinara-Style [3]	M	G	29	1.92
Shop Rite [3]	M	G	32	1.05
Contadina Fresh Marinara [3][5][6]	S	G	15	3.61
Ragù Old World Style	M	G	30	1.90

Product	Size		Oz	Price
A & P Traditional Italian Style	M		26	1.46
Francesco Rinaldi	M		30	1.75
Ragù Old World Style Meatless Marinara [3]	M		30	1.84
Prego No Salt Added [3]	M		29	1.82
Pritikin Original	L		16	2.11
Hunt's Homestyle Traditional [2][3]	M		27	1.04
Sinatra Milano Style Marinara [3]	S		25	2.16
Buitoni Family Style	M		32	2.12*
Kroger Chunky Style With Extra Tomato	M		30	1.89
Sutter Home Italian Style with Zinfandel Wine	L		16	2.92
Town House	M		32	1.38
Kroger Traditional	M		30	1.78

Meat and meat-flavored sauces

Product	Size		Oz	Price
Ragù Thick & Hearty	L		30¾	1.68
Master Choice Bolognese	L		32	1.73
Prego	L		30	1.80
Hunt's [2]	L		27½	1.03
Aunt Millie's [3]	M		26	1.57
Progresso	S		32	1.46
Shop Rite	M		32	1.06
Francesco Rinaldi	M		30	1.73
Weight Watchers [3]	M		15	1.73
Classico D'Abruzzi Beef & Pork [3]	M		26	2.48
Ragù Old World Style	M		30	1.89
Kroger Homestyle	M		48	2.22
Town House	M		32	1.53
Chef Boyardee With Meat [2]	—		15	0.95

1 Product	Cost	Calories	Sodium	6 Sensory comments
			5 Per serving	
Meatless sauces				
Ragù Chunky Gardenstyle Extra Tomatoes	23¢	70	440 mg.	Well-balanced, with notable sautéed-onion flavor; very chunky.
Ragù Slow-Cooked Homestyle Tomato/Herbs	27	110	510	Distinct basil, sweet; chunky.
Ragù Fresh Italian Tomato & Herbs 1	25	90	490	Notable tomato, distinct basil, a bit too sweet; very chunky; seeds.
Hunt's Traditional, A Best Buy 2	15	70	530	Distinct tomato/basil.
Enrico's	36	60	345	Notable tomato, hint oregano/basil; smooth.
Prego Extra Chunky Tomato, Onion & Garlic	25	110	500	Notable sautéed-onion, distinct basil, sweet; very chunky.
Progresso Marinara 3	38	82	472	Slight cheese, mild tomato, hint olive oil; seeds, small chunks.
Aunt Millie's Family Style Italian Spices	25	80	600	Distinct oregano/basil.
Aunt Millie's Traditional 3	25	60	290	Slight oregano, less salty.
Master Choice Pomodoro	22	70	725	Distinct oregano/basil; chunky.
Ragù Thick & Hearty	22	100	460	Long-cooked tomato, basil, a bit too sweet; very thick, chunky.
Aunt Millie's Marinara 3	24	60	320	Mostly tomato; smooth.
Prego	24	130	630	Distinct basil, sweet.
Contadina Fresh Plum Tomato with Basil 3 4 5	98	64	336	Underripe tomato, hint fresh basil and cream; very chunky but watery.
Progresso	19	100	599	Mild tomato, distinct garlic and cheese, hint olive oil; seeds, chunky.
Francesco Rinaldi Marinara	23	70	680	Hint basil and fennel-like flavor; smooth.
Newman's Own Venetian/Marinara	36	70	630	Salty, hint fennel-like flavor; big chunks.
Classico di Napoli Tomato & Basil 3	38	60	340	Slight garlic, no obvious basil, hint olive oil; big chunks.
Prego Marinara-Style 3	26	100	620	Notably sour.
Shop Rite 3	13	70	580	Little herb/spice, hint cheese, salty; smooth.
Contadina Fresh Marinara 3 5 6	96	64	368	Underripe tomato; anchovy, garlic and olive oil; very chunky but watery.
Ragù Old World Style	25	80	740	Little herb/spice, slight cheese, salty; smooth and thin.

				little herb/spice, salty; very smooth
Francesco Rinaldi	23	70	630	Slightly low tomato, little herb/spice, distinct cheese, salty; smooth.
Ragù Old World Style Meatless Marinara [3]	25	80	740	Slightly low tomato, little herb/spice, strong olive, salty; smooth, thin.
Prego No Salt Added [3]	25	110	25	Distinct oregano/basil, a bit "hollow," not salty; chunky.
Pritikin Original	53	60	35	Strong oregano, a bit "hollow," slightly sweet, not salty.
Hunt's Homestyle Traditional [2][3]	15	60	530	Dried-onion/garlic, sour, salty.
Sinatra Milano Style Marinara [3]	35	60	390	Mild tomato, dried-onion, sour; very chunky.
Buitoni Family Style	27	64	680	Slightly low tomato, dried-onion, little herb/spice; chunky.
Kroger Chunky Style With Extra Tomato	25	77	560	Low tomato, dried-onion/garlic, fennel-like flavor; starchy.
Sutter Home Italian Style with Zinfandel Wine	73	100	520	Slightly low tomato, distinct oregano, sour vinegar, bitter; very chunky.
Town House	17	80	710	Slightly low tomato, little herb/spice, "soapy" cheese, salty; smooth.
Kroger Traditional	24	77	760	Low tomato, celery, dried-onion, sour, salty, starchy, congeals.
Meat and meat-flavored sauces				
Ragù Thick & Hearty	22	120	460	Notable tomato, distinct basil; little meat; a bit too sweet; chunky.
Master Choice Bolognese	22	90	721	Distinct oregano/basil, little meat; chunky.
Prego	24	140	660	Distinct basil, little meat, sweet.
Hunt's [2]	15	70	570	Slight processed-meat; some small soft meat bits.
Aunt Millie's [3]	24	60	270	Slight oregano/basil and processed-meat; some soft meat bits.
Progresso	18	100	599	Distinct cheese and garlic, hint olive oil, very low meat; chunky, thin.
Shop Rite	13	90	550	Very slight cheese, very low meat, salty; smooth.
Francesco Rinaldi	23	70	650	Distinct cheese, little meat, salty; slightly greasy-looking; smooth.
Weight Watchers [3]	46	73	646	Distinct black-pepper, slight processed-meat, bitter; thick, smooth.
Classico D'Abruzzi Beef & Pork [3]	38	80	540	Low tomato, processed-meat, salty; thin, chunky, a bit greasy, many soft meat pellets.
Ragù Old World Style	25	80	740	Low tomato, dried-onion, slight processed-meat, salty, thin, smooth, a bit greasy.
Kroger Homestyle	19	85	615	Low tomato, little meat; dried-onion, celery; starchy, thick, congeals.
Town House	19	80	710	Low tomato, "soapy" cheese, little meat, very salty; smooth.
Chef Boyardee With Meat [2]	25	96	642	Little tomato, processed-meat, starchy; a bit greasy and gel-like, with small soft meat bits.

Herbs, and *Fresh Italian Tomato & Herbs* (now called *Fino Italian*). Those three were closely followed by *Hunt's Traditional, Enrico's,* and *Prego Extra Chunky Tomato, Onion & Garlic.* Among the brands rated very good are all three "styles" of sauce—from slightly cooked to long-cooked. You might choose among them by looking for the overall flavor and texture characteristics you prefer.

Note that a brand name alone is no guide: Some *Ragù, Prego,* and *Hunt's* brandmasters (*Ragù Old World Style, Prego No Salt Added,* and *Hunt's Homestyle Traditional*) finished farther down in the Ratings.

Meat sauces fared less well as a class, largely because the meat flavors (such as they were) detracted from the overall taste. Some products had virtually no meat flavor. If you like meat in your sauce, choose a high-rated meatless sauce and add freshly browned meat.

The Ratings list many spaghetti sauces that were considered very good, but that doesn't necessarily mean everyone will like them. The style descriptions and the sensory comments can help you find a product with flavor and texture characteristics you might like. Even the lowest-rated sauce, *Chef Boyardee with Meat,* might be just the thing for someone who was raised on it—although most people would fail to appreciate its greasy, gel-like appearance, starchy mouthfeel, and processed-meat flavor.

The sauces from the stars were not star quality: *Newman's Own* was middling; *Sinatra Milano Style Marinara,* only fair.

A few products have gourmet cachet—and price. The refrigerated *Contadina* sauces come in plastic tubs and cost about $1 per single 4-ounce serving. Only a little less expensive is the sauce from the wine maker, *Sutter Home Italian Style with Zinfandel Wine.* Neither brand is very high in the Ratings.

As if to underscore the point that a good sauce needn't be costly, one top-rated brand, *Hunt's Traditional,* was also among the cheapest: 15 cents per serving. It was judged a Best Buy.

TEA

Nearly all the nonherbal tea we consume in the United States is known as black tea. There are dozens of varieties, from English breakfast to Earl Grey to Darjeeling, not to mention the orange pekoes of perennial top sellers like *Lipton* and *Tetley*. Many black teas have decaffeinated versions meant to capture the market for kinder, gentler tea now served by the herbals, which have no caffeine.

In 1992, *Consumer Reports* expert panel of sensory testers tasted 78 brands of tea—both bagged and loose, with caffeine and without. They concentrated on plain black teas but also looked at flavored black teas—citrus, mint, and Earl Grey varieties. They didn't neglect herbal teas, spice-and-herb blends such as citrus, chamomile, and mint. And they also tasted some powdered instant teas and iced-tea mixes.

The Perfect Cup

Some tea purists insist that you can't get a good cup of tea from a tea bag. *Consumer Reports* tasters disagree. They found half a dozen or more very good tea-bag teas, including *Red Rose, Crown Colony* (a Safeway store brand), *Lipton, Salada, Twinings Orange Pekoe, Celestial Seasonings Organically Grown*, and *Nestea*. That's not to say bagged tea is always best, though. The highest-scoring Darjeeling was a loose tea, *McNulty's Golden*, from a specialty shop in New York City.

Sometimes real differences were found between bagged and loose versions of the same brand. The loose *Tetley* was a much better product than *Tetley* in bags. The bagged *Tetley* was variable: Some samples were slightly ashy, and the floral and tea notes dipped and peaked. But both the *Lipton* and the *Twinings* regular teas tasted very good in both bag and loose form.

Evidently it's easier for tea formulators to cope with lemon flavor than orange. Typically, the orange in an "orange and spice" variety was overwhelmed by the brown-spice flavors.

Decaffeination takes a toll, too. Almost all of the decaffeinated versions of regular black teas had less flavor and a weaker body than the original. The flavored-tea selection turned up a notable exception: Among Earl Grey teas, the decaffeinated *Twinings* in bags tasted better than *Twinings Earl Grey* with caffeine, whether the tea was loose or bagged.

RATINGS

As published in the July 1992 issue of Consumer Reports

Tea

Listed by types; within types, listed in order of overall sensory quality. Products within a few points of each other were similar in overall quality, though not necessarily close in flavor. Products with equal scores are listed alphabetically.

1 Style. Either loose (L) or in bags (B).

2 Sensory index. On a scale of 0 to 100. None was excellent, but many were very good. Testers used different criteria of excellence for each type of tea, so the scores for black tea, say, are not directly comparable to those for herbal tea.

3 Package size. For loose tea, the ounces in the bag, box, or tin were listed; for bagged tea, the number of tea bags per box.

4 Cost per cup. A calculation based on the cost of one teaspoonful for the loose teas and one tea bag for the bagged teas. Figures are derived from national average prices paid in 1992, except those marked with an *, which are derived from prices paid by Consumer Reports.

5 Sensory comments. An excellent black tea should have a slight to moderate sweet, fermented tea aroma and flavor with slight floral top notes. A barely perceptible green, grassy note or aroma of citrus or perfume is acceptable as long as it's well blended with the base tea flavor. The tea should have a full body (not seem watery) and be slightly to moderately bitter and astringent. It shouldn't exhibit such defects as an ashy, earthy, vegetative, or other foreign flavor.

Darjeeling tea should be further distinguished by more notable floral top notes and a subtler base

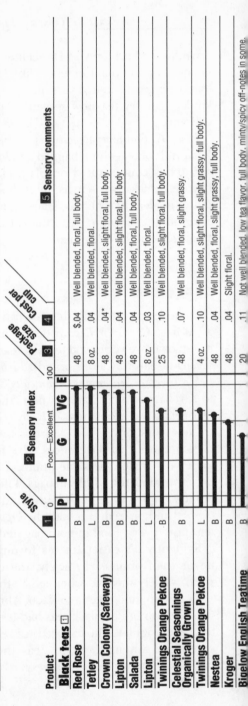

Product	1 Style	2 Sensory index	3 Package size	4 Cost per cup	5 Sensory comments
Black teas 1					
Red Rose	B		48	$.04	Well blended, floral, full body.
Tetley	L		8 oz.	.04	Well blended, floral.
Crown Colony (Safeway)	B		48	.04*	Well blended, slight floral, full body.
Lipton	B		48	.04	Well blended, slight floral, full body.
Salada	B		48	.04	Well blended, floral, full body.
Lipton	L		8 oz.	.03	Well blended, floral.
Twinings Orange Pekoe	B		25	.10	Well blended, slight floral, full body.
Celestial Seasonings Organically Grown	B		48	.07	Well blended, floral, slight grassy.
Twinings Orange Pekoe	L		4 oz.	.10	Well blended, slight floral, slight grassy, full body.
Nestea	B		48	.04	Well blended, floral, slight grassy, full body.
Kroger	B		48	.04	Slight floral.
Bigelow English Teatime	B		20	.11	Not well blended, low tea flavor, full body, minty/spicy off-notes in some.

254

Product	Type	Rating	Size	Price	Comments
Our Own [2]	B		48	.02*	Slight ashy flavor in some samples.
Tetley	B		48	.04	Variable floral and tea, some samples slight ashy.
Lipton Decaf	B		48	.06	Not well blended, earthy/vegetative.
Red Rose Decaf	B		48	.06	Earthy/vegetative.
Pathmark	B		50	.02	Low tea taster, slight grassy, some samples slight earthy.
Tetley Decaf	B		48	.05	Not well blended, earthy/vegetative, weak body.
Our Own Decaf [2]	B		48	.05*	Earthy/vegetative, weak body.
Celestial Seasonings Organically Grown Decaf	B		48	.07	Earthy/vegetative.
Pathmark Decaf	B		48	.05	Slight sweet aromatic in some, weak body.
Salada Decaf	B		48	.05	Weak body.
Luzianne Decaf	B		48	.05	Not well blended, vegetative, weak body.
Bigelow Decaf	B		16	.14	Not well blended, vegetative, weak body.
American Classic	B		20	.09	Off-flavor like almond extract.
Luzianne	B		48	.04	Not well blended, ashy off-flavor.
Kroger Decaf	B		48	.05	Not well blended, weak body, slightly earthy/vegetative.
Darjeeling teas					
McNulty's Golden [3]	L		8 oz.	.12	Well blended, floral, some slight grassy, full body.
Master Choice [2]	B		25	.08	Well blended, citrus/floral, slight grassy, full body.
Jackson's	L		4 oz.	.09	Well blended, citrus/floral, slight smoky, full body.
Bigelow	B		20	.11	Well blended, floral, full body.
Jackson's	B		25	.07	Well blended, floral, some slight smoky, full body.
Twinings	B		25	.10	Well blended, floral, full body.
English Breakfast teas					
Celestial Seasonings	B		24	.09	Well blended, "hearty," floral.
Jackson's	B		25	.08	Well blended, "hearty," some with ashy flavor.
Twinings	B		25	.10	Well blended, "hearty," floral.
Lipton	B		48	.05	Well blended, "hearty," floral.
Master Choice [2]	B		25	.07	Well blended, "hearty," slight floral, smoky, slight grassy.
Twinings	L		8 oz.	.09	Well blended, floral, astringent, full body, some smoky.
Stash [3]	B		20	.11	Ashy, astringent, not well blended.
Twinings Decaf	B		18	.14	Earthy/vegetative, not well blended, some "painty."

Ratings
Continued

tea aroma and flavor. English Breakfast tea should be what we call "heartier" (more bitter, astringent, and full-bodied) than regular black tea.

The added flavor in mint, citrus, and Earl Grey teas should be clean and full; it should be identifiable but should not overpower the basic tea aro-

matics. The bergamot in Earl Grey, for instance, should be a balanced blend of citrus, floral, and piney rather than mostly piney.

Except as noted, all black and flavored black teas had a moderately intense tea aroma and flavor, were slightly to moderately bitter and astringent, and were moderate in body and in blendedness. Except as noted, decafs were low in flavor, bitterness, and astringency.

An excellent herbal tea has a slightly to moder-

ately intense clean and balanced flavor, with slightly weak body. It is slightly astringent but not bitter. The primary flavor—lemon or whatever—is clean and prominent but not overwhelming. Any mix of flavors should blend well. Except as noted, all herbal teas were slightly astringent but not bitter, moderately well blended, and fairly weak-bodied.

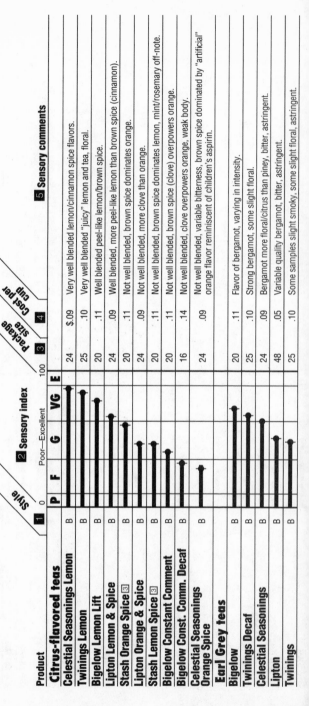

Product	1 Style	2 Sensory index (Poor—Excellent)	3 Package size	4 Cost per cup	5 Sensory comments
Citrus-flavored teas					
Celestial Seasonings Lemon	B		24	$.09	Very well blended lemon/cinnamon spice flavors.
Twinings Lemon	B		25	.10	Very well blended "juicy" lemon and tea, floral.
Bigelow Lemon Lift	B		20	.11	Well blended peel-like lemon/brown spice.
Lipton Lemon & Spice	B		24	.09	Well blended, more peel-like lemon than brown spice (cinnamon).
Stash Orange Spice ③	B		20	.11	Not well blended, brown spice dominates orange.
Lipton Orange & Spice	B		24	.09	Not well blended, more clove than orange.
Stash Lemon Spice ③	B		20	.11	Not well blended, brown spice dominates lemon, mint/rosemary off-note.
Bigelow Constant Comment	B		20	.11	Not well blended, brown spice (clove) overpowers orange.
Bigelow Const. Comm. Decaf	B		16	.14	Not well blended, clove overpowers orange, weak body.
Celestial Seasonings Orange Spice	B		24	.09	Not well blended, variable bitterness, brown spice dominated by "artificial" orange flavor reminiscent of children's aspirin.
Earl Grey teas					
Bigelow	B		20	.11	Flavor of bergamot, varying in intensity.
Twinings Decaf	B		25	.10	Strong bergamot, some slight floral.
Celestial Seasonings	B		24	.09	Bergamot more floral/citrus than piney, bitter, astringent.
Lipton	B		48	.05	Variable quality bergamot, bitter, astringent.
Twinings	B		25	.10	Some samples slight smoky, some slight floral, astringent.

Tea				Comments
Stash [3]	B		20	.11	Low bergamot, slight fermented apple off-note.
Bigelow Decaf	B		16	.14	Variable bergamot, slight vegetative, low tea, weak body.
Jackson's	B		25	.08	Slight ashy/smoky, low bergamot, bitter.
Twinings	L		8 oz.	.08	Intense bergamot, more piney than citrus, not well blended.
Master Choice [2]	B		25	.07	Very low bergamot, bitter, astringent.
Mint-flavored teas					
Lipton	B		24	.10*	Well blended spearmint/peppermint, bitter.
Bigelow Plantation	B		20	.11	Well blended spearmint.
Celestial Seasonings	B		24	.09	A bit more spearmint/peppermint, less well blended.
Citrus herbal teas					
Lipton Lemon Soother	B		24	.08	Well blended, peel-like lemon, slight sour.
Celest. Seas. Lemon Zinger	B		24	.09	Well blended, slight peel-like lemon, slight sour.
Lipton Gentle Orange	B		24	.08	Orange peel, slight grainy, brown spice, not well blended.
Bigelow Orange & Spice	B		20	.10	More brown spice than orange, not well blended.
Celestial Seasonings Mandarin Orange Spice	B		24	.09	Strong clove, slight orange, sharp sour note, not well blended.
Good Earth Orange Spice	B		30	.08	Strong clove, slight grainy, very slight orange, not well blended.
Chamomile herbal teas					
Celest. Seas. Chamomile	B		24	.09	Well blended, slight chamomile (applelike), slight grainy.
Master Choice Chamomile [2]	B		20	.09	Well blended, slight chamomile, slight grainy.
Stash Chamomile [3]	B		20	.12	Well blended, slight chamomile.
Lipton Quietly Chamomile	B		24	.09	Slight chamomile, slight grainy, slight citrus/orange peel.
Mint herbal teas					
Stash Peppermint [3]	B		20	.11	Very well blended peppermint, cooling mouthfeel.
Celest. Seas. Peppermint	B		24	.09	Very well blended peppermint, cooling mouthfeel.
Celest. Seas. Sleepytime	B		24	.09	Slight chamomile and spearmint, very slight grainy.
Bigelow Mint Medley	B		20	.10	Slight peppermint, slight musty, not well blended.

[1] Many characterize themselves as pekoe, orange pekoe, pekoe cut, and the like.
[2] Available at A&P, Food Emporium, Waldbaums, Super Fresh, and other stores.
[3] Available by mail order. McNulty's: 800-356-5200; Stash: 800-826-4218.

Caffeine

Black tea contains approximately 60 milligrams of caffeine per 6-ounce cup, compared with 100 milligrams or so for a cup of brewed coffee. Decaffeinated regular teas contain about 7 milligrams per cup—a negligible amount. (Herbal teas contain no caffeine at all.)

Tea is decaffeinated by methods similar to those used for coffee, which nowadays usually involves treating the leaves with pressurized carbon dioxide or a natural solvent that draws out the caffeine. Neither process leaves a harmful residue.

There's a popular notion that you can limit the caffeine in tea by limiting the brew time, but that's not realistic. In *Consumer Reports* food lab, a bagged tea was brewed and tested for caffeine at 30-second intervals. It turned out that 75 percent of the caffeine was infused out of the leaves within the first 30 seconds and 95 percent within two minutes. Since it takes three to five minutes to brew a decent cup, withholding the tea doesn't cheat the devil.

Cost

Tea is not a costly commodity. *Consumer Reports* found supermarket brands (*Pathmark* and A&P's *Our Own*) selling for as little as 2 cents a cup. At the other end of the spectrum were some upscale names like *Twinings* and *Bigelow* that worked out to 14 cents per cup.

Plenty of good-tasting teas, including most of the top-rated brands, cost 4 or 5 cents a cup—still not exactly a budget buster. Buying in bulk usually saves money, but since tea doesn't stay fresh for long, don't buy more than you plan to consume in a month or two. Keep your tea in an airtight container away from heat.

CANNED TUNA

Canned tuna consistently tops the charts as the most-eaten seafood in America, far ahead of the runners-up, shrimp and cod. The quality of canned tuna, however, has dropped in recent years. High bacterial counts are not a problem; canning's high processing temperatures kill virtually all bacteria. And mercury, a potential hazard in swordfish, is generally within a safe range in tuna. But about half the samples tested for a 1992 article in *Consumer Reports* were contaminated with filth, primarily debris from insects, rodents, and birds—"extraneous matter" that the industry had virtually eliminated when *Consumer Reports* last tested tuna in 1979. Although this contamination does not pose a clear health hazard, it does suggest that overall sanitation in tuna canneries—most of which are now outside the United States—is not up to snuff.

For the tests, *Consumer Reports* shoppers bought 41 cans of tuna from around the country; solid and chunk, white and light, in oil and in water. (White tuna, the more expensive variety, is pure albacore, whereas light tuna is a mixture of different species of tunafish.) In addition to the three big national tuna brands— *Bumble Bee, Chicken of the Sea,* and *StarKist*—smaller brands like *Carnation, Empress, Geisha,* and *3 Diamonds* were sampled, as well as several supermarket labels. Besides testing the fish for cleanliness, the samples were evaluated for appearance and taste.

Tuna Nutrition

Canned tuna has much to recommend it nutritionally.

It's very rich in protein. Three ounces of solid white tuna in water—about half a can—supplies more than 20 grams of protein. That's close to half a day's requirement for an adult. If the tuna is packed in water, that serving will contain only about 100 calories, roughly 85 percent of them from protein. (Chunk light tuna in water typically contains slightly less protein and fewer calories than solid white, because the space between chunks makes for a bit more liquid and less fish.)

When the processor adds vegetable oil, however, the calories and fat increase. Tuna in water supplies just a gram or two of fat per serving, roughly 10 to 15 calories' worth. By contrast, three ounces of chunk tuna in oil, drained, contains eight grams of fat, which account for nearly half of the serving's 155 calories. If you eat the oil-packed tuna *undrained*, though, you'll get 235 calories, close to 70 percent of them from fat. Draining a can of oil-packed tuna and then adding a tablespoon or more of mayonnaise per serving, as many people do, will make the fat and calorie count higher than it would be if it hadn't been drained at all. (A serving of any canned tuna also provides about 35 milligrams of cholesterol, roughly one-tenth of a day's recommended intake.)

Even without oil, tuna does contain some natural fat, but that fat may be beneficial. The fat of tuna, like that found in sardines and salmon, supplies omega-3 fatty acids, which research suggests may benefit the heart and circulatory system. White tuna is an especially rich source, supplying 650 milligrams per serving; light tuna offers only one-fourth as much. By comparison, fish-oil capsules typically supply only 300 to 500 milligrams of omega-3.

Tuna can contain a significant amount of sodium. In a spot check of several products, *Consumer Reports* found that a serving of regular canned tuna supplies anywhere from 160 to 375 milligrams of sodium, with considerable variation from can to can of the same product. People who must follow a sodium-restricted diet may want to try a special low-sodium brand. The no-salt-added "diet" tunas checked supply only about 30 milligrams of sodium per serving; the reduced-salt *StarKist Select*, about 80. But rinsing a serving of regular tuna will also generally remove most of the sodium, although you'll lose some B vitamins as well.

Mercury: How Great a Risk?

Mercury, a toxic metal that can damage the brain and nervous system, is dispersed throughout the oceans. (The metal gets there from natural and industrial pollution of the atmosphere and rivers.) Background levels of mercury in the open ocean, where tuna live, tend to be extremely low, about 50 parts per *trillion* of water. Nonetheless, mercury can work its way from plankton up the food chain to concentrate in tuna flesh, just as it concentrates in other fish, like swordfish, that are also high on the food chain.

Swordfish typically have much higher mercury levels than do tuna. But because Americans eat more tuna than any other fish, canned tuna is a greater source of exposure than other seafoods, and greater, for most of us, than any other item in the diet.

Three samples of each canned tuna were sent out for testing

to see how much mercury they contained. The U.S. Food and Drug Administration (FDA) has set an acceptable limit on mercury in marine fish at 1 part per million (ppm) and, from health studies, has determined that a person's total daily intake should be no more than 30 micrograms of mercury (a little more than one-millionth of an ounce) from all sources.

The findings are fairly reassuring. The average level of mercury detected was 0.16 ppm, one-sixth of the government's limit. If you eat half an average can of tuna, you'll consume just 15 micrograms of mercury, which is only half the acceptable daily maximum.

The results represent averages. Six of the 123 cans analyzed had more mercury per serving than the 30-microgram intake limit—but an occasional dose that size is not enough to worry about. No product was found with high mercury levels in all three cans tested, and no brands, individual products, or types of tuna were consistently higher or lower in mercury than others. So even if you eat tuna regularly, your *average* mercury intake should be below the maximum safe level. And since mercury does its damage only over a long period of exposure, the average dose is what counts.

Considering advice from authorities on mercury toxicity, *Consumer Reports* believes the amount of mercury in the typical American diet—even a diet that includes a serving of tuna practically every day—poses virtually no risk to the average healthy adult. But two groups need to be prudent: pregnant women and young children. They should eat canned tuna only occasionally, because the developing nervous systems of fetuses and small children are extremely sensitive even to very low doses of mercury.

Contaminants in the Can

The FDA is authorized to ensure that processed food is free of extraneous matter such as rodent hairs and insect parts. Nevertheless, the government considers a low level of such contaminants to be unavoidable because some filth originates in nature and it can't always be entirely removed.

Consumer Reports sent three samples of each tuna product purchased in 1991 to a lab that specializes in such testing. Scientists

there wash the filth from the fish and examine it under a micro-
scope. About half the 123 samples contained things that
shouldn't have been there. Extraneous matter turned up in at
least one sample of each brand tested.

This wasn't the first time that tests had found such contamination. In 1974, *Consumer Reports* found a similarly high rate of
filth in tuna. Following that report, the industry appeared to
clean up its act; in 1979, less than 2 percent of the cans examined
contained extraneous matter. So it is possible for the industry to
produce clean canned tuna. In the last several years, however,
laxity seems to have set in once more.

Detritus from rats, birds, and insects won't necessarily make
canned tuna unsafe to eat, since the canning process should kill
bacteria the contaminants may carry. But this extraneous matter
could be an indicator of tuna-processing conditions that are generally unsanitary. In any case, contamination puts material in the
food that has no reason to be there at all.

The government takes extraneous matter seriously in the tuna
it purchases for the U.S. military and for federal food programs.
At the request of government agencies, the National Marine Fisheries Service, a part of the U.S. Department of Commerce, tests
tuna before the government buys it. The Fisheries Service will
reject an entire lot of tuna if its labs find extraneous matter in
even a small fraction of the cans of tuna they test.

If Uncle Sam demands a high level of cleanliness in the tuna
it buys, then its consumer watchdog, the FDA, should do what's
necessary to give the rest of us better than 50-50 odds of getting
a clean can of fish. Better sanitation at the processing plants
would keep out most of the insects and rodents, and would help
wash off the feathers, insect parts, and rodent hairs that still find
their way onto fish. And more frequent FDA inspection of canneries would help motivate the industry to eradicate the filth.

Taste

In the 1992 *Consumer Reports* taste tests, the white tunas generally beat out the competition—and by a considerable margin.
Although none was scored excellent, many came close and were

scored as very good. White tunas in oil tended to rack up the highest scores of all, probably because fat helps to round out and enhance the flavor and makes the tuna less dry. *Bumble Bee* topped the list, with the two other major brands, *Chicken of the Sea* and *StarKist*, close behind. There were also very good white tunas packed in water. *Bumble Bee* led again, followed closely by *Lady Lee, Empress,* and *Chicken of the Sea.*

As a group, the light tunas—whether in oil or water—scored at least a notch below the whites. None was judged better than good on the sensory index. The light-meat tunas generally had an "unclean" flavor: Most had at least a slight sour, bitter, or metallic taste. They generally weren't much to look at, either; the cans contained some grated fish and were sloppily packed. Two supermarket brands topped the lights: *Kroger*, packed in oil, and Safeway's *Captain's Choice*, canned in water.

The low-salt tuna and the three diet tunas—two white, two light—were rated lowest of all in taste within their types. Blandness and dryness were the main reasons.

Because tuna is a natural product, a certain amount of variation from can to can was expected, so the sensory index is necessarily a composite score for each tuna. And you cannot generalize about the big-three brands. *Bumble Bee* and *StarKist*, each capable of canning such a good white tuna, turned out mediocre-tasting light tunas. Results for *Chicken of the Sea* were also mixed.

Recommendations

Canned tuna is an excellent, low-cost source of protein. Depending on how it's canned and served, it can also carry a significant amount of fat. If you're concerned about your fat intake, you'll get much less fat and fewer calories from water-packed tuna than from tuna packed in oil. However, there are no major nutritional differences between light and white tuna, or between solid and chunk, if you drain the can. The expensive "diet" tunas, too, offer no nutritional advantage over other water-packed tunas besides their low sodium content—and you could lower sodium just as well by buying any water-packed tuna and rinsing it.

The taste differences between white and light tuna may not be worth the extra cost of white, unless you take your tuna straight or lightly dressed. Although white tunas generally scored higher in the *Consumer Reports* taste tests, adding a lot of mayonnaise, onions, and spices would likely overwhelm the flavor differences we noted. So if you mix your tuna into tuna salad or bake it in a tuna-noodle casserole, save some money and buy light, not white. Light tuna is often half the price of white or less. Even so, the sour, bitter, and "unclean" taste of many light tunas means you might well want to look for products near the top of the Ratings.

For tuna connoisseurs, *Bumble Bee Fancy Albacore*, a solid white tuna in oil, tasted best in its class and contained nary a blemish. For those avoiding fat, *Bumble Bee Albacore*, a chunk white tuna in water, also tasted very good, as did *Lady Lee* and *Empress* brands, both solid white tunas in water.

CARBONATED WATERS

A 1992 study by researchers at Harvard University and the Medical College of Wisconsin produced new evidence of a link between chlorinated drinking water and rectal and bladder cancer. Although alarming, the risks today aren't as great as they were 20 years ago, when levels of chlorination were typically higher than they are now. But chlorination is still the main method used to disinfect municipal water, and its by-products—formed when chlorine reacts with trace organic compounds naturally present in the water—may still pose some risk.

Whatever the current risk, you will not necessarily avoid it by switching from tap water to bottled water. Despite steps taken by bottlers to remove contaminants, spot checks by *Consumer Reports* in 1992 indicated that bottled beverages made with municipal water could contain the same chlorinated organic compounds as the tap water from which they came.

Among the most commonly occurring and thoroughly studied chlorination by-products are trihalomethanes, or THMs, a group that includes chloroform. The U.S. Environmental Protection Agency (EPA) has set a limit of 0.1 milligram per liter, or 100 parts per billion (ppb), for total THMs in municipal drinking water. The California Department of Health Services and the

(*continued on page 270*)

RATINGS

*As published in the **February 1992** issue of Consumer Reports*

Canned tuna

Listed by types; within types, listed in order of overall sensory quality. Products that are within a few points of each other are similar in sensory quality; those with identical scores are listed alphabetically.

1 Pack. Solid pack (**S**) should contain one piece of fish cut crosswise. Chunk pack (**C**) contains smaller chunks and slightly more liquid.

2 Price. Unless noted, for a $6^{1}/_{8}$-ounce can. Prices were the estimated national average for 1991.

3 Sensory index. Based on measurements by trained sensory panel. See text for "typical" profile of white and light tuna and criteria for excellence.

4 Appearance. Unless otherwise noted, white tunas had a fairly uniform light color with a few blemishes and little grated fish; lights were darker and less neatly packed, with more grated fish.

5 Sensory comments. Comments indicate distinctive characteristics of each product.

Ratings
Continued

Better ● ◐ ○ ◑ ● Worse

Product	1 Pack	2 Price	3 Sensory index (Poor–Excellent, 0–100)	4 Appearance
White tuna in oil				
Bumble Bee Fancy	S	$1.57		◐
Chicken of the Sea Fancy	S	1.55		○
StarKist Fancy	S	1.54		◐
3 Diamonds Fancy	S	1.38		○
White tuna in water				
Bumble Bee	C	1.28		○
Lady Lee (Lucky Stores)	S	1.21 ⊡		○
Empress Fancy	S	1.28		◐
Chicken of the Sea Fancy	S	1.53		○
Bumble Bee Fancy	S	1.53		○
Kroger Fancy	S	1.49		◐
StarKist Fancy	S	1.60		◐
3 Diamonds Fancy	S	1.42		○
Carnation Fancy	S	1.31		○
Geisha	S	1.32		○
A&P Fancy	S	1.12		○
Albertsons	S	1.33		◐
StarKist Select, 60% Less Salt	S	1.55		○
Chicken of the Sea Dietetic Fancy	C	1.63		◐

Light tuna in oil

		Price	Rating
Kroger	C	.58	○
3 Diamonds	C	.78	○
Chicken of the Sea	S	.78	○
A&P	C	1.15	○
Bumble Bee	C	.76	○
Captain's Choice (Safeway)	C	.78	○
StarKist	C	.76	◑

Light tuna in water

		Price	Rating
Captain's Choice (Safeway)	C	.72	◑
Chicken of the Sea	C	.77	○
A&P	C	.73	◑
Lady Lee (Lucky Stores)	C	.60	◑
Carnation Hi-Protein	C	.83	◑
Geisha	C	.71	○
Empress	C	.66	◑
StarKist	C	.77	◑
Pathmark	C	.79 ①	◑
Albertsons	C	.56	○
3 Diamonds	C	.79	◑
Bumble Bee	C	.80	○
Kroger	C	.54	◑
Shop Rite	C	.59 ①	◑
Chicken of the Sea Diet	C	1.35	◑
StarKist Diet	C	1.39	◑

① 6½-oz. can.

267

Ratings
Continued

Product	🔄 Sensory comments
White tuna in oil	
Bumble Bee Fancy	Uniform white color, mostly solid; mild, full flavor, chickenlike.
Chicken of the Sea Fancy	Mostly solid; a bit dry; chickenlike flavor.
StarKist Fancy	Uniform white, mostly solid (though much fish is grated in some cans); chickenlike flavor.
3 Diamonds Fancy	Mostly solid; a bit dry, tough; mild fish flavor, chickenlike taste. One can had rancid-oil taste.
White tuna in water	
Bumble Bee	Sloppily packed (many flakes, much grated fish); moist; full fish flavor.
Lady Lee (Lucky Stores)	Blemished areas; some cans with much grated fish; full fish flavor with chickenlike flavor.
Empress Fancy	Neatly packed; full fish flavor.
Chicken of the Sea Fancy	Light white but with blemished areas; some cans with much grated fish. Full flavor, chickenlike.
Bumble Bee Fancy	White color, neatly packed; but with blemished areas; some grated fish.
Kroger Fancy	Light white uniform color; mild fish flavor.
StarKist Fancy	Light white uniform color, relatively blemish-free; mild fish flavor, chickenlike; some cans with little saltiness.
3 Diamonds Fancy	Blemished areas; a bit sour, bitter, with tinny off-taste.
Carnation Fancy	Beige; mild fish flavor, a bit sour, bitter, with tinny off-taste.
Geisha	Neatly packed small chunks; a bit dry; mild flavor.
A&P Fancy	Neatly packed chunks; a bit dry; some cans with little saltiness.
Albertsons	Neatly packed chunks; a bit dry; mild fish flavor; a bit sour, bitter with tinny off-taste; some cans with little saltiness.
StarKist Select, 60% Less Salt	White; sloppily packed (many flakes); dry; bland, with sourness, little saltiness, and tinny off-taste.
Chicken of the Sea Dietetic Fancy	White; many flakes; dry, tough; very bland; a bit sour; not salty, with slight petroleum off-taste.

Light tuna in oil

Kroger	Very light; sloppily packed (mostly flakes); relatively blemish-free; mushy texture; full flavor.
3 Diamonds	Sloppily packed (mostly flakes); mild fish flavor.
Chicken of the Sea	Dark beige; sloppily packed (but relatively blemish-free); full flavor, with sourness.
A&P	Sloppily packed (mostly flakes); slight organ-meat taste, sour, tinny off-taste.
Bumble Bee	Some chunks, grated fish; mushy texture; sour, and slight bitter, tinny off-taste.
Captain's Choice (Safeway)	Sloppily packed (mostly flakes); relatively blemish-free; mushy texture; sour, salty, and slight bitter and tinny off-taste.
StarKist	Color varied; sloppily packed (mostly flakes); mushy texture; mild fish flavor; slight bitter and tinny off-taste, plus iodine off-taste in some cans.

Light tuna in water

Captain's Choice (Safeway)	Neatly packed chunks.
Chicken of the Sea	Sloppily packed (mostly flakes).
A&P	Relatively blemish-free.
Lady Lee (Lucky Stores)	Sloppily packed (mostly flakes). Some cans with little saltiness.
Carnation Hi-Protein	Sloppily packed (mostly flakes); some cans with much grated fish, blemishes; salty, with tinny off-taste.
Geisha	Dark beige; more chunks; relatively blemish-free; tinny off-taste.
Empress	Dark beige; more chunks; relatively blemish-free; sour taste.
StarKist	Sloppily packed (many flakes); many cans with excessive grated fish; sour taste.
Pathmark	Sloppily packed (mostly flakes); bitter, some cans with iodine off-taste.
Albertsons	Pink; sloppily packed—some cans with much grated fish—but relatively blemish-free; excessively fishy taste.
3 Diamonds	Dark beige; sloppily packed (mostly flakes); some cans with much grated fish, some fat globules; organ-meat taste, bitter, with tinny off-taste.
Bumble Bee	Dark beige; sloppily packed; slight organ-meat taste.
Kroger	Dark beige; more chunks; salty and bitter, with tinny off-taste.
Shop Rite	Relatively blemish-free; slight organ-meat taste.
Chicken of the Sea Diet	Light color; more chunks; relatively blemish-free; dry; very bland; a bit chickenlike flavor; not salty.
StarKist Diet	Light color; more chunks; dry; very bland, a bit chickenlike, not salty, less sour and bitter.

EPA, using data from various sources, have estimated the theoretical cancer risk from a lifetime of drinking a quart or so of water a day containing 100 ppb of chloroform. That level of intake, their calculations show, could produce 9 cancers per million exposed people.

Although not a huge risk, that's still far above the one-in-a-million that's considered "negligible" and that serves as a general guideline for limiting carcinogens in food and water. The standard for THMs allows more than negligible risk, the EPA concedes, because of the unacceptable health hazards of prohibiting chlorination and the high economic costs of eliminating all of its by-products from municipal water supplies.

The U.S. Food and Drug Administration has applied the EPA's municipal-water standards, including the THM limit, to bottled waters, but there's no need to allow high THM levels in bottled waters. In a bottling plant, filtration with activated carbon can eliminate the by-products of chlorination at minimal cost. The California Department of Health Services has recommended a standard of no more than 6 ppb for soft drinks, including seltzer.

In 1992, *Consumer Reports* tested 27 sparkling waters, mineral waters, and seltzers—flavored and unflavored—for THMs and other chemicals. The tests showed no significant contamination of any product with industrial or agricultural chemicals. Most of the tested products made with municipal water contained at least some THMs, generally chloroform. Seven products, all calling themselves seltzers, had average levels at or above 50 ppb.

All but one of the waters containing THMs were manufactured at more than one bottling plant, using different municipal water supplies. Even at a single plant, THM levels in the water can vary from day to day. Levels in the products are therefore likely to vary, and the two or three samples tested of each brand could differ from samples bought at other times or in other cities.

Until bottlers take effective steps to reduce THM levels, the only way to be sure you're avoiding THMs completely is to avoid products that use municipal water. The Ratings chart shows the water source for each product tested by *Consumer Reports* and identifies those that had more than a trace of THMs in the samples tested.

The tests also measured levels of substances other than THMs.

Sodium

Sodium in fresh water comes not just from salt (sodium chloride) but from other sodium compounds. Most of the tested mineral waters had higher levels than the other products. The highest was *Apollinaris Naturally Sparkling* mineral water, with 99 milligrams per 8-ounce glass. That's a fraction of the 2,400 milligrams recommended as a maximum daily sodium intake for those adults who must watch their sodium, but it was enough to make *Apollinaris* taste slightly salty.

Fluoride

Many municipal water supplies contain added fluoride to combat tooth decay, generally at a level of 1 part per million (ppm). At higher than recommended intakes, fluoride can cause discoloration of tooth enamel in children and, over decades, produce bone changes in adults. In the past, *Consumer Reports* has found some mineral waters with excessive fluoride levels. In its 1992 tests, however, most mineral and sparkling waters had even less than 1 ppm. Seltzers and other products made with municipal water were either fluoridated at about 1 ppm or contained essentially no fluoride, depending on the fluoride content of the water where they were bottled.

Arsenic, Lead

Lead levels were all well below EPA limits for tap water.

Total Dissolved Solids

If you boiled away all the water from any of the products, you'd be left with what are called "total dissolved solids." They don't generally supply minerals in nutritionally significant amounts, but they do give mineral water its distinctive taste. The mineral waters tested generally had total dissolved solids of at least 500 ppm, a respectable score for such products. *S. Pellegrino* and *Apollinaris* had levels of more than 1,000 ppm.

LISTINGS

As published in the September 1992 issue of Consumer Reports

Carbonated waters

Listed by flavor types; within types, listed in alphabetical order.

1 Product type. Sparkling mineral waters (**SMW**) contain dissolved minerals and typically have a distinctive mineral flavor. Products labeled sparkling water (**SW**) may derive from natural or municipal sources. Carbonation may be naturally present or added from natural or manmade carbon dioxide. Products labeled seltzer (**S**) are typically filtered and carbonated tap water.

2 Cost per serving. The estimated average for an eight-ounce serving, based on prices paid nationally in 1992 for a bottle as close to 1 liter as was available. An * denotes a serving cost based on the price *Consumer Reports* paid (a national average wasn't available).

3 Water source. Products derived from municipal water supplies (**M**) are likely to contain trihalomethanes such as chloroform, a suspected carcinogen. Those that come from a spring (**S**), well (**W**), or geothermal pool (**GP**) lack THMs. The THM content will vary from sample to sample, especially for products that are bottled at more than one plant. The Comments call out products with an average THM level of 5 or more parts per billion in the two or three samples tested and those bottled at more than one plant.

4 Bottle. Both glass (**G**) and PET plastic (**P**) are recyclable, though glass is accepted at more recycling centers.

5 Sensory comments. Except as noted, all the products were moderately fizzy (mineral waters a bit less so); slightly sour; and very slightly sodalike, astringent, salty, and bitter. All the unflavored products bottled in plastic had a slight fruity flavor in some

samples. All the flavored products had moderate citrus flavor.

Features in Common
Except as noted, all: ● Have artificial carbonation. ● Have less than 13 mg. sodium per serving. ● Are not available throughout the United States.

Key to Comments
A—THMs were detected at greater than trace amounts in the samples we analyzed.
B—From more than one bottling plant; THM, fluoride, sodium, and mineral levels vary depending on where water was bottled.
C—Naturally carbonated.
D—Sodium: 39–55 mg. per serving.
E—Sodium: 99 mg. per serving.
F—Sold nationwide.

Brand	1 Product type	2 Cost per serving	3 Water source	4 Bottle	Comments	5 Sensory comments
Unflavored waters						
A&P	S	9¢	M	P	A,B	—
Apollinaris	SMW	37	S	G	C,E	More sodalike, salty; slightly soapy; trace of mineral flavor.
Bel-Air (Safeway)	S	10	M	P	A,B	Very fizzy.
Calistoga	SMW	27	S	G	D	Trace of mineral and fruity flavors.

Canada Dry	S	19	M	P	A,B	—
Canada Dry	SW	19	M	P	A,B	—
Crystal Geyser	SMW	29	GP	G	D	More salty; distinct mineral flavor; medicinal/iodine flavor in some samples.
Golden Crown (Kroger)	S	15	M	P	A	Clean flavor, very fizzy.
La Croix	SW	22	W	G	F	—
Perrier	SMW	33*	S	G	F	Clean flavor.
Poland Spring	SW	20	S	P	—	—
Quibell	SW	25	S	G	—	Clean flavor.
S. Pellegrino	SMW	42	W	G	—	Less fizzy; mineral flavor; trace of stale and soapy flavors.
Schweppes	S	19	M,W	P	B,F	—
Seagram's	S	17	M	P	A,B	—
Vintage	S	8	M	P	A,B	—

Orange-flavored waters

Calistoga	SMW	27	S	G	D	Hint of mineral flavor; bitter; orange, citrus, lemon/lime flavors with peel notes; a bit candylike.
Canada Dry	S	18	M	P	A,B	Tangerine/mandarin flavor with peel notes; hint of juice.
Canada Dry	SW	18	M	P	B	Tangerine/mandarin and orange flavors with peel notes; hint of juice.
Crystal Geyser	SMW	29	GP	G	D	Hint of soapy, orange, citrus, lemon/lime flavors with peel notes; candylike.
La Croix	SW	22	W	G	F	Less total citrus flavor; orange flavor with peel notes; hint of juice.
Perrier	SMW	34*	S	G	F	Lots of orange flavor; candylike; peel notes.
Poland Spring	SW	22*	S	P	—	Some orange flavor, mostly peel.
Quibell	SW	25	S	G	—	Tangerine/mandarin, a bit of orange, lemon/lime flavors and peel notes; hint of juice.
Schweppes	S	20	M,W	P	B,F	Orange flavor with peel notes.
Seagram's	S	15	M	P	A,B	Orange flavor with peel notes; a bit candylike.
Vintage	S	8	M	P	A,B	Tangerine/mandarin flavor with peel notes; hint of juice.

Recommendations

The differences from one brand of unflavored fizzy water to another, the *Consumer Reports* tasters found, were subtle. Poured over ice, mixed with another beverage, or adorned with a slice of fruit, these products would taste pretty much the same—which is to say, pretty good. The orange-flavored waters were fairly good, too, although the orange flavor wasn't always up to par. Both groups are listed alphabetically, along with descriptive comments from the *Consumer Reports* taste tests.

If you like the taste of mineral water, choose one of the three unflavored products that the tasters found had a mineral flavor. If you like mineral water without a mineral taste, choose *Perrier*. It was also lower in sodium than the other mineral waters. Among orange-flavored products, fruity-tasting ingredients tended to drown out any mineral taste.

If you're concerned about the risk posed by THMs, avoid any of the products listed as coming from a municipal water supply. For the most part, that means avoiding seltzers and club sodas and limiting your choice to the sparkling or mineral waters.

YOGURT

When the Dannon Company started up in the United States in the 1940s, it sold its yogurt as a diet food. But Americans didn't like the tart, tangy dairy food as much as, say, Bulgarians did. To please the local palate, the Dannon Company added strawberry preserves to its product.

Over the years, the sugar-coating of yogurt led to an explosion of sweetened yogurt products. Flavors range from French vanilla to strawberry to banana to piña colada. Forms now include frozen, liquid, and in the cup (which may be "sundae style," with the fruit on the bottom; "Swiss style," with the fruit blended throughout; or "custard style," a thicker, sweeter blended product).

For a report published in 1991, *Consumer Reports* purchased some 40 products representing all these types, including national brands such as *Dannon*, *Yoplait*, and *Light n' Lively*; regional brands such as *Colombo* and *La Yogurt* in the Northeast and *Moun-*

tain High in the West; and various supermarket brands. The two most popular flavors—strawberry and plain—were chosen.

The Tang of Yogurt

In its simplest form, yogurt is nothing but milk fermented by certain bacterial strains. Over the years, all kinds of milk have been used—from cows, goats, buffalo, even camels and yaks—a diversity that betrays yogurt's origins and popularity in the Middle East and central Asia.

The milk is typically inoculated with starter cultures and incubated several hours at around 110°F. As the bacteria do their work, they digest most of the milk sugar, or lactose, converting it to lactic acid. The acid curdles the milk and adds the tartness.

A good-tasting yogurt, therefore, tastes mainly of soured milk, with echoes of dairy products like buttermilk and sour cream. The dairy taste should be full and complex, not flat and one-dimensional, with flavor notes so balanced and intertwined it's difficult to pick out this note or that.

What sets yogurt apart from other dairy products, especially sour cream, is the special tanginess that expert tasters call "green" flavor, a quality associated with green apples. Yogurt's acidity, however, should be moderate, neither faint-hearted nor overpoweringly sour. Plain yogurt may even have a hint of sweetness. Strawberry yogurts are sweeter and may have less of a dairy flavor. In either case, there should be no off-tastes—yeasty, cheesy, or fruity notes from improper processing, cheap ingredients, or poor handling.

In texture, an excellent yogurt should have a smooth, creamy consistency that may range from thick to thin. The product should not be pasty, runny, chalky, or overly lumpy, although some graininess is allowed.

Yogurts rated low by *Consumer Reports* often had a poor consistency. They were either too runny, too gelatinous, or too gummy, the last from added pectin, gelatin, vegetable gums, and starches. The expert panel tasters nearly always detected aspartame in low-calorie yogurts because of the artificial sweetener's characteristic taste—an intensifying, lingering sweetness. Some low-rated strawberry yogurts were also a garish, almost neon pink (some brands jack up color with beet juice or artificial coloring).

Consumer Reports food specialists mixed their own fruit yogurt, combining the top-rated *Colombo* plain yogurt with a dollop of *Smucker's* strawberry preserves, a jam among the best in the last test of jams. That combination tasted even better than the best-prepared strawberry products.

The Nutrition of Yogurt

Yogurt is a good food. It offers high-quality protein in good quantity, a generous amount of calcium, and supplies other vitamins and minerals including riboflavin, vitamin B_{12}, phosphorus, and potassium. Essentially, these are the nutrients you'd get from milk.

Consumer Reports food scientists relied on nutrition labeling, called companies for additional data, spot-checked values, and ran lab tests for nutrients seldom noted on packages.

An 8-ounce cup of milk supplies about 8 grams of protein. Often the yogurt packs a few grams more, from added milk solids (nonfat dry milk).

Similarly, a glass of milk supplies about 300 milligrams of calcium, nearly 30 percent of the 1,000-milligram daily quota for adults. A serving of some plain yogurts supplies 300, 400, or even 450 milligrams, depending on the amount of added milk solids.

Even plain yogurt contains some sugar, in the form of lactose (milk sugar). Although most of that is converted into lactic acid as part of the yogurt-making process, some remains, and more comes from those added milk solids.

Flavored yogurts, with their added jam, contain much more sugar. The jam takes up room in the container that would otherwise be taken up by yogurt, so sweetened products typically provide less protein, calcium, and other nutrients than does plain yogurt.

The typical jam-sweetened strawberry yogurt contains about 35 grams of sugar per cup, equivalent to nearly 9 teaspoons. That's almost as much sugar as in a can of *Coke*. Some products have more. Half or even two-thirds of a strawberry yogurt's calories can come from the sugar.

As the Ratings show, low-fat strawberry yogurts pack an average of 240 calories a cup, about 100 calories more than plain. Aspartame-sweetened products save those sugar calories. Flavors that don't use jam—coffee, lemon, and vanilla, for example—tend to use less sugar and thus have fewer calories. So do *Dannon Fresh Flavors*, which use fruit juice instead of jam. Some companies offer fewer calories per container by shrinking the container from 8 to 6 ounces.

The other key source of calories is fat, of course. When made from whole milk, yogurt typically contains 3½ percent milk fat, just like the milk. Made from low-fat milk, it typically contains 1½ percent fat. Made from skim milk, the resulting nonfat yogurt generally contains less than 1/2 percent fat.

These differences look small but can add up to extra calories: A serving of plain nonfat yogurt can carry as few as 90 calories; a serving of plain whole-milk yogurt, as many as 200. But, as the Ratings show, the differences aren't always that dramatic. Even the fat in the fattiest yogurt can easily fit into a balanced diet: A serving has only 9 grams of fat, about what's in a one-ounce slice of American cheese. Most yogurts have less than that.

The cholesterol content of yogurt is no cause for worry, either. At most, these products supply 25 milligrams per serving; most are in the 5-to-15-milligram range. That's a trivial amount compared with an egg's 213 milligrams. The government has recommended a 300-milligram daily maximum.

Recommendations

Yogurt makes a nutritious snack or dessert, or the core of a quick lunch, but some yogurts are more nutritious than others. Unless artificially sweetened, strawberry yogurts tend to derive many or even most of their calories from sugar—at the expense of extra protein and calcium that the same amount of plain yogurt delivers. And strawberry yogurts pack more calories. If you add a little of your favorite jam to plain yogurt, you can control the amount of sugar you eat and the result may even taste superior to what you can find in the dairy case. Or you can slice in fresh fruit.

The best plain yogurt in the *Consumer Reports* tests was *Colombo* whole-milk yogurt, with a smooth, creamy texture and a full dairy taste. It has a little more fat than most low-fat yogurts tested (7 grams versus 4), but the taste may be worth it. *Dannon* low-fat yogurt and *Mountain High*, a whole-milk product, were runners-up. If you eschew fat, try *Colombo* nonfat, the best-tasting product of its kind.

Of the strawberry yogurts, the tastiest were *Colombo* whole-milk and *Pathmark* low-fat yogurts. The *Colombo* has the fruit on the bottom; the *Pathmark* has it blended throughout. Both offer satisfying, full dairy taste, which comes through despite the fruit.

The aspartame-sweetened products didn't score well. The sweetener saves calories, but it adds a characteristic taste that some people find unpleasant.

RATINGS

*As published in the **May 1991** issue of Consumer Reports*

Yogurt

Listed by flavors; within flavors, listed in order of overall sensory quality. Products within a few points of each other are very similar in overall quality. Products with identical scores listed alphabetically.

1 Type. By federal regulation, whole-milk yogurt (**W**) must contain at least 3¼ percent milk fat. Low-fat yogurt (**L**) must contain between ½ and 2 percent milk fat. Nonfat yogurt (**N**), made from skim milk, must contain less than ½ percent milk fat.

2 Sensory index. Overall sensory quality, on a 100-point scale, based on evaluations by a trained panel. Products lost points to the extent they deviated from *Consumer Reports* criteria for excellence.

3 Cost. What was paid per ounce. Plain yogurt was purchased in large sizes (16 or 32 ounces) and strawberry yogurt in individual-serving cups, generally 8 ounces or, where noted, 6 ounces.

4 Nutrients. Nutritional data are standardized per eight-ounce serving and are from labels, manufacturers' data, and supplementary analyses. The first figure under **fat** gives the grams per serving; the second figure, the percentage of a yogurt's calories that the fat contributes. A dash indicates less than one gram of fat per serving.

5 Sensory comments. An excellent yogurt has a smooth, creamy texture with a full, balanced taste of dairy, moderate sourness, and some "green" quality (a flavor reminiscent of green apples). Excellent strawberry yogurts are sweeter, possess appropriate fruit flavor of fresh fruit or fruit jam, and may have somewhat less dairy taste. Unless otherwise noted, quantity of fruit was slight to moderate.

Ratings
Continued

Product	Type [1]	Sensory index [2] (Poor—Excellent)	Cost/oz. [3]
Plain			
Colombo	W	E	9¢
Dannon	L	VG	7
Mountain High	W	VG	7
Yoplait Original [1]	L	VG	12
A&P	L	VG	5
Colombo	N	VG	6
Yoplait	N	G	6
Kroger	L	G	7
Axelrod	L	G	5
Breyers All Natural	L	G	6
Dannon	N	G	7
Albertsons	L	G	4
Lucerne (Safeway)	L	F	5
Weight Watchers	N	P	8
Strawberry			
Colombo	W	E	10
Pathmark All Natural	L	E	7
Dannon Original	L	VG	10

Product		Value
La Yogurt [1]	W	9
Yoplait Original [1]	L	11
Breyers	L	8
Colombo Lite	N	10
Lucerne Pre-stirred (Safeway)	L	4
Dannon Fresh Flavors	L	10
Mountain High	W	9
Yoplait Fat Free [1]	N	12
La Yogurt	N	7
Dannon Light [2]	N	10
Mountain High Honey Light	L	9
Kroger Lite [2]	N	5
Light n' Lively	L	9
Superbrand Swiss Style (Winn Dixie)	L	5
New Country [1]	L	8
Yoplait Light [1] [2]	N	10
A&P Swiss Style	L	6
Axelrod Swiss Style	L	10
Light n' Lively [2]	N	10
Weight Watchers Ultimate 90 [2]	N	10

[1] Individual-serving container holds 6 ounces, not 8 ounces.
[2] Sweetened with aspartame artificial sweetener.

281

Ratings
Continued

Product	Calories	4 Nutrients per 8 oz.			5 Sensory comments
		Protein, g	Fat, g/%	Calcium, mg	
Plain					
Colombo	150	9	7/42%	350	Smooth, creamy texture, with full dairy flavor.
Dannon	150	12	4/24	400	A bit low in sourness; a bit chalky.
Mountain High	200	12	9/41	400	Creamy texture; some samples very sour.
Yoplait Original [1]	173	13	4/21	400	Very smooth and creamy, like pudding; a bit low in yogurt flavor and sourness; a bit sweet.
A&P	150	12	4/24	400	Very sour.
Colombo	110	11	—/6	400	A bit chalky.
Yoplait	120	13	—/4	450	Thick and a bit chalky; low yogurt flavor and little sourness.
Kroger	140	11	4/26	400	Very sour.
Axelrod	140	12	2/13	400	A bit chalky; very sour.
Breyers All Natural	140	12	3/19	400	Very lumpy, grainy, a bit chalky; some samples very sour.
Dannon	130	13	—/4	350	A bit chalky; low yogurt flavor and little sourness.
Albertsons	140	11	5/32	350	Gel texture; cooked-milk flavor; very sour.
Lucerne (Safeway)	160	12	5/28	400	Thin, with gel texture; little dairy flavor.
Weight Watchers	90	10	1/11	350	Thin, with gel texture; not well balanced; little dairy flavor; very sour.
Strawberry					
Colombo	230	7	6/23	250	Creamy texture, with full dairy flavor.
Pathmark All Natural	270	10	2/7	350	Full, blended dairy and distinct yogurt flavor.
Dannon Original	240	9	3/11	350	Lumpy, with distinct yogurt flavor.
La Yogurt [1]	253	9	5/19	333	Smooth and thin, with little fruit, mild strawberry.

	253	11	4/14	333	Creamy texture.
Breyers	250	9	2/7	300	Very lumpy, with distinct yogurt flavor and many fruit pieces; very sweet.
Colombo Lite	190	8	—/3	300	Perfumey strawberry aroma.
Lucerne Pre-stirred (Safeway)	260	10	4/14	350	A bit gelatinous and sour.
Dannon Fresh Flavors	200	10	4/18	400	Smooth, like pudding, with no fruit pieces; candylike strawberry.
Mountain High	220	10	6/25	350	Distinct yogurt taste with honey but little strawberry; pruney note; not very sweet; sour; brownish color.
Yoplait Fat Free [1]	200	9	—/1	333	Slightly gummy texture; many fruit pieces.
La Yogurt	190	8	—/2	300	Slightly gummy texture.
Dannon Light [2]	100	9	—/3	300	Slight artificial-sweetener taste.
Mountain High Honey Light	190	9	—/5	300	Distinct yogurt flavor with honey but little strawberry; pruney note; not very sweet; sour; brownish color.
Kroger Lite [2]	120	10	—/3	350	More peach than strawberry; artificial-sweetener taste; very sour.
Light n' Lively	240	9	2/8	250	Smooth, like pudding, with candylike strawberry; very sweet; bright pink.
Superbrand Swiss Style (Winn Dixie)	240	8	3/11	300	Candylike strawberry; bright pink.
New Country [1]	200	7	3/12	200	Smooth, like pudding; little dairy flavor; candylike strawberry with little fruit; a bit sour.
Yoplait Light [1] [2]	120	9	—/2	333	Smooth and thin, with little dairy flavor; candylike strawberry, cherry, slight artificial-sweetener taste; brigh pink.
A&P Swiss Style	260	10	2/7	350	A bit gummy but smooth; slight candylike strawberry with little fruit; bright pink.
Axelrod Swiss Style	240	8	2/8	300	Gel texture; little dairy flavor; slight, candylike strawberry with little fruit; a bit sour; bright pink.
Light n' Lively [2]	100	8	—/4	300	Smooth and thin, with little dairy flavor; candylike strawberry, slight artificial-sweetener taste.
Weight Watchers Ultimate 90 [2]	90	10	—/4	300	Thin with gel texture; little dairy flavor; slight, candylike strawberry, slight artificial-sweetener taste; flavors not well balanced.

INDEX

A&P supermarket chain, 24
Acme supermarket chain, 24
Acorn squash, 88
Additives, 171–72
   in sausages, 58
Advertising, 5–6
   of cereals, 127
Aflatoxins, 166
Agriculture, U.S. Department of
   (USDA), 20, 31, 40, 47, 51, 53,
   54, 58, 71–73, 93–94, 114,
   123, 124, 135, 171
American cheese, 115–18
American Heart Association, 124,
   143
Animal feed, drugs in, 170–71
Animal rights, 50
Anise, 73–74
Antibiotics in foods, 170–71
Apples, 94–97
Apricots, 97
Aquaculture, 64
Aromatic rice, 131–32
Artichokes, 74
Artificial sweeteners, 171
Asparagus, 74
Avocados, 97–98

Bacon, 60–61
Bacteria, 160–63
   in well water, 176

Bamboo shoots, 91
Bananas, 98
Banana squash, 88
Barbecue sauces, 178–83
   Ratings, 180–83
Basmati rice, 132
Beans, 75–76
Bean sprouts, 91
Beard, James, 30
Beef, 42–50
   cooking methods for, 48–49
   cuts of, 44–47
   grades of, 48
   inspection of, 47
Beets, 76–77
Bell peppers, 84
Bel Paese cheese, 120
Berries, 98–100
Blackberries, 99
Blueberries, 99
Blue cheese, 120
Bok choy, 91
Bonus clubs, 6
Borden's, 150, 234
Bottled water, 154–57
   tap water versus, 175–76
Boursin cheese, 120
Bovine growth hormone (bGH),
   170
Boysenberries, 99
Brains, 62

Brand-name products
  advertising and marketing of, 5–6
  fats and oils, 144
  new, 7–8
  peanut butter, 137
  placement of, 8
  potato chips, 138
  Ratings. *See specific products*
  store brands versus, 9–13
Brie cheese, 120
Brine curing, 52
Broccoli, 77
Brown rice, 131, 133
Brussels sprouts, 77
Buckwheat flour, 130
Butter, 114, 142–43
Buttercup squash, 88
Butter-flavored spreads, 144
Butterhead lettuce, 82
Buttermilk, 113

Cabbage, 77–78
Caffeine, 172
  in tea, 258
California Department of Health Services, 264
Camembert cheese, 120
Campylobacter bacteria, 160
Cantaloupe, 103
Capons, 39–40
Carbonated water, 155, 264, 270–74
  Ratings, 272–73
Carrots, 78
Casaba melon, 104
Cauliflower, 78
Cayenne peppers, 84
Celery, 78–79
Cereals, 125–28, 179, 184, 192
  Ratings, 185–91
Cheddar cheese, 118, 120
Cheeses, 115–21
  bacteria in, 163
  natural, 118–21
  process, 115–18
Chemical contaminants, 163–65
Cherries, 100

Chicken, 31–38
  cooking methods, 36–38
  grading, 31–32
  parts, 32
  precooked, 34–35
  pricing formulas for, 32–34
  stewing, 35–36
Chick-peas, 76
Chili peppers, 84
Chinese cabbage, 78
Ciguatoxin, 166
Citrus fruits, 100–105
  juices, 108–11
Clams, 69
Club soda, 155
Coca-Cola, 153, 192, 193, 196
Coffee
  decaffeinated, 146
  ground, 144–48
  instant, 148–51
Colas, 153–54, 192–96
  Ratings, 194–95
Colby cheese, 120
Cold storage, 93
Commerce, U.S. Department of, 262
Condensed milk, 114
Contaminants, 159–73
  additives, 171–72
  animal antibiotics, 170–71
  bacteria, 160–63
  of canned tuna, 261–62
  from cooking, 166–68
  irradiation, 172–73
  metals, 168–70
  natural toxins, 165–66
  pesticides, 163–65
Convenience foods, 157–58
Corn, 79
Corn flour, 130
Cornish game hens, 38–39
Cos, 82
Cost per pound, 18–19
Coupons, 6–8
  for cereals, 127
CPC International, 234
Crabs, 69
Cranberries, 99
Cream, 113

Crème fraîche, 113
Crenshaw melon, 104
Crustaceans, 69
Cucumbers, 80
Cured meats, 52–53
Cutting boards, 169

Dairy products, 112–24
  cheeses, 115–19
  eggs, 119–24
  milk products, 112–14
Dannon Company, 274
Design of supermarkets, 8
Discounts, taking advantage of, 23
Downgrading, 22
Dry milk, 114
Duck, 38
Dyes, 171

Edam cheese, 120
Edwards supermarket chain, 24
Eggplant, 80
Eggs, 119–24
  bacteria in, 160–63
  freshness and quality of, 122
  grading of, 121–23
  substitutes, 124
Electronic price scanners, 14–15
Environmental Protection Agency
    (EPA), 176, 264, 270
Evaporated milk, 114
Extracts, 156

Factory-farming techniques, 50
Fats, 140–44
Feta cheese, 120
Finast supermarket chain, 24
Fish, 63–70
  comparative cost of, 68–69
  contamination of, 160–64,
    166–68
  demand versus supply of, 63–64
  fresh, how to buy, 64–65
  frozen, how to buy, 65–66
  mislabeled, 14
  shellfish, 69–70
  smoked or salted, how to buy, 66
  varieties of, 66–68
Flatfish, 66

Flavorings, 156
Flours, 128–30
Food and Drug Administration
    (FDA), 20, 171, 172, 261, 262,
    270
Food Lion supermarket chain, 23
Food poisoning, 160
Food storage, 173–74
Frankfurters. *See* Hot dogs
Free-range chickens, 34
Frozen desserts, low–fat, 114–15,
    196–204
  Ratings, 199–203
Frozen light entrées, 204–12
  Ratings, 207–11
Fruit, 92–111
  canned and frozen, 94, 95, 105,
    106
  grading of, 93–95
  juice, 108–11
  packaging of, 93
  pesticides in, 164
  price-quality relationship for, 16
  ripening of, 92–93
  seasonal price fluctuations for, 15
  types of, 94–107

Garbanzo beans, 76
Garlic, 80–81
General Mills, 127
Giant supermarket chain, 24
Goat cheese, 120
Gorgonzola, 121
Gouda, 121
Grading
  of beef, 48, 54
  of butter, 114
  of chicken, 31–32
  of eggs, 121–23
  of fruits, 93–94
  of lamb, 51
  of nuts, 135
  of turkey, 40
  of vegetables, 71–73
Graham flour, 129
Grand Union supermarket chain,
    24
Grapefruit, 100–101
  juice, 111

Grapes, 101–2
Green beans, 75–76
Grilled foods, contaminants in,
166–67

Ham, 52–53
Harris-Teeter supermarket chain,
23–24
Harvard University, 264
Heart, 62
Herbal teas, 153
Herbs, 156
Hershey, 234
Heterocyclic amines (HAs), 167
Honeydew melon, 103
Hormones in animal feed, 171
Hot dogs, 57–60, 212–20
Ratings, 215–19
Hubbard squash, 88

Iceberg lettuce, 81–82
Ice cream, 114–15
Impulse buying, guarding against,
17
Inner city supermarkets, 24
Irradiated foods, 172–73

Jewel supermarket chain, 24
Juices, fruit, 108–11

Kellogg, 127
Kidney beans, 76
Kidneys, 62

Labeling regulations, 20–21
for cooking meat, 49
Lactose-reduced milk, 113
Lamb, 50–52
Layout of supermarkets, 8
shopping strategy and, 18
Lead, 168–70
in tap water, 175–76
Leaf lettuce, 82
Leeks, 81
Leftovers, 22–23
bacteria in, 162, 163
Lemons, 102
Lettuce, 81
Lima beans, 76

Limes, 103
Listeria bacteria, 160, 163
Liver, 62
Lobsters, 69
Loss leaders, 14
Low-fat milk, 113
Lucky supermarket chain, 23, 24

Macaroni products, 133–34
Margarine, 114, 143–44
Mark-downs, 13
Marketing, 5–6
Mayonnaise, 144
Meats, 43–62
bacon, 60–61
beef, 42–49
contamination of, 160, 161, 164,
167, 168, 170–71
cost per pound of, 18–19
inspection of, 47
lamb, 50–52
microwaving, 56–57
mislabeled, 14
pork, 52–53
reducing shrinkage in, 53–56
sausages and frankfurters, 57–61
sausages and frankfurters, 57–61
seasonal price fluctuations for,
15–16
variety meats, 61–62
veal, 49–50
Meijer supermarket chain, 23
Melons, 103–4
Mercury, fish contaminated with,
68, 170
canned tuna, 260–61
Metal contaminants, 168–70
Micromarketing, 5–6
Microwaving, 174–75
meat, 56
poultry, 37–38
Milk products, 112–14
drugs used in production of,
170–71
Mineral water, 155
Mislabeling, 13–14
Mold, 173–74
toxins produced by, 166
Mollusks, 69

Monosodium glutamate (MSG), 171
Monterey Jack cheese, 121
Muenster cheese, 121
Mushrooms, 82–83
Muskmelon, 103
Mussels, 69

National Institute of Environmental Health Sciences, 172
National Marine Fisheries Service, 262
National Research Council, 143
Navy beans, 76
Nectarines, 106
Nestlé's, 150
New products, coupons for, 7–8
Nutrition
    of cereal, 179, 184–85
    of cheese, 117–18
    of eggs, 119
    of frozen desserts, 198
    of frozen light entrées, 204–5
    of fruit juices, 110–11
    of hot dogs, 213–14
    of milk products, 112
    of peanut butter, 136–137
    of potato chips, 139–40
    of rice, 133
    of snack food, 139
    of spaghetti, 240–41
    of spaghetti sauce, 245–46
    of tuna, 259–60
    of yogurt, 276–77
Nuts, 134–35

Oat flour, 129
Objective product evaluation, 17
Oils, 142, 143
    See also Olive oil
Okra, 83
Olive oil, 143, 220–23
    Ratings, 224–25
Onions, 83
Orange juice, 108–11
Oranges, 104–5
Oysters, 69

Pancakes, 223, 226–27
    Ratings, 228–31
Pancake syrups, 227, 232–34
    Ratings, 235–39
Parasites, food-borne, 160
Parmesan cheese, 121
Pasta, 133–34
    See also Spaghetti
Pathmark supermarket chain, 23, 24
Pea beans, 76
Peaches, 105
Peanut butter, 136–37
    toxins in, 166
Pears, 106–7
Peas, 84
Peppers, 84
Pepsi, 153, 192, 193, 196
Persian melon, 104
Pesticides, 163–65
Pimentos, 84
Pineapple juice, 111
Pineapples, 107
Pinto beans, 76
Plums, 107
Polychlorinated biphenyls (PCBs), 68, 164
Polycyclic aromatic hydrocarbons (PAHs), 166–67
Pork, 52–53
Potato chips, 138–40
Potatoes, 84–86
    toxins in, 165–66
Potato flour, 130
Poultry, 29–41
    capon, 39
    chicken, 31–38
    contamination of, 160–62, 164, 167, 168, 170
    Cornish game hen, 38–39
    duck, 38
    mislabeled, 14
    seasonal price fluctuations for, 15
    storing and preparing, 30
    turkey, 40–41
Powdered milk, 114
Preferred-shopper programs, 6
Pricing practices, 13–16
Process American cheese, 115–18

Produce. *See* Fruit; Vegetables
Product differentiation, 8
Product placement, 8
Prune juice, 111
Publix supermarket chain, 24

Quality, relationship between price and, 16

Radiological Health, U.S. Bureau of, 174
Radishes, 86–87
Radon, 176
Range-growth birds, 34
Raspberries, 99–100
Rice, 130–33
Rice flour, 129
Romaine, 82
Romano cheese, 121
Roundfish, 66
Rutabagas, 90
Rye flour, 129

Safeway supermarket chain, 24
Salad dressing, 144
Salmon, 68
Salmonella, 160, 172
Santa Claus melon, 104
Sausages, 57–61
    contents of, 57–58
    locally produced, 58–59
    specialty and ethnic, 60–61
    supermarket, 59–60
Savoy cabbage, 78
Scallop squash, 88
Scanners, 14–15
Scombrotoxin, 166
Seafood. *See* Fish
Seasonal price fluctuations, 15–16
Seeds, 156
Self-basting turkeys, 40
Seltzer, 155
Shell beans, 76
Shellfish, 69–70
    bacteria in, 161–63
    pesticides in, 165
    toxins in, 166
ShopRite supermarket chain, 23
Shortenings, 141–42

Shrimp, 69–70
Skim milk, 113
Snack foods, 138–40
Snow peas, 91
Sodium nitrite, 171–72
Soft drinks, 153–54
    See also Colas
Solanine, 165–66
Sour cream, 113
Soybeans, 91
Soy flour, 129
Spaghetti, 133–34, 234, 240–41
    Ratings, 242–43
Spaghetti sauces, 241, 244–52
    Ratings, 247–51
Spaghetti squash, 88
Sparkling water, 155
Special pricing, 13
Spices, 156
Spinach, 87
Squash, 87–88
Stem lettuce, 82
Steroid hormones, 171
Stewing chickens, 35–36
Still water, 155
Storage, 173–74
Strawberries, 100
Stuffing for poultry, 30
Sulfites, 171
Supermarket Ratings, 25–27
Sweetbreads, 62
Sweet potatoes, 88, 90
Swiss chard, 91
Swordfish, 68

Teas, 151–53, 252–58
    Ratings, 254–57
Texmati rice, 132
Tie-ins, 12
Tomatoes, 89, 90
Tomato juice, 111
Tongue, 62
Toxins, natural, 165–66
Trihalomethanes (THMs), 175, 264, 270
Tripe, 62
Tuna, 258–64
    fresh, 68
    mercury in, 170, 260–61
    Ratings, 265–71

Turkey, 40–41
  thawing frozen, 162
Turnips, 90

Variety meats, 61–62
Veal, 49–50
Vegetables, 71–91
  canned, 72, 74
  fresh, varieties of, 73–91
  frozen, 72, 74
  grading of, 71–73
  pesticides in, 164
  price-quality relationship, 16
  seasonal price fluctuations for, 15
  specialty, 91
Viruses, food-borne, 160
Vons supermarket chain, 24

Warehouse price clubs, 7
Water, bottled, 154–57
  See also Carbonated waters
  tap water versus, 175–76

Water chestnuts, 91
Watercress, 91
Watermelon, 104
Wax beans, 75–76
Wheat flour, 128–29
White beans, 76
Whitefish, 68
White rice, 131
Whole grain cereals, 125–28
Whole milk, 112–13
Whole wheat flour, 129
Wild rice, 132
Wisconsin, Medical College of, 264

Yams, 88
Yellow squash, 87–88
Yield, 18–19
Yogurt, 113, 274–78
  frozen, 197, 198; *see also* Frozen
    desserts, low-fat
  Ratings, 279–83

Zucchini, 88